Oil, power and a Sign of Hope

Of corporations and the
human right to clean water

Klaus Stieglitz
with Sabine Pamperrien

Translated by
Terry Swartzberg

This book is dedicated to
the people in South Sudan whose great suffering is due to
the activities of the oil industry, and, in the final analysis,
to our hunger for energy.

First edition Spring 2016
All rights reserved
Copyright © 2016 by rüffer & rub Sachbuchverlag GmbH, Zurich
info@rrufferundrub.ch | www.rrufferundrub.ch

Typefont: Filo Pro
Printing and binding: Books on Demand GmbH, Norderstedt
Paper: Creme white, 90 g/m²

ISBN 978-3-907625-96-5

TABLE OF CONTENTS

Libya

Egypt

Red Sea

Chad

SUDAN

DARFUR

Khartoum ●

Eritrea

Bentiu ●

Ethiopia

● Raga

Central African
Republic

Rumbek ●

SOUTH SUDAN

Juba ●

Democratic Republic
of the Congo

Uganda

Kenya

PROLOGUE

Powerless people

July, 2012. Sarnico, a town in northern Italy. Throngs of paparazzi. George Clooney is shooting a commercial for a luxury version of Mercedes-Benz's E-class of cars. The commercial covers the star's determined attempts to get a close-up on the car. This entails him initially grabbing an aquaplane, which then follows a silver-colored model of the car as it winds its way down the spectacular road hugging the banks of the Lago d'Iseo. Clooney's next step is to grab a speedboat, which flies him up close to the object of his desire. Great chase scene. The commercial's message: the new model of Mercedes causes this womanizer to mobilize all of the well-known determination and charm that he normally displays when wooing an exquisitely attractive woman.

Clooney relaxes during the breaks between shooting by enjoying a bit of joshing with his fans, and by bringing food to the members of the crew. He lets himself be photographed while doing such. The world's media snap up the photos.

Clooney makes an announcement during the day of shooting. He is going to auction off his 2008 Tesla Signature 100 Roadster, which has only 1,700 miles on its clock. And he is going to donate the proceeds to a project of assistance in Sudan.

August, 2012: $US 99,000. That's the amount raised by the auctioning of Clooney's four years old car. The funds go to the

Satellite Sentinel Project, which Clooney helped found and which operates in Sudan.

*

It was sometime around 60 A.D. that the Emperor Nero decided to split off two of his centurions and their centuries (companies) from his legions stationed in Rome's province of Egypt, and to send them south. The mission's purpose was to scout the unknown lands stretching down to the sources of the White Nile, and to claim them for Rome, which would thus gain new, sub-Saharan lands. Nero was greedy for the gold supposed to be lying around for the picking in these lands, which comprised the ancient kingdom of Meroe. It was located in what is today's Sudan. In the interests of maximizing his cost-benefits ratio, Nero gave his scouting party a clearly-defined mission: find out whether or not these unknown lands had any resources at all worthy of exploitation.

Overcoming and surviving unimaginably-challenging obstacles, the Roman legionnaires managed to reach Lake Victoria, the source of the White Nile. One of these obstacles was so challenging that it put an end to any visions of lasting conquest of the region: the "Sudd". This gigantic, contiguous expanse of wetlands—nearly 6 million hectares in size—is located in Southern Sudan, and is one of the largest of its kind in the world. The Sudd is comprised of the White Nile's countless arms and of the land between them. These streams are too shallow to be navigated by ships. The rest of the region is covered by such aquatic plants as papyrus and other reeds. These preclude any attempts at wading through it.

Seneca, the Roman historian, bequeathed us a telling description of the Sudd wetlands. It constitutes the first firmly-

The Sudd is one of the largest wetlands in the world. Slight rises serve inhabitants as a place of settlement. The photographs are of swamps in the southern reaches of the state of Unity.

documented mentioning of the region. "Sudd" stems from the Arabic "Sadet", which means "barrier" or "dam".

*

In May, 1847, Johannes von Müller, a researching botanist from southwestern Germany, embarked upon an expedition in Africa. He was accompanied by his secretary and trusty helper Alfred Brehm, who was the son of an ornithologist. The expedition started in Egypt. Its plan was to traverse the entire continent of Africa, and to research its fauna in the process. In January, 1848, von Müller and Brehm arrived in Sudan, which was un-der the control of the Ottoman Empire in those days. The Ottoman had expanded their sway over the Sudan from their base in Egypt ten years previously. Brehm made a copious amount of notes about and sketches of the people encountered in his travels. Brehm was especially moved and distressed by the slave trade, which was widespread in the Sudan of those days. Especially distressing to him was the exacting and unscrupulous treatment of the slaves by the Europeans living in the Sudan. During Brehm's sojourn in the Sudan, he was witness to the arrival of slaves from a march that had started in the south of the region. The state of the dark-skinned humans, who were member of the Dinka ethnic group, especially bothered Brehm: "It was a ghastly sight, one that no words suffice to describe. It remained in my soul for weeks—as the epitome of horror. It took place on January 12, 1848."[1] As Brehm noted: "This fate of being regarded as objects of sale applies to all the ethnic groups of Abyssinia, including the Galla, Shewa, Makate, Amhara, [...], the Shilluk, Dinka, Takhallaui, Darfuri, Sheibuni, Kik and Nuer."[2]

In his notes, Brehm described the cycle of violence and counter-violence prevailing in Africa. According to Brehm the former stemmed from the whites, who employed slavery as one of their means of ruthlessly oppressing the people of Sub-Saharan Africa. This oppression produced a widespread hostility towards whites—an attitude that Brehm found completely understandable—among the Africans. This hostility prevented von Müller and Brehm from proceeding upon their travels in Southern Sudan. As he noted resignedly: "The hunting for slaves bars the way for researchers seeking to explore the central lands of Africa."[3]

*

Daniele Comboni was a Catholic priest. In 1857, he embarked upon his first trip to Africa. He was accompanied by five other missionaries. Their trip brought them to Southern Sudan, where he experienced first hand the misery and the enslavement of Africans. These experiences led him to found a mission. Comboni's main objective was to put an end to slavery. His approach to missionary work sounds like it could have been formulated today: "Enabling Africa to rescue Africa."[4] Overcoming strong objections from within the ranks of his own church, Comboni recruited women and laypersons to participate in missionary work.[5] The greatest difference between Comboni's approach and those of previous missions was that he granted Africans full respect by viewing them as equals, ones well capable of being responsible for the managing of their affairs. One of Comboni's main principles was that the Europeans could well support and teach their counterparts—but should not patronize striving to form Africans according to European model.[6]

Comboni's missionary work proved to be a huge success. The ethnic groups living in Southern Sudan are cultures highly open to the Christians' visions of divinity. The effects have proved lasting. Southern Sudan is still the realm of nature-based religions and of Christianity—in contrast to northern Sudan, in which Islam predominantly prevails.

*

June 11, 1955, 4 pm. The start of the famous 24 Hours of Le Mans. The weather is hot and humid. A thunderstorm is in the offing — as shown by the dark clouds crowding the horizon. The sun is still, however, shining over the race course.

More than 200,000 spectators are lining the 13 kilometers of the race course, which is, on non-race days, comprised of normal-use roads. Case-in-point: the long straightaway. It is part of the road connecting Le Mans and Tours. The fastest cars reach speeds of nearly 300 kilometers an hour on the straight-away. Not surprisingly, this is the most popular place from which to watch the race. These "Populaires" are cheap. That's because fans have to stand. The "Populaires" are located in front of the more expensive bleachers. The former offer, however, the best views of the starting positions and the pits. The crowd in the Populaires gets to hear the yelling of the race managers and the mechanics, and gets to sample the odor of fuels and of abraded clutches and brakes. The crowd is comprised of thousands of people, all thronging the race course, from which they are separated only by a nearly one meter-high fence made of bales of hay and of planks. The crowd is enjoying itself. The race is being covered on-site by the world's media, many of which are reporting live from Le Mans. Among the media are film teams, which are shooting full-color, Cinemascope news flashes for the weekly reports shown in cinemas.

174 minutes after the race has commenced, several race cars zoom into the narrow stretch in front of the bleachers. The crowd cranes to get a good view. This is because the race's lead-

ers are in the pack. Among the leaders: the UK's Mike Hawthorn, who is driving a Jaguar, and the drivers of both of the Mercedes "Silver Arrows". These three are in a neck-on-neck battle for victory. The cars' manufacturers —Jaguar and Mercedes—are contending for both the World Cup's drivers' and manufacturer's championships. Mercedes is under pressure. It has to notch a victory in Le Mans if it plans on retaining its opportunity to win the title.[7] At first glance, this battle is about prestige and about gaining incentives that convince potential buyers to purchase the manufacturers' vehicles. These incentives constitute powerful, not-to-be-under-estimated advertising. A victory in Le Mans showcases the technical superiority of the manufacturer's products—in an era in which the automobile industry is embarking upon its boom.

This battle is also about something more, something deeper. World War II concluded a scant ten years previously. This battle is thus between the UK and Germany.[8] Mike Hawthorn's nationalism is well-known. During the days preceding the race, Hawthorn repeatedly proclaims that he will never allow himself to be beaten by a German. The flanks of his Jaguar D-Type are emblazoned with the national emblems of the British army. There are those who still remember that the Mercedes Silver Arrows were vehicles for the Nazis' propaganda in the pre-World War II era.[9] The Nazis were the main sponsors of the Sliver Arrows[10], providing millions of marks to the racing department of the Stuttgart-based manufacturer of automobiles.[11] The Nazis viewed car racing as a "kind of mental armament, one preparing the people to wage war".[12] Headed by Albert Neumann, the Mercedes team had been highly successful in the pre-World War II era. Once the war was over, the team—featuring the same personnel—set forth its successes. The only difference: it had "converted to democracy", as Guido

Knopp, a historian working for Germany's "ZDF" national broadcaster, described it in a work published several decades subsequently.[13]

Mercedes' managing board has given its racing team unmistakable marching orders. The team is to win both titles in Formula 1—the driver's and the manufacturer's championships. Mercedes has backed these plans with generous funds and other resources. The company has founded a dedicated racing department, and has hired what has come to be more than 200 persons to staff it. This staff consults with a further 300 specialists—who work for other departments at Mercedes.

It has taken the Mercedes team a mere four years to transform models from the prewar era into high-performance race cars. Nineteen fifty four was the newly-revamped Silver Arrow's first Grand Prix season. The team's first race comes in the middle of the season. It is the Grand Prix of France, which is held on July 4, 1954 in Reims. It turns out to be a historic day for the Silver Arrows—and for Germany's national football team. In a match played in Bern, Switzerland, the team wins the world championship. At Reims, the Mercedes team gains both titles. Thanks to these victories, July 4, 1954 becomes for many Germans a turning point in the history of the newly-constituted Federal Republic of Germany. It marks the end of the era of disgrace and obscurity, and the beginning of a new dignity and identity.[14] An English newspaper calls July 4, 1954 "Der Tag for Germans".[15]

Mercedes' record of success in the sports car races also commences in 1954. Mercedes broadcasts a commercial in 1954 and 1955. Under the name "Pioneers of Progress", the film is shown in the UK and in the USA. A highlight of the film is the raising of the German flag (which is comprised of the colors of black, red and gold) in honor of Mercedes' great victory in

France. The flag symbolizes the ties binding all of Mercedes' staff members working on and for the racing team. The flag also expresses their aspirations.[16]

Britain's press would continue until the 1980s to cultivate World War II-caused anti-German sentiments. These mean that Mike Hawthorn was by no means the only person who viewed the duel on the race track as being a continuation of the war, only this time on another venue.[17] The spectators at Le Mans on this June 11, 1955 have been observing how Mike Hawthorn is implementing this policy of "no surrender" ever since the start of the race. The young Briton has already twice disregarded the signs issued by his team that it is time for him to come to his pits to fill up. Hawthorn is obviously determined to keep his lead at all costs.

Never has this race been so hotly contested so early on. Juan Manuel Fangio is hot on Hawthorn's heels. To get there, the legendary Argentinian race driver has played an incredible game of catch-up. To overcome his awful start, Fangio has floored his Mercedes Benz, and, risking life and limb in the process, has managed to erase Hawthorn's lead of two rounds. While competing with each other, Hawthorn and Fangio have achieved average speeds of 200 kilometers an hour. These have left the rest of the pack far behind, with the two leaders already having lapped a number of the other drivers. Driving at such top speeds is absolutely nonsensical so early—a mere two and a half hours after the starting gun—in a race that lasts for 24 hours.

Hawthorn and Fangio are facing a straightaway in which, once more, slower race cars are ahead of them. Driven by Lance Macklin, a Briton, an Austin Healey is proceeding along on the right of the track at a speed of 190 kilometers an hour. About to pass Macklin is another Silver Arrow, this one driven by Pierre

Levegh. Although already lapped by Hawthorn and Fangio, Levegh also plans to overtake the slower Austin Healey.

The recruiting of Levegh to its team represents a PR coup on the part of Mercedes. Levegh is an amateur driver who is highly popular in France. His joining the highly-successful team from Germany is designed to be a symbol of the reconciliation between the two countries. Mercedes is thus sending a team featuring a Frenchman—in addition to such stars as Fangio and Stirling Moss—to compete in the most important car race in France.[18] Mercedes has other reasons for recruiting Levegh, whose daytime job is being a jeweler based in Paris. The nearly 50 year old has repeatedly and successfully competed at Le Mans. In the 1952 staging of the 24 Hours of Le Mans, Levegh was the only driver to stay at the wheel for the race's entire 24 hours. Up until the very end of the race, Levegh had a commanding lead. A mere 15 minutes prior to the end of the race, his gears failed, robbing him of a certain victory in the process. This tragedy left him the moral victor, and made him the much-loved "hero of Le Mans".

Levegh is also flooring his car in the moments prior to the accident. Maintaining the high speeds of Hawthorn's Jaguar, the race's leader, Levegh's Mercedes tears along the very left of the track. Macklin sticks to the right. In a stretch immediately in front of the pit lane, Hawthorn's Jaguar passes—taking the middle of the track—his fellow-countryman's Austin Healey. Hawthorn then zooms to the right. At this point, he is in front of the Austin Healey. But instead of continuing to speed away from the car, Hawthorn brakes sharply, so as to leave the track on the right, and to head for a pit stop. His sudden and unexpected braking unleashes a horrifying chain reaction. His Jaguar is the only car that has disk brakes. The Austin Healey has drum brakes—and thus a much longer braking path. Macklin is forced to abruptly swerve to the left to avoid a collision with Hawthorn. This puts him in the path of Levegh's Silver Arrow, which is approaching him at a speed of 240 kilometers an hour. Levegh's car nicks the left rear fender of the Austin-Healey. Acting as if it had been launched from a rocket pad, the Mercedes veers to the left, bounces against a concrete wall, from which it is spun against the barricade separating the race tracks from the spectators. Levegh is jettisoned from his car and dies at the site of the accident. His car is smashed to pieces and starts to burn. Its axles, wheels, brakes and sections of its chassis are catapulted into the crowds thronging the track. The spectators standing in this area are mowed down by the debris flying in their midst. Heads, arms, entire torsos are cut off in the process. It is a scene of absolute horror.

The collision with the Silver Arrow causes Macklin's Austin-Healey to skid. Its plunges into the pits, running over three people in the process, only to then be sent flying across the track, running into the barricade protecting the bleachers. It comes to a stop there. Macklin is able to free himself from his wrecked car.

The accident lasts no more than four seconds. Its consequences are catastrophic. The accident remains the worst ever experienced in automobile racing. The only reason why TV viewers in Germany and France are spared a live transmission of the dreadful catastrophe was the broadcasters' schedules of programming. These schedules cause the TV channels to interrupt during the late afternoon their live coverage of the race, so as to show other programs.[19] Notwithstanding this, the horrible details of the accident are filmed. Working for a French TV network, two cameramen are using a 16 millimeter cine camera to shoot shorts for inclusion in later reports. The cameramen have stationed themselves in front of the pits,[20] so as to shoot scenes conveying the race's atmosphere. Then the accident takes place. Immediately upon the crash of Levegh's Silver Arrow, the cameramen point their cameras to the scene of the accident. The images that they record are so horrifying that the only thing ever to be shown of them are several excerpts.

The accident kills 84 people. One hundred more suffered injuries. Hundreds, perhaps even thousands, are left traumatized. Notwithstanding all this, the thousands of spectators located at other areas of the racetrack hardly—if at all—notice the accident. Accidents are in any case part of automobile racing's daily fare. The fact that the drivers are continuously putting themselves in danger by driving at their vehicles' technical limits and by undertaking daring maneuvers produces racing's especially strong appeal to the spectators. They love the kick arising from the rush of speed. They seem to revel in racing's "flair", which includes the pillars of smoke spiraling up from vehicles on fire, and of the sight of dead drivers. Immediately after the accident at Le Mans, two laps of low speeds are imposed upon the drivers at the race. The race itself is not called off. After a brief period, it is, rather, permitted to proceed as normal. Most of the people attending it learn of the magnitude of the catastrophe only from the following day's newspapers.

Juan Manuel Fangio escapes the inferno unscathed. He subsequently reports that Pierre Levegh had warned him—via a hand signal—of the dangers ahead. The Frenchman has thus saved his life. This adds yet another chapter in automobile racing's long history derring-do, camaraderie and other legendary deeds.

The accident gives rise to another legend. For decades, conventional wisdom linked it to the end of the era of Silver Arrows. To be noted is that all other teams at Le Mans in 1955 did not stop racing at it afterwards. Mercedes did in fact decide during the night of June 12, 1955 to withdraw its team. A few days after the catastrophic accident, Fritz Könecke, Mercedes' boss, announced that Mercedes would no longer take part in automobile racing. The message emanating from this decision is capable of being understood to be that the "price to be paid for the achieving of sporting successes and of the prestige associated with it is not worth the price, which was paid in human lives". Mercedes thus abruptly left the sport that it had come to dominate during its short return to it. Its racing team had in fact already rapidly met the ambitious goals set for it by the company's executive board. Mercedes' decision did not at all diminish the aura emanating since the pre-WW II era from the Silver Arrows. The aura maintained itself throughout the years of Mercedes' refraining from participating in racing. Since the withdrawal of 1955, racing fans have bemoaned the lack of "their" Silver Arrows. Their attitude has almost been to treat the results of each subsequent race as being incomplete, since, of course, no Silver Arrow was there to compete in them.

The fact is that Mercedes' decision to withdraw from automobile racing was caused by business reasons. This decision was actually made prior to the commencement of the 1955 racing season. Racing consumed the funds needed to develop standard vehicles.[21]

Mercedes had provided all of the funds needed to finance its race team. There were no sponsors in those days. They arrived on the scene in 1968, in which the ban on placing advertisements on race cars was abolished.[22]

*

One month after the accident at Le Mans, an uprising breaks out in Southern Sudan's garrison city of Torit. Forming part of the UK's Sudan Defence Force, which is charged with maintaining Britain's colonial dominance of the country, the Equatorial Corps is stationed in this small city, which is located near the Sudan's border with Uganda. The Corps includes soldiers from Southern Sudan. On August 18, 1955, they rise in mutiny. They refuse to let themselves be replaced by soldiers from northern Sudan. The uprising is fueled by fears of the oppression expected to be experienced by Southern Sudan upon the granting of independence on January 1, 1956 to the regions of Southern Sudan and Northern Sudan by the British-Egyptian Condominium controlling the areas.

Since the creation of the British-Egyptian Condominium and its extension to comprise the Sudan, northern Sudan was run by a British-Egyptian administration. Southern Sudan was managed as a British colony.[23] In 1922, the Egyptians were compelled to withdraw from Sudan. This caused the British to introduce a form of indirect rule in northern Sudan.[24] British administrators supervised the operations of native and locally-based responsible parties.[25] This move was caused by the Britons' wish to cut costs of administration.[26] The British attributed the move, however, to their wish for "modernization".[27] The British regarded Southern Sudan as not being ready for such a "modernization". They thus set up a dedicated administration in the region.[28] By doing such, they pursue a policy designed to isolate Southern Sudan.[29] It resulted in the cementing of the partition of Sudan into two cultural, ethnic and linguistic regions.[30]

The cultivation of and trading in cotton gave northern Sudan a modicum of prosperity. Under the guidance of the British, the region and its education and health care systems were developed, as was its infrastructure. The region's population, which is predominantly Arab, was inculcated in the precepts of participation in politics and its ramification upon public life. This caused nationalism to arise in northern Sudan in the post-World War I era.[31] As was the case in those Arab regions that allied themselves during World War I with the UK, France and the USA as a way of putting an end to the 500-year domination of the Ottoman Empire, northern Sudan experienced a mushrooming of Muslim sects. Akin to the Arab regions, nationalism's goal in Sudan was also the achieving of independence. Northern Sudan's nationalists' vision for the future state: it was to retain its Islamic nature.[32] In World War II, the Sudan Defence Force prevented Italy's Fascist armies from conquering the region. It was only after the war that negotiations on independence were launched.[33] A conference was staged in 1947 in Juba, a city in Southern Sudan. At it, the British and North Sudanese negotiators presented the Southern Sudanese with a fait accompli. They had resolved that northern and Southern Sudan were to be joined into one country.[34]

Southern Sudan was underdeveloped and backward, in every definition of the terms. This was due to the colonial administration's failure to do anything to develop the region's economy, education system or infrastructure. This was in sharp contrast to the UK's actions in northern Sudan. The Southern Sudanese were quite aware of this situation. They felt themselves—quite correctly so—to be ostracized and oppressed. Southern Sudan's rejection of the jerry-built national structure being imposed upon them grew with each day that independence approached.

Major protests broke out in Southern Sudan in 1955. Being protested were northern Sudan's dominance and the neglect of the interests of the south resulting from it. Southern Sudan's population began to assert its rights to such. The above-described mutiny in Torit led to the initial, violent expression of the frustration that had built up over the decades. This outbreak of violence caused the death of hundreds of northern Sudanese in Torit.[35] The day on which the mutiny in Torit began is now known as "Torit Revolution Day". It has been celebrated as a national holiday since South Sudan gained its independence in 2011. The rebels of Torit are now regarded as national heroes.[36] The outbreak of violence in 1955 has become the stuff of legend-building.

The Southern Sudanese were not very well organized. This lack enabled the northern Sudanese to rapidly quell the rebellion. They imposed death sentences upon 250 Southern Sudanese, most of them Christians and intellectuals.[37] The North's massive repression caused Southern Sudanese to flee in large numbers to neighboring countries. These refugees soon founded resistance groups. They began waging war with their opponents from the North. This civil war began prior to Sudan's gaining of independence. It ended only in 1972, the year in which Southern Sudan was granted partial administrative autonomy. This civil war was to be followed by another. The wave of forced emigration from Southern Sudan was also only the first of many.

*

In 1974, Chevron, the American oil corporation, acquired the rights to prospect for oil in Sudan, and to exploit any findings of such. The company's prospecting was successful. Test drilling conducted in 1978 in Southern Sudan paid off. The finding of oil gave Sudan, one of the world's poorest countries, the prospect of being lifted out of poverty. While not as large as those of Saudi Arabia or Iraq, Sudan's oil reserves are comparable in size with those of such oil producers as Brunei or Colombia.[38] Had it been prudently managed, the oil could proved a benefit for the country.[39] As will be shown, Sudan's oil has been anything but that for the country. The oil has enriched a small elite. For the rest of the country, the finding of oil has not improved life. Quite the opposite. It has proven a curse. The oil has given rise to warfare, despoliation, depopulation and environmental destruction.

*

A war is launched in 1983. It is against a part of the country's own population. It is being waged by the regime in Khartoum. Cloaking its aggression in the dogma of radical Islam, the regime starts asserting its hegemony over the non-Islamic and non-Arab parts of the population. The resulting war of cultures is to be viewed from today's vantage point as being a forerunner of the today's phenomenon of Islam being used an instrument of the violence-based, state-organized assertion of control. For many years, the world takes scant notice of the Sudan's regime brutal oppression, whose underlying and true motive is the gaining and maintaining of dominance over resources—and specifically over the oil.[40] The ensuing conflict causes a complete collapse of all order in Sudan, be it state or traditions-imposed. Sudan is a home to a multiplicity of ethnic groups. As such, it has always been subject to tensions among them, with resources repeatedly proving a source of such strife. This strife had, however, been kept under control until the recent past by mechanisms of conflict resolution adhered to by both nomadic Arabs and non-nomadic Africans engaged in trading with each other.[41] During the resulting conflict, all parties perpetrate despicable acts of barbaric violence upon the civilian population.

*

At the beginning of the 1980s, Daimler-Benz's managers start thinking about the company's returning to automobile racing.[42] This idea gains support. Daimler-Benz has a problem — a bad image. Its cars are viewed as not having an adequate level of quality.[43] The managers view automobile racing as being a "hot button" for purchasers of cars, who tend to transfer the image arising from race cars—high levels of performance, dynamism, advanced technologies and internationalism—to standard vehicles. Daimler wants and needs to profit from this transferring.[44] In 1988, the corporation resolves to return to car racing. Its initial fields of re-entry are touring cars and sport prototypes.[45] This re-entry produces mixed results. Daimler's management is by no means unanimously convinced of the efficacy of the investments made in this area.[46] Also planned by the company is a return to Formula 1. But efforts to do such run into a number of bumps.[47] The return does have its impact upon standard models: silver is the favorite color of the Mercedes purchased.[48]

★

While all this was going on, the exploitation of the oil found in the Sudan was being pursued. The regime in Khartoum and Chevron concluded agreements foreseeing the marketing of oil from the country by 1984. The attack by rebels on Chevron facilities—resulting in the death of several of the company's staff members—caused the postponing of such plans.[49] Many in Southern Sudan viewed Chevron as being an ally of the Khartoum-based repressive regime. It, in turn, distrusted Chevron, and didn't accept its reasons for halting the exploitation.[50] The regime's assumption was that Chevron welcomed the rebels' attack, as it gave them an excuse not to have to live up to its commitments in a time of falling oil prices.[51] The regime's assumption was that the Americans actually intended to wait until the exploitation of oil in Sudan returned to making business sense.[52] Once Chevron ran out of reasons to delay production and upon Khartoum's increasing of the pressure to live up to agreements, the US oil giant ceased all activities in the country. This was expedited by the lack of support forthcoming from the USA for the company's activities in Sudan.[53]

Chevron's withdrawal from the country causes the regime in Khartoum to divide the concession. Created are several "blocks"—areas of oil exploitation and production. The licenses to develop these are awarded on individual bases. The regime in Khartoum's experience with Chevron leads to its striving to attract smaller-sized oil companies to the country.[54] The idea is that such companies are more interested in forging personal relationships, and that, through these, the government can exert more control over them.[55] Khartoum's plans meet with enthusiastic response. Oil companies from Canada and Europe are joined by those from Asia—including the China National Petroleum Corporation (CNPC) and Malaysia's Petronas (Petroliam Nasional Berhad)—in striving to enter what they view as being Sudan's promising oil industry. The Canadians rapidly shelve such plans. One key reason is the public pressure ensuing from the link between doing business in Sudan and being involved in the violation of human rights there.[56] The regime in Khartoum has proven itself willing to do anything to remove obstacles that would prevent foreign companies from making investments in the country. The regime has employed violence to drive the population from regions in which oil fields are to be exploited.

Documented in detail has been what happened in "Block 5A". This area of concession is located in Unity state. It contains the Thar Jath[57] oil fields. To provide unimpeded access to them and to thus expedite their exploitation, thousands of persons were killed and tens of thousands forced to flee. A large-scale investigation subsequently confirmed the suspicion such non-Sudanese oil companies as Sweden's Lundin Oil, the Malaysian government's Petronas and Austria's OMV were not only prepared to accept these forced flights, but that, in fact, it was these investors that actively pressured the regime in Khartoum to pursue them.[58] One fact is apparent. Such oil companies immediately benefited from the "scorched earth" policy implemented by the regime in Khartoum against Southern Sudan, a policy yielding so many refugees.[59] The especially close relationship between Khartoum and this Malaysian company is also no doubt due to both countries' being Islamic.[60] Petronas' involvement in Sudan comprises its participation in consortia that are exploiting oil fields. The Malaysian company also maintains gas stations in the country. It is, further, the main supplier of the kerosene used by the country's civil and military aviation sectors[61]. Petronas has also built a refinery in the country. This investment has come to a billion dollars.[62] Petronas is an ambitious company. To realize these ambitions, it has selected Sudan to be its venue of operation outside Malaysia.[63]

*

The decades of conflict cause the deaths of some 50% of the people in Sudan as a whole, and the flight of four million refugees since 1983.[64] The countryside has been ravaged. This applies to fertile regions whose cultivation would have the potential to feed the entire nation. The millions of refugees are housed—often under miserable conditions—in camps. The refugees are dependent upon the assistance provided by international organizations.

*

The Comboni friars have been operating missions in Sudan for all of the last 150 years. This longevity makes the friars important sources of contacts and counsel to and major partners of the relief organizations setting up shop in the Sudan. The founders of the Comboni congregation developed a depiction of humanity that still informs their work today. This "mission statement" also guides the assistance supplied by organizations in the country that are not religious in nature. One of the organizations providing assistance and helping protect human rights in Sudan is "Sign of Hope". This interdenominational NGO is headquartered in Konstanz, a city located in southwestern Germany. The thrusts of its work are the protection of human rights and the provision of assistance.

*

At the beginning of June 1994, Reimund Reubelt, staff member of Sign of Hope, traveled to Southern Sudan, which was being racked by a civil war in those days. He arrived in a small airplane. It was full of assistance supplies that Reimund had procured in Kenya. The airplane's pilot was nervous. This was because he didn't know—the rebels or the government's forces—who controlled the airstrip at which they were going to land. He said: "If people start running at us, that's a bad sign. We will have to immediately take off again." The tall and haggard people waiting at the airfield approached the airplane in a slow and dignified pace.

The event, which took place more than 20 years ago, marked the beginning of Sign of Hope's work in the country, in which more than 75% of the people cannot read or write, and in which more than half live below the poverty level. Since that time, Sign of Hope has organized and carried out on a regular basis transports of humanitarian goods to the dangerous, crisis-ridden region. One first step was the forging of working relationships with on-site clerical partners.

Klaus Stieglitz is also a staff member at Sign of Hope. He can still clearly recall the details of a meeting with an elderly gentleman during one of Stieglitz' frequent visits to Southern Sudan. This took place a couple of years after Reubelt's visit. Reimund Reubelt's colleague Stieglitz says: "The man was dressed in clothing that looked worse for wear. He had bright white hair. He was old, and a former teacher. He recounted tales out of his life, and we listened attentively. After a while, he asked us where we came from. He said that he knew Germany well from radio broadcasts. For many years, he had listened to the short wave broadcasts of the BBC to keep abreast of what was going on in the world. Something that had made him especially sad was the building of the wall throughout Germany in 1961. This was because it would separate the people living there. He prayed since that event every day for the fall of the wall, even though he had never seen it. This came to pass in 1989. Although living in one of the most remote corners of what is today South Sudan, this man was able to show us that the injustice symbolized by this wall had moved him. And that he had done whatever he could to stand up for his fellow human beings in Europe. He had prayed. At this moment, we felt ourselves to be loved deeply by this man. It was a moment that, once more, conveyed the import of our personal credo to us: We help people. We work with them, and we protect their rights."

Over the following decades, our rendering of humanitarian assistance in Southern Sudan was joined by the conducting of development projects and of missions to protect human rights. This joint thrust—when carried out in crisis regions—generates tension: This is because helping people assert their rights automatically means raising your voice against the powers that be. As is the case in other countries run by potentates, it is precisely those in power that get to decide whether or not you will be allowed to speak with the people. Notwithstanding this, Sign of Hope places importance on supplying people with food, water, medicine and education (through the building of schools)—and on attacking the roots of their problems—the lack of respect of their human rights. Klaus Stieglitz and Reimund Reubelt share the conviction that "our wish to form onsite true partnerships of respect with the disadvantaged requires our ensuring their getting their rights. What's at stake: protecting human dignity."

*

In 2006, Sign of Hope was accorded consultative status by the United Nation's Economic and Social Council. This fostered Sign of Hope's work to publicize violations of human rights in Southern Sudan.

*

At the end of 2007, problems with drinking water were brought to the attention of Sign of Hope. The German organization was told of the contamination being found in the water available for drinking in certain regions of Southern Sudan. The initial tests made of the water confirmed the assumption that this contamination stemmed from the extraction of oil. Sign of Hope commissioned the conducting of a comprehensive, scientific study.

It found that this connection in fact existed. This book tells the story of Sign of Hope's attempts to get the oil companies to adhere to internationally-applicable standards. The story tells the chronology of the organization's push to enable the 180,000 affected residents to assert their human right to have clean water to drink. Another thrust of this push is the attempt to conserve one of the world's largest wetlands and its unique biodiversity. This book will also depict the mechanisms employed by a newly-founded state to rule. These mechanisms have turned the country's oil reserves into a curse for its population. This chronology also reveals, by way of contrast, something gratifying. There are buttons for outsiders to push. And pushing them can in fact affect the decisions reached by the liable parties—if the pushing is undertaken on a lasting and thoroughgoing basis.

The cattle camps are the venues of
social, cultural and economic life
of the semi-nomadic peoples living
in Southern Sudan.

2008

A Suspicion

For more than 20 years, Southern Sudan has been the focus of Sign of Hope's work. The rendering of assistance in an area repeatedly roiling with crises requires the careful selection of partners, ones capable of pursuing projects even in times of great difficulty. South Sudan (which was formerly part of the country of Sudan) is one of the poorest countries in the world. As such, it requires a wide variety of assistance: in helping supply its people with food, potable water, medical treatment (via "bush" clinics and other parts of a dedicated infrastructure) and education. Requisite to set up a resilient organization is the dispatching of own staff to the region. They then work with local players. Sign of Hope accordingly has deployed up to 80 staff members to South Sudan. Their jobs include the facilitation of mother-children projects, of the building of village day care centers, and of the operation of two bush clinics.

*

Sign of Hope received at the end of 2007 an alarming message from Southern Sudan. It stated that a trustworthy person living in the region had been receiving over the past few weeks and months ever-more frequent and disturbing reports of there being something wrong with the water found in the vicinity of the oil rigs ringing Thar Jath. Worried mothers were complaining about its bitterness. It was being said that the water was so salty that children were immediately vomiting after drinking it. Cases of stomach aches and diarrhea were reported to have become more and more common. Along with children, the elderly and the weak were suffering from this. Livestock were dying in unusually large numbers. According to the herders, this was due to the bad water. The people in the region viewed the cause of the water's contamination as being the wastes produced by the oil industry. The wastes contained chemicals that were probably being deposited in the ambient environment. As the message stated, there were no hard facts. Our contacts in the region issued a desperate plea. They had neither funds nor any ways of conducting an investigation. So they were asking Sign of Hope to do such. The organization was surely capable of helping from its base in Germany?

*

The staff working for Sign of Hope's Sudan Project are equally as alarmed. Access to safe water has become in any case a main concern of many of the world's human rights activists. On December 23, 2003, the 58th General Assembly of the United Nations called "Water for Life" into being. This was to be an International Decade of Action.[1] The Decade commenced on March 22, 2005, which was World Water Day. The Decade was to end on March 22, 2015.[2] The Decade was to be employed to make the world's decision-makers and the general public aware of the importance of water. A thrust of this program was pushing to ensure that commitments made were lived up to.[3] The program's objective was to halve by 2015 the number of people that do not have access to safe water and to appropriate sanitary facilities.[4] Another objective: putting an end to unsustainable ways of using water.[5]

The right to consume clean water still hasn't been officially approved and to thus take legal force. The world is, however, increasingly aware of the water-related emergencies facing its peoples—and of the ever-more apparent ramifications of these. This awareness is yielding action. Such human rights organizations as Sign of Hope regard the human right to have clean water as being indisputable.

No one knows what we at Sign of Hope will discover in the Sudan. Perhaps the reports of bad water are nothing more than unfounded rumors. That has been known to happen. Speaking against this is the verdict rendered by our contact, who enjoys our complete trust. He regards the situation as being very serious. That is why there is only one decision to be reached. We have to see whether or not the fears are in fact based in fact. But how are we to go about this? We could takes samples from the oil fields, to see if they are contaminated. We are currently preparing our next trip to the Sudan. Its purpose is to ascertain the state of human rights. We have put the areas of oil extraction on our itinerary. Sign of Hope has never gathered samples of water. Our operating maxim also, however, applies to this case: anything practical will be done.

The first step is easy. Klaus Stieglitz is friends with a staff member of a water testing laboratory. It is located in the vicinity of the Lake of Constance. Stieglitz' friend shows him to gather samples of water, and how to perform quick tests of it. He also instructs him in the preparation of the samples for being investigated in laboratories. Another laboratory—also located in the same region—is to be commissioned with the carrying out of the requisite further analyses. Bottles for the transporting of samples are then provided to the organization, which drafts forms to be used in the forthcoming collection of samples.

→ Further information:
The South learns how to assert its interest

A land experiencing a chaotic disruption, one caused by the strife among its groups and interests: that is the general picture of the Sudan. Contradicting this depiction of a country tearing itself part are the clearly-established guidelines that have been established in the Sudan. They apply to the handling of oil reserves. These guidelines mandate this processing's conforming to societal and environmental principles. Due to these, no one can claim lack of awareness of the perils arising from the failure to adhere to these.

While the peace talks were being conducted between the conflicting parties, a meeting held in Kenya in January 2004 had established that the exploitation of Sudan's natural resources would observe standards of sustainability. The Basic Memorandum signed on January 7, 2004 would go on to become Chapter III of the Comprehensive Peace Agreement of 2005.[6] Subscribed to by the parties, the Memorandum's Point III. 1.10 stated that the sharing of prosperity would be the principle informing the responsible treatment of the resources available. The Point stated: "that the best-known method of the sustainable utilization and control of natural resources shall follow."[7] What this meant: the exploitation of the country's natural resources was to adhere to international standards.

The principles governing the utilization of oil resources were listed discretely in sub-point 3 of this Memorandum. Precisely-formulated requirements were created. They were designed to make the oil exploration and exploitation environmentally and socially compatible. As this shows, representatives of the government and of the rebels were aware at this time of the drilling for oil's being associated with especially-grave disruptions in the habitats in which flora and fauna live—and of the need to keep this in mind. According to this agreement, the preservation of national interests and public welfare were to be given highest priority when prospecting for and extracting oil[8]. To be accorded the same importance were to be, in addition, the interests of regions involved[9] and of the local population[10]. The listing of the principles also included the preconditions governing the reaching of all further decisions, the need to adhere to national environmental regulations, the directives for the preservation of biodiversity, and the principles for the protection of the cultural heritage.[11] The Agreement gave rise to the National Petroleum Commission (NPC). Its board was to be comprised of representatives from both parties—on an equal basis. The Commission was charged with the responsibility for creating a body of rules implementing the above points and to be adhered to by the oil industry.[12] The NPC was also to negotiate the contracts with extractors of oil.

The Agreement thus brought an end—at least on paper—to the era in which the people of Southern Sudan were at the mercy of the schemes of the North, in which the former could be exploited, expelled or massacred as so wished by the latter. A variety of cease-fire agreements notwithstanding, conflicts kept on breaking out until 2003 between the government's troops and the rebels. The era was also marked by the full-scale attacks perpetrated upon the country's civilians. These conflicts were motivated by the will to maintain or obtain control over oil fields. The government's chief reason for waging war was, however, to enable its contractual partners' undisturbed drilling for oil. Human rights organizations started reporting in 1999 on attacks being carried out against civilians. These were being carried out to drive them from the catchment areas of sources of oil.[13] Although interrupted from time to time, the prospectors for oil did manage to overcome the disturbances ensuing from the civil war and to set forth their test drilling. These resulted in the pumping of oil.

In a first in the country's history, the Comprehensive Peace Agreement (CPA) elevated the Southern Sudanese to being equally-entitled partners. Representatives of the rebels' party gained unimpeded access to the contracts concluded with oil extraction companies. They were empowered to commission technical experts with the assessment of the ramifications of these contracts.[14] Regarded as being especially important was the evaluation of impacts already having taken place. These agreements were worth more than the paper they were printed on. In 2006, the Sudan People's Liberation Army (SPLA) commissioned Norwegian experts with the compilation of an appraisal of the effects of oil extraction upon Southern Sudan. The appraisal was also to present the consequences of these, in view of the further expansion of the oil industry expected to occur.[15]

In 2007 and 2008, a team of experts from the Norwegian Directorate for Nature Management traveled throughout Sudan. The experts held talks with representatives of the government and with other officials in Khartoum and Juba. The team then visited industrial facilities and waste disposal facilities. This enabled them to get a picture of the effects of and challenges posed by the drilling for and extracting of oil in Southern Sudan. When compiling this evaluation, the team used as criteria the applicable international standards and the experiences gained in other countries in dealing with the risks known to arise from comparable on-shore drilling. The team also factored in the special conditions prevailing on site. It did not gather samples of the water, soil or living beings found in the vicinity of oil drilling and transportation facilities. This procedure was normal. The prime objective of the evaluation was to detail the parameters from which further, concrete measures were to be derived. The team's evaluation thus constituted a beginning, albeit one that came in a period in which the drilling for oil was well advanced in Southern Sudan.

On February 6, 2008, two staff members of Sign of Hope embark upon a 10-day trip to Southern Sudan. They are accompanied by two influential journalists. One is a Kenyan who works for the "Agence France Presse" ("AFP") news service. He joins the group in Nairobi. "AFP's" office in Nairobi is staffed by experts who are very interested in developments in Southern Sudan. The reporter writes an article that is carried on the wires of "AFP", which is one of the world's largest news agencies. The other reporter is German who works for "Schwäbische Zeitung", a daily based in the southwest part of the country. He too will go on to publish his impressions of the trip.

After stops in Nairobi and Juba, Sign of Hope's group arrives on February 8, 2008 in the town of Raga. The group's five-hour delay is due to their plane's, a chartered bush aircraft, not being ready to fly. Raga's "airport" is a long sandy trail. The "airport terminal" is a container. Raga has some 20'000 residents, making it one of the largest settlements in Southern Sudan. The town is located close to the (in those days) virtual border to northern Sudan. Its region is called Western Bahr el Ghazal.[16] The town is the headquarters of the Commissioner for the County of Raga.

We make camp in Raga on a ground that is located within a secured area. The campground is in the immediate vicinity of traditional tukuls. Our group sleeps on foam rubber mats. We use camping cartridges to cook. Wandering animals are occasional visitors, with this especially occurring during the evening. We find a spider the size of a human palm. It must have hitched a ride in a rolled up pant leg. There is no other explanation for its suddenly making its present known in the middle of the night by noisily climbing up the tent—from the inside. In an instinctive move, one of us captures it using a coffee cup, which is then used to send the gigantic insect on its way in the great outdoors. From now on, pant cuffs are going to be subject to intensive inspection. From time to time, we hear the local residents' yells. This signals the sighting of a poisonous snake. Nobody pays any attention to a waran, although this lizard is a meter and a half in length, as it meanders through the little settlement. A waran is not dangerous. It shows absolutely no interest in us as it waddles right past us, displaying no fear in the process.

In 2007, Sign of Hope set up an assistance project in Raga. Since then, one of the Comboni Missionaries has been heading an educational project. In 2001, the friars had been forced to flee the war. The conclusion of conflict allowed them to return to their base of operations. The friars rebuilt their schools, which had been badly damaged. Separated by genders, 1,200 children are taught at two elementary and one high school. Most of these children are from large and very poor farmer families. Sign of Hope's donation amounts to € 20,000. It goes for the food provided to the children every day, for educational materials, and, in this year, for small-scale repairs. In addition to the schools, the Comboni friars maintain a large number of day care centers.

We travel on the following day to Boro Medina, which is 100 kilometers to the west of Raga. It takes five hours. There is a refugee camp in the town, and it was there that Sign of Hope's work in the area started in 2007. The camp is home to people fleeing from war and floods, and to those returning to the region. We brought 200 first response packages during our first visit. To date, our assistance amounts to 1500 sacks and 75 tons of relief goods. In this trip, we are bringing 125 sacks, each containing 50 kilos of relief goods. These goods comprise basic food, blankets, plastic tarpaulins, cooking equipment, mosquito nets, soap and hoes. These goods go to families. Conditions have not improved since the previous year. The number of refugees has risen from 1,000 to 2,100.

A 40 year old woman belongs to the Borge, an ethnic group living farther to the north. There was fighting in her homeland. It caused her to flee in April of the previous year. She walked 15 days to get to the camp. "I was afraid, so afraid," she says. "We were bombed by a plane, and shot at on the ground."

The camps' residents get very little support. The camp does not have any sanitary facilities. Nor does it have any housing capable of withstanding the elements. There is no medical care. The residents' biggest foes are, however, hunger and thirst. Many of the people that we talk to complain about not having anything or very little to eat. Another problem: there is no water—and certainly no clean water—in the vicinity of the camp. This forces most of the women to trudge 40 minutes to the Boro river. Refugee families have recently arrived in the villages of Minamba and Deim Jalab. We deliver 45 sacks of relief goods there, with the rest going to Boro Medina. Sign of Hope donates € 20,000 for this delivery of goods. The organization plans to deliver a further € 40,000's worth of goods.

We return on February 11, 2008 to Raga, where we confer with paramilitary and other soldiers. The civil war featured a number of battles and massive attacks upon civilians in the region. Many of these attacks were carried out by militia fighting for North Sudan. The Comprehensive Peace Agreement (CPA) of 2005 foresaw the disarming of all militia. The army serving the regime in Khartoum and the SPLA rebels were joined by a variety of militias in fighting for the two sides. Several of the militias' commanders can be aptly described as warlords. They were prone to changing sides. This propensity made the security situation in the regions involved virtually incomprehensible. A monopoly on force exerted by a legitimatized government did not exist. Might makes right—that was the principle in the region. If you have a gun, you can get your way. That is why one of the most important objectives of the CPA is to disband these "OAGs" ("other armed groups"), or to integrate them into the SPLA or the government's army. To achieve this, a team of observers has been dispatched. It is being led by the USA's military, and is supposed to ensure the protection of civilians. Sign of Hope is an NGO. As such, we are entitled to report our observations to this team. In fact, we frequently receive from our on-site contacts reports of armed gangs and of conflicts in South Darfur and points farther away in Southern Sudan.

*

Our expedition in 2007 enabled us to prove that two militia were illegally stationed in Raga, notwithstanding the security arrangements forming part of the CPA, which had been ratified two years previously. We were able to speak to both militias' commanders. Major Hassan Mohammed Abo commanded the Quot al Salam militia, which had stationed 3,750 troops in the city. Major Hamdan Ahmed al-Momim headed the Fursan militia, which had 1,320 soldiers.

Our contacts tell us during our expedition in 2008 that the Quot al-Salam militia has lived up to the CPA and has decamped. The Fursan militia is said, although three years have elapsed since the CPA, to still be in the city. In fact, it is supposed to have retained all of its arms. The only difference is that the original commander is no longer there. We have to verify this information.

The barracks that housed the Quot al-Salam militia in the previous year is empty. Except for the empty cartridges strewn all around the barracks' sandy ground, there are no visible signs of the militia. Our trips through Raga also reveal no members of the militia. The Fursan are, however, still around. We confer with the current warlords. They are situated in the same headquarters in which we had spoken with the previous year's commander. The militia's emblem, a tin sign, is still posted on the building's entryway. The commanders state that their army numbers 1,623 soldiers, of which 500 to 600 fighters are in Raga, where they are working as traders in the market or as herders. According to the commanders, all of the soldiers are fully-armed with G3 rifles and Kalashnikov assault rifles. These were purchased for the militia by the regime in Khartoum, which continues to pay them for their services, and to which they are loyal. For this reason, they are prepared to hand over their weapons only to representatives of the Khartoum regime. They would expect to be paid for such. The militia do not want to show us their guns, because they had done so for the UNMIS (United Nations Mission in Sudan), whose representatives had then taken photographs of them.

The militia's heads refer to themselves as "Amir". They tell us that they have heard that a large SPLA unit is making its way from Wau to Raga, so as to disarm the Fursan. They are not prepared to accept that. "We will not hand over our weapons to them. If they want to conduct talks with us, we are not going to say anything. If they want to, we will fight." It is a danger-fraught conflict. Should the SPLA in fact let itself be drawn into fighting with the militia, the ones suffering will be, once more, the civilians.

In addition to the Fursan militia, there are other soldiers in Raga. Two regular battalions are stationed in the city, each manned by 350 soldiers. The battalions belong respectively to the Sudan Armed Forces (SAF)—the army of the Khartoum government and to the SPLA, which used to be the rebels' armed forces. Together, these two battalions comprise a "Joint Integrated Unit" (JIU). This "merger" seems to be working out. We set up a meeting with the commander of the SAF (the Khartoum regime's army). He tells us that the relationship between the two units is good, the fact that they were enemies until January 9, 2005 notwithstanding. He reports that the two commanders sometimes eat together. "There are no tensions between the soldiers of the JIU," he states, "and if there are, it's only when they are drunk." The two battalions have formed a football team. It occasionally competes against other teams from Raga, the commander says. It is as if he wants to show us how normal daily life has already become, despite the decades of civil war. He is also worried about the problem posed by the Fursan, and by the facts that their presence and their being financed by the Khartoum regime represent grievous breaches of the peace agreements. The JIUs have, however, not been given the mandate to disarm the militia.

The successful refusal by the Fursan militia to let themselves be disarmed is an unmistakable indication that the state's authority—and its legitimate monopoly upon force—is not respected in this part of Sudan. The peaceful departure of the militia would help stabilize the region. The Janjaweed mounted militia are still fighting in the Darfur region, and the situation there is accordingly dramatic. The Khartoum regime had equipped the Arab nomadic tribals in the region with modern armaments, and trained them in their use, so to enlist them in the fight against the African ethnic groups rebelling against the regime. These moves were motivated by the regime's views that the Southern Sudanese' demands for rights in and to their lands are unacceptable. The Janjaweed are doing more than fighting against armed rebels. They are oppressing the entire population—through the perpetration of mass murders, plundering and rape.[17]

Khartoum is completely closing its eyes to the countless cases of violations of human rights being committed upon ethnic groups not enjoying their favor. The regime is well aware of the traditional disrespect accorded by the Arabic nomad groups for the peoples of Southern Sudan. This is due to the latter's having other religions and another skin color. It is also due to their being farmers. Khartoum is now ruthlessly exploiting this dislike, in order to pursue its interests. Darfur is home to Arab and African ethnic groups. The latter's religion is a mix of Christianity and of animism. This tradition of coexistence is now to be shattered by the Arabs' purging of the Africans and of their "wrong religions" and "wrong ethnic" ties. This "cleansing" is obviously supported by the regime. It puts an end to the conflict resolution mechanisms that the various ethnic groups had so successfully employed in the era prior to the creation of the nation of the Sudan.[18] The regime in the north was able to sit back and relax, while the uncontrollable violence (or so it was made to seem) was being unleashed against the civilians in the south. To put the situation in a nutshell: the regime in Khartoum opened the hunting season upon these civilians.[19]

In the course of our talks in the refugee camp in Boro, we meet large number of eyewitnesses to the assaults carried out by the Sudanese army and by their paramilitary allies. A number of women from the village of Dafak report having been the objects of a bombardment carried out on May 12, 2007 by the Sudanese air force. This attack forced the women to flee.

A 25 year old woman and her four children have fled. They arrived at the camp only 25 days ago. They belong to the Meziriyah group, and lived in the village of Jokan, which is located in the county of Buram. Mariam and her family departed from their village on the night of the first Monday in the first week in January. She reports that her village was attacked in the night. "They came late in the evening. They were on foot and in cars. They shot most of the villagers, and then burned the village down. We had no one to help us. I took my children and ran away. The attackers shot at me." We asked her if she could describe the attackers in more detail. She said that they wore green uniforms with insignia of rank, and, as well, dark blue caps. The particular targets of their attacks were the Zaghawa, a African ethnic group. The assault had robbed the woman of her 30 livestock and all of her stores of grain. Shortly after our interview with this woman, we were able to speak to her eight year old daughter. The child remembered running away at night, with her mother holding her hand. She also recalled hearing shots.

Several days subsequently, on January 18, 2008, the village of Malaaka, which is located in the vicinity of Rudom, was reportedly attacked. We learn of the assault from another young mother. She fled, along with her three children, from the village to the camp. The woman states that the Janjaweed had attacked the village in the early morning. As she says: "They came at three in the morning. I heard their shooting. I put one of my children on my back and one on my chest. I grabbed the hand of the third one. And we ran away." The woman later learned of her brother's having been shot in his chest.

Eyewitness accounts constitute important evidence. They will thus form part of the report that we will submit to the Human Rights Council of the United Nations on the ongoing violations of human rights by both the militia and by the Sudanese army.

*

What is putting the salt in the region's drinking water? Our search for answers starts in the Thar Jath oil field. We fly on February 12, 2008 from Raga to Leer, which is where we set up our new camp. It serves as our base for our research into the source of the contamination of water. On our day of arrival, we travel from Leer to Adok, which is a port on the Nile. It is a transport node. It joins the roads coming from the oil fields with the waterway to the north. An excellently-maintained (at least until Bentiu), all-weather gravel road links Adok to Bentiu, the capital of Sudan's Unity state. This road makes the oil fields easily accessible. The previous residents of the area have had to pay a high price for the building of this road. Lundin Oil is based in Sweden. In 2000, the company was undertaking sample drilling in the region. Lundin Oil lodged at the time a complaint with the Khartoum regime: the bad roads found in its region of concession would cause delays in its operations. Conducted during the dry season, the next campaigns waged by the regime's troops were against the population in the area. Their settlements stood in the way of the construction of the road. The region was thus efficaciously "cleansed" for this purpose. Tens of thousands of people were either killed or forced to flee. Their villages were destroyed.[20] In 2003, Human Rights Watch submitted a nearly 600 page report on the relationships among these events, and on the causes of the civil war in Sudan.[21] Our enjoyment of this road—after all the bumpy trails that we had been forced to endure—and of the speed it enabled thus gave us a strange feeling.

We proceed on the following morning along the road to the Thar Jath oil field, in which the contamination of the environment was said to exist. We travel northwards down the broad road, enjoying the overwhelming views of absolutely unspoiled nature. The area on whose edge we are now traversing is one of the world's largest contiguous wetlands. The Nile's dividing itself into rivulets whose currents are scarcely perceptible has created a huge delta. With its actual size depending on the amounts of rainfall and of water conveyed from the lake serving as the source of the Nile, these wetlands—the "Sudd"—covers an area of up to 5.7 million hectares. This is the size of Belgium. During the dry season, herders let their large herds of cattle and goats graze in the meter-high grass growing on the fertile ground. The diversity of fauna existing in this gigantic habitat of marsh and flood plain has been compared by experts to that of the Serengeti.[22] Birds decked out in the brightest colors imaginable accompany us on our way. A bald eagle perches directly on the road. Species of birds unknown to us—each more colorful than the one previously—join a lizard about a meter long that is lying bored in the blindingly hot sun in imparting an interesting impression of the diversity found in the region.

In conjunction with the international Ramsar Convention,[23] the Sudd was incorporated on World Environment Day into the list of wetlands of worldwide importance.[24] This made the Sudd the second habitat in Sudan to be accorded this honor, which was conferred in an official ceremony staged in Khartoum. This honor was due to the exceptional importance of these wetlands, which are the fourth largest in the world. The Sudd fulfills all of the criteria foreseen for being conferred such a classification. These criteria are laid down in the Ramsar Convention.[25] The awarding of the status of being a protected area—as narrowly defined—does not, however, ensue from this incorporation. The Sudd's protection is the responsibility of the Sudanese government, which is now called upon to create an appropriate body of rules and control mechanisms.[26]

The Sudd is gigantic. It is comprised of a variety of ecosystems, with these including open water and its underwater vegetation; floating vegetation found on the edges of expanses of water; classic marshes; woods flooded on a seasonal basis; grass hollows irrigated by rain and by floods; meadows; and bush brush. The Sudd is the winter home of species of birds whose protection is of both regional and of international importance. They include the white pelican, whose wings can attain a span of up to 3.6 meters, white storks, crowned cranes and sea swallows. The wetlands are full of plants, fish, birds and mammals. The latter include the endangered Mongalla gazelle, the eland, the African elephant, and the shoe bill stork. Giant herds of peripatetic mammals subsist upon the grass growing in the wetlands during the dry season.[27]

Recently-compiled scientific studies help get a grasp of the biodiversity found in this region. In 2007, the regime in Southern Sudan and the USA-based Wildlife Conservation Society jointly published and presented at inventory—the first compiled in 25 years—of the biodiversity found in Southern Sudan. One of the American researchers involved reported that his first encounter with this richness of flora and flora left him rubbing his eyes.[28] "I thought I was hallucinating," he told the New York Times.[29] The researchers' counts were extrapolated to yield a total of nearly 1.5 million gazelles and antelopes. Among the latter: healthy populations of white-eared kobs, which are found only in this region and in Uganda. The researchers took to the air to observe closely-packed herds of animals covering an expanse of 80 kilometers in length and 50 kilometers in breadth.[30] Sighted in the region were even the oryx antelopes, which had been regarded as being extinct in this area, along with herds of elephants, giraffes, lions and leopards.[31] Crocodiles and hippopotamuses throng the region's lagoons and lakes.[32]

The civil wars in Mozambique and Angola allowed poachers to all but wipe out the wild animals. The researchers thus approached their expedition to Sudan with grave trepidations.[33] The animal population found in northwestern area of Southern Sudan turned out in fact to have been ravaged by poachers. This was also the case in Boma national park, which is located in the southeast of the area. The gigantic herds of buffaloes and zebras had been completely decimated.[34] Reports were received on a frequent basis of the Jajanweed's slaughtering of entire herds of elephants—for their ivory—found in neighboring countries.[35] The Sudd is impassible. And that obviously hindered the region's penetration by poachers. The swamp became the shield protecting the animals of Southern Sudan.[36]

The roads leading to the oil fields intersect the animals' traditional paths of migration. This was a concern of the nature protectors. It took seemingly a miracle to protect the animals from destruction during the war. The animals saved by this miracle are now threatened with being the victims of the post-war era. The Sudd serves another purpose. It makes the region absolutely indispensable. Viewed hydrologically, the Sudd is a huge filter that monitors and normalizes the quality of the water passing through it. The Sudd is like a huge sponge. It thus stabilizes the water's flowage. The wetlands are the main source of the water needed by humans and animals. It is also a rich source of fish. The Sudd's inhabitants belong mostly to the Dinka, Nuer and Shilluk ethnic groups. Their lives, livelihoods and cultural activities are completely dominated by the seasons, and particularly by the alternating between dry and wet weather. The rainy season enables the recovery of the meadows on which the cattle graze. The local people leave their homes upon the commencement on the dry season.

Above | The oil processing facility at Thar Jath, as seen from the air. The facility's main job is separating the oil from such unwanted additives as salt water and sand.
Below | Klaus Stieglitz collects samples of water. The analyses made confirm that the use of ground water in Thar Jath is making people throughout the region sick.

These homes are located in the highlands. They and their livestock migrate to the lowlands. The beginning of the rainy season, which generally comes in May or June, causes them to return to their villages.[37] One of the reasons for the civil war between north and south's breaking out once more was the plan to dry out the Sudd. This would have been done through the building of a canal. It would have enabled the Nile's water to flow to the north.[38] This would have stripped the south's people of the wellspring of their lives. It was as early as 2006 that the exploitation of oil reserves was recognized to be a threat to this unique ecosystem. The pumping of oil was launched for the first time in the same year. Has this peril in fact become—so very quickly—a reality? We are going to look at the mater in depth.

The first evidence of the change takes the form of the rusted signs placed on the side of the road. They indicate the presence of oil fields. The next sight is—fully unexpectedly—the appearance of high voltage lines. We pass every more frequently oil pumps protected by rings of barbed wire. We are now in the middle of the Thar Jath oil fields. And suddenly, from out of nowhere, six smokestacks appear in front of us. Each has a pattern of red and white rings. They form part of the refinery whose construction has been completed a couple of months previously. The refinery has been commissioned a few weeks earlier. Issuing from two of the stacks are dark clouds of pollutants. The unpainted metal expanses found on pipes, tanks and buildings reflect the blinding sunlight. The facility is fenced in. The watchtowers placed on the corners are scary.

We drive past the facility. Six and a half kilometers down the road is Rier, where we meet with lots of the local residents, and takes notes of these discussions. This Rier is new. The old village was destroyed to make room for a facility for the pumping of oil. The town's 3,500 residents were forced in 2005 by the Khartoum regime to immediately leave. The residents say that North Sudan was in control of their region until the beginning of the year. They received neither indemnification nor assistance in the construction of their new homes.

The new Rier feels like a refugee camp. It has hardly anything of a time-crafted homeland. In contrast to other communities, the first step in the building of this one was not the construction of the tukuls—the abode huts—and then the laying out of the paths connecting the clumps of houses. In the "new" Rier, the streets were first laid out in a strict grid. Hutches for the residents were then constructed along these roads. The expelling of these people from their town is yet another alarming breach of basic human rights.

One special source of concern is the quality of the water available for drinking. A hand-operated pump is supposed to transport the water out of the ground. But the residents of Rier do not use this water any more. They assume that the water has been contaminated by the chemicals released by the oil companies. A young girl reports: "The water is bitter. We don't even wash our clothes with it, because the water attacks the colors and destroys the fabric." She thus confirms many accounts of the matter. It was these that caused our contact in the region to voice his growing concerns to us.

We take in Rier our first sample of water on February 13th. It is of the water brought up by this hand pump. We then travel to Koch, which is 23 kilometers away from the refinery. Many of the people we talk to report that their livestock have died and that the water is bad. They are afraid of being called to account for such statements. For that reason, they refuse to tell us their names. "They made all sorts of promises to us: schools, road, supplies. And what have they delivered? Do you see any schools here? What we need is healthful land and clean water, so that we can let our herds graze," says a young man.

We subsequently have a meeting with Colonel Peter Bol Ruot, the Commissioner of the county of Koch. He is holding court in a nicely-furnished and extended tukul. His "court" is strangely old-fashioned. The hut is very clean and neat. An acacia occupies the center of the yard, providing shade. We are offered places to sit—on plastic chairs bleached by the sun. The chair of the lord of the manor has been placed behind a small table. A satellite telephone lies on it. This is the status symbol in this remote region. We feel like we are being received by royalty.

The Commissioner answers our questions in a friendly way. His answers are alarming. In 2006, he states, 27 adults and 3 children died from drinking water contaminated with chemicals. At this moment, up to 1,000 persons have fallen sick due to the water, which has also killed large numbers of livestock. The Commissioner reports having gathered the local residents' complaints and having relayed them to the oil consortium which is the licensee for Block 5A—the local oil field. In three cases, indemnification was paid—"without recognition of culpability on the part of the operator", in the words of another official representative when speaking to the "AFP". No other amends were made, the large number of cases notwithstanding.

Shortly after the meeting with the Commissioner, we encounter a man[39] who works for one of the oil companies. He speaks openly about staff members' wearing of gloves and face masks while they go about tossing chemical wastes into pits that have been dug for that purpose. As the man says, it's now the dry season. In the rainy one to follow, these pits will be flooded. We take samples of the water in the wells in Koch and in that of the marshes along the road from Koch to Thar

Jath, which goes around the refinery. We also do the same in the wells found in the town of Mirmir and in the swamp there. The least distance between the places of sampling and the suspected source of the contamination—the refinery—is 600 meters; the greatest, 32.7 kilometers.

We then bring the samples back to Leer, where we confer with the Commissioner[40] there. Immediately after that, we meet, quite by accident, Dr. Riek Machar Teny and his wife Angelina Teny. Dr. Teny is the controversial vice president of Southern Sudan, which was accorded autonomy in 2005. Ms. Teny has been since 2005 the Minister of Energy in the joint regime set up in 2005 to unite Northern and Southern Sudan on an interim basis. It is a strange encounter. Riek Machar chats a bit with us. He inquires into our fact-finding mission. Notwithstanding this, we have the impression that we are banging our heads against a wall. What we have to say doesn't really interest him, or so it seems. One reason for our skepticism may well be his ostentatious display of power, which reminds us of the suffering of the people in Southern Sudan.

Riek Machar's wife is a highly regarded politician. She stated at a conference in 2006, held in Juba, that there was a problem with the produced water produced by the extraction of oil. As she mentioned, this crisis was particularly pronounced at the old drilling sites in the north. Companies launching operations in the South were on their ways to handling this.[41] That might have thus been one possible reason for her having kept quiet while we related our suspicions.

On the following day, we fly back to Nairobi, where we hold on the subsequent day a press conference. At it, we present the preliminary findings of our expedition and call upon the government of Sudan to take effective action. The statements given by eyewitnesses that we have gathered suffice to prove the existence of a massive damaging of the health of local residents and the environment.

We then return to Germany, where we deliver on February 18th the samples of water to a renowned laboratory, which is to scientifically analyze them. The results confirm our assumption. The water taken from the wells in Rier turns out to be strongly contaminated. The analysis revealed a total amount of salt of 6,600.50 milligrams per liter of water (mg/l) and its contamination with strontium of 6.7 mg/l. The water in this sample evinces nitrates amounting to 81.6 mg/l. The USA's Environmental Protection Agency's recommended ceilings[42] for the total amount of salt permissible in potable water has been set at 500 mg/l. The sample investigated thus exceeds this ceiling 13-fold. The ceiling for nitrate has been established to be 10 mg/l and has thus been exceeded 8-fold. A concentration of nitrates in such amounts can cause infants to take seriously ill. The failure to treat these illness can lead to death. The findings from points of sample collection further afield do not give rise to concerns.

The result is terrifying, since the commercial-scale production of oil in the region has after all just been launched. It has yet to be fully ramped up.[43] The failure to take countermeasures will give rise to a horrible environmental catastrophe in this area. The results of the analysis of the water samples are presented in a press release that forms the subject of a large number of reports in the media in Germany and abroad.

★

→ Further information:
Where does the contamination come from?

Water is of elementary importance in drilling. It serves as the basis for rinsing solutions.[44] This drilling fluids plays a key role in the drilling process because it ensures a disturbance-free pursuing of it. "Drilling fluids" refer to the liquids circulating during the drilling of the hole. These liquids transport the "cuttings" upwards. They also cool the drill bit and shaft, and secure the wall of the drill hole against collapsing. Chemicals are added to the rinse solutions when drilling in non-firm sediments, which in turn characterize the area being described.[45] These chemicals force the formation of a filter crust that seals the porous layers of the rock.[46] This prevents a collapsing of the drill hole. The amount of drilling fluids is to be minimized. The solution permeates the porous layers until the point that they are sealed. The solution has another function. It is to preclude an uncontrolled seepage of fluids or gases from the rock into the drill hole. Reasons of costs also dictate the configuration of the solution's accordance with the respective geological conditions.

To prevent the corrosion of the drill shaft, an oxygen-free environment has to be maintained. The danger of corrosion of steel is negligibly small at pH values of between 10 and 12.5. To accordingly increase the pH values, sodium, calcium and potassium alkalis are added to the solution. In cases in which the pH values are lower in the solution, phosphates, borates, chromates or special tensides have to be added to the solution. The alkalis include KCl (stabilizes clay) and potashes (K_2CO_3).

A number of solution additives have two or more functions to fulfill. The drilling fluids' composition accordingly varies according to the material being drilled: be it bedrock, loose rock, sediments or sedimentary rock. Clay and argillaceous rock are found in and around Thar Jath. This requires the stabilization of drilling holes through the addition of sodium chloride, calcium chloride or potassium sulfate. These additions replace the sodium ions found in clays with potassium or calcium. The result is the reduction of the clays' absorption of water. Potassium-based drilling fluids are especially important when drilling in clays and argillaceous rocks. This is because they optimally prevent the absorption of water—due to the anti-osmotic characteristics of potassium ions—in formations whose makeup is unknown.

The extremely great potential dangers emanating from the use of chemicals in drill drilling fluids cause it to be strictly regulated by internationally-applicable guidelines. Augmenting this peril is another technique employed when extracting oil. Highly-concentrated salts-containing solutions are injected into the oil deposits, so as to increase the pressure in them. The crude oil and the previously-injected salts-containing solutions are pumped to the surface, where the crude oil is separated from the so-called "produced water". The extraction of each liter of crude oil requires the employment of from 3 to 9.5 liters of produced water[47]— an incredible amount. This produced water often has a higher content of salt than does ocean water. The produced water also often contains noxious metals and radioactive materials.[48] The general practice is to inject the produced water—via another injection hole—deep enough into the ground, with this meaning its being transported to layers of rocks that are far away from potable water.[49] Should, however, the produced water be disposed of via in-feeds into surface waters, or via shallow drilling into layers containing ground water, the risk arises that this polluted water will—via wells—be incorporated into humans' food cycle.

That Sudan has this problem has been well-known for quite some time. This problem was the topic at a conference held in Juba in 2006. The conference was about revamping the production of oil in the era commenced by the conclusion of the peace *agreement, and marked by a possible participation in the industry by Southern Sudan.*[50] *This conference showed that Chevron, the US petroleum giant, used the proven—but expensive—procedure ensuring the safe disposal of produced water upon its drilling of Sudan's first oil wells in the period until 1983. Chevron injected the contaminated water into deeply-laying layers of ground. It was Chevron's successors in the country's oil industry that developed the methods yielding the damaging of the environment now becoming apparent to all.*[51] *The oil field at Thar Jath is estimated to contain 149.1 million barrels.*[52] *A barrel of oil is comprised of 159 liters. Taking a mean of 7 liters of produced water per liter of oil, and extrapolating that to account for the entire potential of oil to be transported yields the figure of 1,659,483.3 million liters of waste water to be disposed of.*

*

On March 18, 2008, Sign of Hope sends a letter to the operator of the refinery in Thar Jath. The letter requests the operator to make a statement presenting its position on the results of the tests. This operator is the White Nile Petroleum Operating Company Ltd. (WNPOC). This consortium is based in Khartoum. Some 67.875% of its shares are held by Petronas Caligari Overseas, a subsidiary of Petronas, a company owned by the government of Malaysia; with 24.125% being owned by the India-based Oil and Natural Gas Corporation (ONGC) Videsh Ltd.; and 8% by Sudapet (Sudan National Petroleum Corporation), the Southern Sudan state oil company.[53] Petronas' holding of two thirds of the consortium's equity arose from its acquisition in 2003 of the shares held by Lundin, a Swedish company.[54] Petronas is the most important partner of the government of Sudan in the area of oil production and processing. This applies to all areas of licensing. The company is thus the most influential stakeholder in oil in Sudan.[55]

Sign of Hope's letter courteously requests the operators to comment upon the results of the collection of samples of water, and to elucidate how the wastes arising in the production process are disposed of. The operators are also called upon to detail the measures they plan to institute to provide the residents of Rier with safe water. The operators do not respond.

*

On March 28th, in response to urgings by Spain and Germany, the Human Rights Council of the United Nations publishes a resolution calling for the integration of the rights to have safe drinking water and proper sanitary facilities into the catalog of human rights. The resolution is in response to a report issued by the UN High Commissioner. It states that more than a billion people in the world have been denied access to safe water, and that 2.6 billion people have to endure not having sanitary facilities. The UN High Commissioner has issued an urgent call for the recognition of the right to have clean water as a human right.

An independent expert panel was commissioned to compile a listing of the best practices employed in the procurement of safe and clean water and the arrangement of sanitary facilities. The commission was for three years. It comprised the pursuing of a dialogue with all political and societal stakeholders, with these to include national governments, the UN, and academic institutions and NGOs—and, in this case, especially on-site ones.

Experts on water have been fighting for decades for the recognition of the human right to clean water. These experts view the resolution as constituting an important step towards the achievement of this right.[56] The outcome of the process of identification of rights—now that it has finally been instituted—is to be a legally enforceable right to clean water for each person on this planet.

*

Sign of Hope commissions in July, 2008, Hella Rüskamp, a hydro-geologist, with the conducting of a study on the causes of the contamination of drinking water in the Thar Jath and Mala regions of oil prospecting. The objective of the study is to document or refute the possible connection between the activities of companies that are prospecting for oil (test drilling, treatment and disposal of produced water) and the contamination of groundwater by primarily salts and heavy metals.

*

Everyone expects the final race of this year's Grand Prix season, to be held on November 2nd in Sao Paulo, to produce a world championship for Lewis Hamilton. Hamilton's car is a McLaren-Mercedes. Hamilton is in fifth place during most of the race. This will suffice to put Hamilton atop the year's rankings of the drivers in Formula 1, and thus past Felipe Massa, a Brazilian driver who is leading this race in his Ferrari. The race is somewhat boring—until the second to last round, in which it experiences an unexpected development. Rain starts to fall, causing the most of the drivers to change their tires. While this is occurring, Sebastian Vettel, a German driver, guns his Toro Rosso past Hamilton, surprising him in the process. Goodbye, world championship! Hamilton's best result will now be to rack up the same total points as Massa, who has, however, achieved a greater number of victories this year. This means that Massa is on track to nab the world championship. Hamilton dogs Vettel meter-by-meter, but he doesn't have any way of re-passing the Vettel, who is an incredibly strong driver. Is his dream really over? Ferrari's team in the pits is getting ready to celebrate. One hundred thousand spectators are cheering on their country-person Massa. But then, in what is practically the very last moment of the race, Hamilton and Vettel race past Timo Glock, whose Toyota was in fourth place. Hamilton goes from being sixth to fifth—and thus wins the world championship. He is 23 years old. This makes him the youngest world champion in Formula 1 history. His victory represents the first time since 1999 that a car with a motor manufactured by Mercedes has won the championship.[57]

*

At Sign of Hope we are working at top speed to prepare a further documentation of the contamination found and of its causes. This documentation is to back up the findings of the previous one. The organization's research includes monitoring the Internet. It causes us to encounter the Facebook page of a person working for Central Processing Facility (CPF) in Thar Jath. The page shows us that the gigantic facility—which we thought was a refinery—is actually a plant processing crude oil. At it, the crude is separated from the produced water and sands. The crude is then pumped down a pipeline to refineries in the north, at which it is further processed. An evaluation of the satellite photographs reveals that there are some 70 oil wells in the oil field. They feed the oil to the CPF. This does not include abandoned drill holes, next to which are also to be found pits containing the hazardous drilling fluids.

Sign of Hope has a discussion with one of Hella Rüskamp's staff members. The staff member and Klaus Stieglitz have to travel to Thar Jath as soon as possible. The samples have to be gathered this time by an expert, so as to preclude the arising of any doubts as to the conclusive nature of the samples of water. The forms to be used for the logging of the collection of samples are thoroughly and precisely prepared. We use the GPS data on the sites of the samples made in February to decide where we want to gather them this time. Our approach is to take samples from other wells yielding potable water, from swamps and from sites containing produced water. All of these are to be in or near to the CPF. We also start looking for the waste pits that a worker in the oil fields had described to us in February.

We land on November 12th on a bumpy bush runway in Southern Sudan. Accompanying us on this trip is a correspondent of the "Deutsche Presse Agentur" ("dpa") news agency. Our area of investigation starts north of the city of Leer and extends some 75 kilometers northwards from there. The White Nile forms the eastern geographic and hydrological border of our area. The first sample will be taken some 55 kilometers from the Nile. Scheduled is the taking of samples from a total of 12 wells, and, as well, the gathering of seven samples of surface waters. Of these, it is to be assumed that they might contain residual contaminants. Four of these surface waters are located in the immediate vicinity of the Central Processing Facility (CPF) of Thar Jath.[58] In the case of several wells, the complaints voiced by local residents as to the water occasioned our taking of samples. The hand-operated pumps are also subjected to an appraisal. This reveals that they were all of a kind common in India, that they are all sealed against permeation from outside, and that they all have been placed in a concrete base. A direct contamination from the surface of the well itself is thus to be excluded. The results show that the level of salt found in the wells markedly increases as you move from east to west.

The analysis of the samples taken from potable water pumps in Rier on November 14, 2008 shows their having a total salt content of 6,420 and 6,170 milligrams per liter of water (mg/l). The USA's Environmental Protection Agency has set a ceiling of 500 mg/l. These samples thus exceed this limit 12-fold. A salt content this high drains the body of its water. The resultant dehydration can be deadly. Required to survive it is the immediately supplying of clean water to the body. The samples of water taken in Rier also evince strontium; with one sample also containing lead and traces of cadmium.

But where is this clean water supposed to come from? Many of the residents of Rier, which has a total population of 5,000, fetch water—a moldy stinky swill—from the swamps. They say that it's better than the salty water produced from the wells. "This water tastes salty and causes throat aches," says a local resident in Rier. "You get skin rashes and diarrhea," reports this mother of three children.

A tanker truck containing water comes around occasionally—often less than once a week. This is paid for by the oil companies. The truck holds up to 20,000 liters of water. Twenty thousand liters for 5,000 people translates into 4 liters per person per week—at temperatures of 40 degrees in the shade. The arrival of the tanker truck often causes fights to break out among the people. A woman points to her chin and relates: "This is where I got hit. I wanted to get some water from the tanker truck. People really fight for the water." Everybody wants to get some of the precious liquid for her or his family. And everybody is ready to wrestle, hit and kick for it. This horrible sight is the result of machinations of the oil industry.

The two wells in Rier are not the only ones causing problems. All of the 12 wells from which we took samples showed contamination. Of them, five are so seriously contaminated that they should be closed down or remediated. These five are the two wells in Rier, the one near Mar, and the ones in Bouw and Duar.

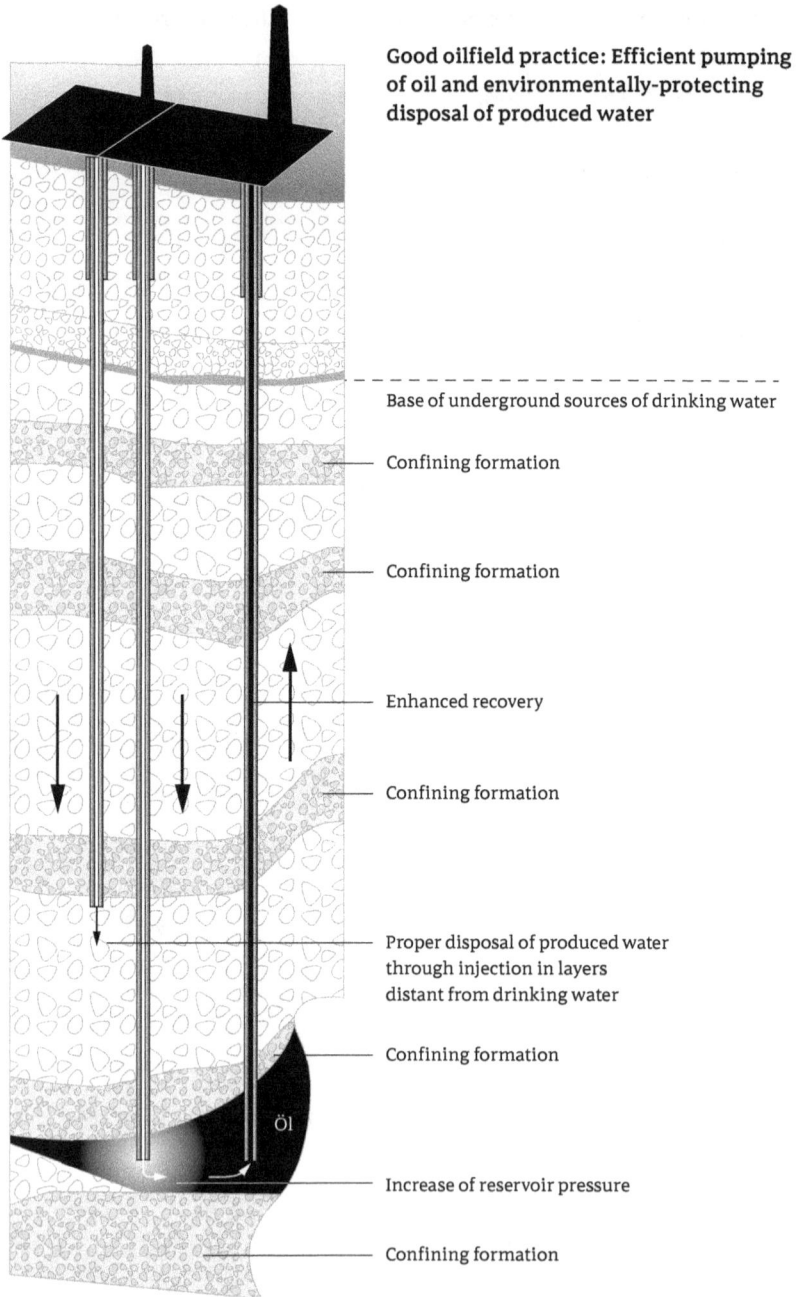

Brine disposal   Oil and gas recovery

Good oilfield practice: Efficient pumping of oil and environmentally-protecting disposal of produced water

- -
Base of underground sources of drinking water

Confining formation

Confining formation

Enhanced recovery

Confining formation

Proper disposal of produced water through injection in layers distant from drinking water

Confining formation

Öl

Increase of reservoir pressure

Confining formation

2009

Questions for an oil consortium

In January, 2009, the Norwegian Directorate for Nature Management submitted its report—also know as the "The Trondheim Report"—on the "Environmental and Social Impacts of the Petroleum Industry in Southern Sudan"[1] to the Southern Sudanese commissioning party. The experts' findings caused them to appeal to the party to conduct as soon as possible a full-scale strategic environmental impact assessment.[2] Their audit of the situation found the treatment of produced water to be especially worrisome: "Our findings are in general consistent with experience in similar environmental circumstances elsewhere, apart from the fact that the volume, viability and sustainability of produced water handling schemes are uncertain.[3] Southern Sudan's biodiversity is both rich and poorly documented. The effects of oil activity on virgin landscapes (especially wetlands) and on plant and animal species are a major concern. Thus arguably of equal importance as a Social Impact Assessment is our recommendation for a major effort to survey and map flora and fauna of the region. We therefore call for a full Strategic Environmental Assessment as soon as possible."

It is for that reason that a comprehensive audit is required. It is to encompass the consequences upon society and upon nature. Produced water, the contaminated by-product of oil production, is dangerous. Several ways in which this water damages and endangers people and animals are clearly apparent. Others are unknown or yet to be adequately researched. These include the water's effects upon specific species and upon the chain of nutrition in general. The method of disposing of the waste water arising from the production of oil involve biological treatment facilities, states the report. Bioremediation techniques remain unproven on the scale with which they have been introduced, the experts criticize.[4] Phytotechnologies are used in Sudan to treat produced water. In theory, this method has been comprehensively researched. Tests of small-scale models have been successfully carried out.[5] The facilities set up and commissioned in 2003 in Sudan are said to be the largest in the world.[6]

The question of why an untested process was selected for deployment in a developing country is a matter of guesswork. Oceans is a UK company. It planned the bioremediation facilities in Sudan. In its brochures, the company emphasizes the long-term cost advantages arising from the process.[7] The 2007 edition of Petronas (Petroliam Nasional Berhad) sustainability report cites the process as being a component of the company's worldwide commitment to protecting the environment, which includes projects to save turtles and mangroves.[8] "Bioremediation is a biodiversity-friendly process that cleans up harmful chemical effluents using natural microbes that live in soil and groundwater."[9]

The Norwegian experts do not allow themselves to be swayed by advertising messages. They emphasize in their analysis that there is a lack of research on how ecosystems are altered through the creation of artificial and gigantic bodies of water. Another point: there is no conclusive answer to the questions of how well the system works when removing the toxic components from waste water and how much accumulation there is of components that resist degradation.[10] The experts conclude by demanding the conducting of an appraisal by certified independent auditors. They thus identify the weak point of the process. This is because the lack of transparency is a further key criticism of the experts. This lack basically precludes any effective supervision. Another consideration is that the people living on such sites often lack the awareness of the dangers posed by waste water.[11] They simply do not understand that the residues left from the repeated treatment of the produced water still poses dangers to them and to their animals.[12]

The Norwegians have also formulated specific proposals to remedy this problem: Better communication and transparency regarding the environmental effects of petro-industrial activities could improve relations between local communities and the oil companies. Operators' oil related activities must comply with Sudanese framework regulations and discharge permits and should adhere to the standards and guidelines of the best international oilfield practice. To ensure compliance the authority should improve and increase auditing activities.[13] These proposals give rise to a single possible inference. The conduct shown by the oil companies and by the local administration does not meet these standards. In view of the history of the matter, the latter's failings are not surprising. All of the oil companies—it should however be noted—are corporations that have a great trove of experience on acting on the international level—and that are thus well experienced in meeting the norms applicable to them, with these including documentation and disclosure requirements.

A report issued by the United Nations Environment Programme (UNEP) shows what the reality actually looks like. UNEP sent its experts all throughout Sudan in the era subsequent to the conclusion of the peace agreement of 2005. Their brief was to conduct a comprehensive environmental assessment.[14] The ensuing report views the treatment of produced water as possessing a problem for the environment. The oil processing facility located in Heglig—already in operation—was inspected in March 2006. The inspectors noted the existence of a reeds-based facility for the treatment of produced water.[15] In November 2006, the inspectors were informed by the ministry responsible for the matter that unknown quantities of produced water issuing from this facility had been fed into the environment—without having been treated.[16] Personnel based on-site confirmed these statements.[17] UNEP's inspectors were told that the reason for doing such was that the produced water treatment facilities were too small to treat the quantity of produced water produced.[18] The operator of the facility in Heglig is still the same consortium, in which Petronas, the oil company owned by the government of Malaysia, holds a stake. Petronas is also the owner of a majority of the equity of the White Nile Operating Company (WNPOC). Petronas has cited the water treatment facility in Heglig as being an example of its commitment to environmental protection.[19]

The consortium still has yet to respond to the queries posed by Sign of Hope on the disposal of produced water in Thar Jath. UNEP's inspectors had noticed something special about this oil field. Unlike the other oil consortia in Sudan, the WNPOC has not been placed under the supervision of the Khartoum-based Ministry of Energy and Mining (MEM) of the Government of National Unity (GONU) and of its regulations.[20] The WNPOC, rather, is monitored by the Ministry of Industry and Mining of the Government of Southern Sudan.[21] This government is, in turn, a holder of a minority stake in the consortium via Sudapet, (Sudan National Petroleum Corporation) the state oil company. The evaluation of the activities of the consortia and the performance of the ministry concluded that the consortium is effectively self-regulated.[22]

UNEP's experts issued an urgent recommendation to Sudan's joint government: it should commission UNEP or another independent institution with the compiling of an environment assessment of the extraction of oil[23]. Another recommendation: the results definitely have to be made public.[24]

The Trondheim-based organization also submitted proposals to their commissioning parties—the former Southern Sudan rebel army—calling for the issuing of the report to the general public.[25] This hasn't, however, happened. Experts have had to employ indirect means to gain access to the study issued by the Norwegian Directorate for Nature Management.

*

Sign of Hope re-contacts the WNPOC on February 20th. The organization provides the oil consortium with a paper comprised of several pages. It presents a detailed elucidation of the analysis of the samples of water gathered. It delineates the concrete dangers emanating from the many contaminants found in the water. The paper establishes that the extreme salination identified by the scientific investigation increases the closer one comes to the oil fields. Along with the presence of strontium, heavy metals and PAHs in several samples, this leads to the conclusion that the water in the samples has been contaminated by produced water or by drilling fluids. Sign of Hope accuses the WNPOC of inappropriately treating waste waster. The consortium is also informed that its failure to do such gives rise to both a dangerous threat to the local population and to the prospect of an environmental catastrophe in the Sudd.

"In that context we kindly ask you to fully and unconditionally protect the environment—notably surface and ground water from contamination by toxic chemicals. We would be very thankful if you conducted petroleum operations in accordance with international good oil field practice in terms of health, safety and environmental standards. Drilling water must not be discharged into rivers, swamps and on the ground.

We would also like to point out that your company should feel responsible for improving the quality of drinking water dramatically."[26]

The consortium is also requested in a friendly way to pay indemnification to the residents of the "old" Rier for their having been forcibly relocated. The organization also proposes to the WNPOC its participating in water rehabilitation projects. Sign of Hope also repeats its offer to the oil company. Both could jointly work to identify how the local population could be provided with access to clean drinking water. After having summoned the WNPOC to adhere to the water quality regulations applicable in Sudan, Sign of Hope concludes by demanding information on how the WNPOC is handling the disposal of produced water and of other noxious chemicals. Sign of Hope also requests being briefed on what the consortium is doing to provide the population in Rier and other communities involved with palatable water. The consortium does not respond.

*

Sign of Hope sends in April another team to Southern Sudan. The exclusive purpose of this trip is to investigate water-related problems. One of the team's members is Dr. Hella Rüskamp. The German hydro-geologist requires the taking of further samples for the second phase of her study, which is to distinguish between the chemical makeup of the water found in the region's nature and that of the contaminated liquids. This distinguishing will exclude there being any geological reason for the samples' striking findings. The way in which the chemical make-up of natural bodies of water distinguishes itself from that of the water stemming from wells contaminated with salts is constituted by minerals. Geological conditions can cause the former kind of make-ups to vary. An object of the further scientific investigation is the reduction of hydrogen carbonate. This will enable the identification of chlorides, whose seepage into the upper drinking water aquifer could result from the addition of potassium chloride to drilling fluids and to produced water.

*

→ Further information: geological, tectonic and climatic conditions

Hella Rüskamp has commenced her scientific classification of water by determining the nature of the geological conditions of the area to be investigated. The African continent has a Pre-Cambrian basement. The base of rock is actually the oldest on Earth. It is largely covered by sediments that have been subsequently deposited. This covering rock has a thickness of up to 13 kilometers. In Sudan, this rock is comprised of chalk sediments. These include Nubian sandstone and the deposits made in Tertiary and Quaternary periods.

The area to be investigated is located in the Guit, Koch and Leer regions of Southern Sudan's Unity state. Geological maps indicate the existence of two formations. The first is "Umm Rawaba". It came into being in the late Tertiary and Pliocene (Early Quaternary) period. This formation is comprised of unhardened sands featuring portions of gravel, clay (loam) and shales. The Umm Rawaba has thicknesses ranging up to 3,000 feet (900 me-

ters). The correlation of the lateral spread of this formation is impaired by its tendency to rapidly change its characteristics.

The maps report that the second formation is the "Alluvium". This is an old way of referring to the Holocene, which is the most recent period of the earth's history (Quaternary). The Holocene is comprised in Sudan of wadi fill-ins, terraces, river deltas and swamp deposits. "Wadi" refers to a dry valley that transports water on a temporary basis in cases of strong rains. "Terraces" are formed on riverbeds. As is the case with wadis, they are largely comprised of such sediments as sand and gravel. River deltas and swamp deposits are generally made up of finely-grained sediments. Holocene deposits are unhardened.

Located between the basement and the Umm Rawaba formation are continental clastic sediments of the Cretaceous era. These are produced by the weathering and erosion of rocks[27] and are comprised of sandstone, siltstone, claystone and conglomerates. The Bentiu sandstone is up to 1,550 meters thick (it is also referred to as the "Nubian" sandstone). This oil bedrock dates back to the Cenomanian era[28].

Viewed tectonically, the area of investigation forms an inland trench pond. This pond opened itself from the Early Jurassic to the Late Cretaceous periods. This area, in turn, forms part of the Central African systems of ponds. The opening of the pond enabled the commencement of its filling with continental chalk sediments. The increasing inflow of fresh water caused deposits to form in wadis, swamps, lakes and rivers. This took place in the Tertiary and Quaternary periods. The predominant orientation of clefts and currents is NW-SE, and, in a subordinate role, NE-SW. Groundwater flows in a northeasterly direction in our area of investigation.

Widely-applicable, the geological and tectonic findings enable the compilation of a general profile of the layers in the area of investigation. The actual thicknesses may not accord to this. Also possible is the existence of gaps in the layers. This would entail the area of investigation's lacking the individual layers presented in the generalized profile. A precisely-delineated profile of the layers found in the upper 500 meters, which is where the groundwater is located, has yet to be compiled. This depth of drilling has been set on a preliminary basis. This is due to the assumption that all the wells found in the area of investigation do not come close to exceeding this depth. The layers are comprised of unhardened, clastic sediments of all possible grain sizes. Sand is the main constituent mineral. To be investigated is how these Quaternary and Early Tertiary sediments perform their function of transporting groundwater. There is groundwater in the depths below the Umm Rawaba formation. There is also fossil water in the Nubian sandstone. The tapping of this water requires very deep drilling.

Data on the climate is also required to hydro-geologically assess the region. The area of investigation has a mean temperature of between 26 and 28 degrees Celsius. This temperature give rises to the assumption of a high rate of evaporation. This assumption is confirmed by the fact of there being rain forests, wet savannas and swamps in the region. The tropical nature of this climate is emphasized by the mean annual rainfall falling on the region of 600–800 mm. During the rainy season, precipitation can amount to 1,600 mm. The rainy season is very short. Very little rain falls—sporadically—during the rest of the year. This pattern endangers the groundwater. This is because the compilation of this natural resource is limited in scope. Groundwater that is close to the surface has come into being in the area of investigation through the inflow of water from the Nile and from its flood plains.

*

Sign of Hope's staff members are about to start commence a new activity for us. We will scout for the sources of the contamination. At this point in time, we are not sure exactly what we are searching for actually looks like. Suspicious sites are virtually impossible to identify from the ground, especially since there is so much of this to be covered. We therefore charter an airplane, one whose prime is long gone. The pilot is an old wild Englishman whom we have known for a long time. A cinema fan would say that the setting is reminiscent of the flight scenes in "Out of Africa". To chart the best possible route for our reconnaissance by air, we have spent—at home in Germany—hours at our computers or peering at maps. We want to take a look at the Central Processing Facility (CPF), to see if we can find a place to collect samples of the waste water flowing off the facility. We also want to see if the birds' eye view reveals something unusual in the vicinity of the villages ringing the CPF. We are also still looking for our needle in a haystack—the pit containing chemical wastes.

Our aircraft—a Dornier 228 that is not air-conditioned—flies low—only 200 meters—above the ground. This enables us to search for abandoned bore holes and waste pits. On board is a team from the Reuters news agency. The air in the plane is oppressively hot, thanks to the heat radiating from the ground and from the thermic displacement that it causes. These are bubbles of hot air that rise—invisibly—from the surface. As they do such, they shake the aircraft. A flight marked by tight curves, a hot interior, thermic displacements. And, while enduring this, repeatedly glancing at the map, taking photographs and operating electronic devices. A lot of stomachs quickly have a hard time dealing with all of this. Although arduous, the air-borne reconnaissance enables us to make a range of pertinent findings, ones that traveling by car through the Sudd would not have produced. This is thanks to the high ranks of reeds flanking the area's gravel roads. These reeds serve as walls blocking lines of sight. To overcome this, one has to climb on your car's roof—or board an aircraft.

We ask the pilot to fly as close as possible to the CPF. We get breathtaking photos—close-ups and overhead views of the CPF's complex waste water treatment systems. For each liter of crude oil pumped and transported via a pipeline to the north, the CPF has to separate from an average of 7 liters of other materials—water, chemicals and sand. The produced water has to be disposed of. The first stage of treatment outside the CPF takes place in retention ponds. The fluids in them contain so much oil that the pond's surface has a thick, thoroughgoing layer of oil floating on it (oil floats on water). This oil is fed back by workers wielding vacuum hoses into the CPF, where it is incorporated into the process of separation. Oil is too valuable to be wasted. The produced water in the retention ponds is then fed into the evaporation ponds. The water is evaporated in them. Salts and heavy metals can not evaporate. These materials form a residue on the bottom of the pond. As far as we can see, this pond is not sealed, for example with a plastic lining, and is thus not effectively separated from the ground beneath it. For that reason, we consider the evaporation pond to be nothing more than gigantic seepage pits, from which the noxious components of the produced water make their way into the upper potable water aquifers.

After having inspected the CPF, the aircraft flies for another two hours, along the route prepared by us. Its flight plan repeatedly takes it along a variety of the corridors bisecting our area of investigation. We thus fly along water flowages that are easily recognizable from the air. These flowages are in swamps. Also highly visible are areas in which waste water could be fed into the flowages. Easy to recognize from the air would also be the pits dug by humans. A map of the region on the knee and holding a GPS device, a member of our team sits next to the pilot in the cockpit. Anything unusual is pinpointed on maps using GPS data. This will enable us to find the places marked when we look for them while traversing the area on the ground.

We are still looking for our needle in the haystack—the waste pit that the staff member at the oil plant had told us about during our latest trip to the area. Does this dump actually exist? The flight is almost over. We are sitting in the tight quarters of the Dornier aircraft. We are covered in sweat. We are over the stretch of land north of the village of Koch, and we already preparing ourselves for the landing. Should we put our passengers through another tight curve? We ask the pilot to flight over Koch at a low altitude. Suddenly, a poisonously green pond is to be seen through the plane's window on the right side. The pond's water has a color that is completely different from that of the other ponds. We quickly realize that this has to be an abandoned drilling site. One of our team quickly and instinctively grabs his single lens reflex camera. He rapidly clicks 20 photographs. The important thing is not to forget to enter the GPS data. We expeditiously establish a waypoint. We will make sure to pay a ground-side visit to this abandoned drilling site. It is our first and major opportunity to get a sample from a pit containing drill fluids, and to thus compare it with others. When subsequently looking at the photos, we notice that the drilling site is being neither protected by security personnel, nor does it have a fence around it. The drilling site in Koch will become very important.

We subsequently drive across the region, so as to investigate the possible sources of contaminants marked on our map.

It turns out that many of the pits located next to the roads that we considered to be those containing liquids from drilling are actually borrow pits excavated in the course of building or improving roads. Finding the sources of the contamination of water is a difficult process. Many of the ponds that have the telltale lurid green and that were discovered from the aircraft subsequently turn out to be uncontaminated.

The second phase of the study is designed to resolve several issues, the first of which is: The salt found in the wells' waters display—viewed geographically—an increasing concentration, meaning it rises as one heads westwards from Bouw to Duar, Rier and the CPF. Is the cause of this phenomenon geogenic or anthropogenic? The second issue is our attempt to verify or falsify a link between the waste water produced by the oil industry and the contamination of drinking water, and to scientifically prove such. To achieve this, the compositions of minerals characteristic of various types of water are to be compared with each other. Our field work will lead to our having to compare six types of water with each other: salts-laden well water from the upper aquifer, waters from uncontaminated wells in the upper aquifer, waters from the deep groundwater aquifer, waters from natural surface-level bodies of water (rain-fed and swamp ponds), water from the produced water ponds located in the vicinity of the CPF and water from the pits containing drilling fluids. A third thrust of our work is the assessment of the current state of the peril to which the population is being exposed. Our fourth thrust stems from our decision to conduct an exploratory drilling. This will enable our compilation of a geological profile. This, in turn, will facilitate the planning of the drilling of new potable water wells.

We collect a total of 19 samples during the trip. This starts in the village of Bouw, and is set forth in Pakur, Rier, the CPF,

In order to get a comprehensive picture about the composition of a water sample, the laboratory requires a specific amount of water per sample. The water of one single sample is to be distributed on several vessels. In order to analyze specific parameters correctly the sampler has to add stabilizing agents to some of the vessels. The photograph shows an example of a complete water sample taken by Sign of Hope in the year 2008.

Koch and the site of the exploratory drilling. The area of investigation is to the north of the city of Leer. From there, it extends northwards to the villages of Bouw and Kilo 50. The area forms part of a large-sized swamp and flood plain, and is subject to amounts of precipitation varying strongly with the seasons. This means that a special thrust of the investigation is to be the concentrations of a diversity of trans-regional parameters—such as salts and nitrates—and their variations during the dry and rainy seasons. The samples made in November 2008 were undertaken at the end of the rainy season; the current ones at the conclusion of the dry season. The main causes of the influx of nitrates are to be seen as lack of sewage treatment infrastructure and of sanitary facilities. We inform once more the local population of the need to fence in the wells and to keep livestock away from them, as doing such will prevent feces' landing in the immediate vicinity of the wells, from which it would permeate down to the subterranean structure of the well and to thus to the drinking water.

It is early in the morning of April 24th. The sun is already displaying, however, its ascendant power. We have just returned from a walk around the village of Rier. We are now in our tents.

"Move, it's going to happen," calls our interpreter, a lanky young man who belongs to the Nuer ethnic group, to us. He runs up to us saying. "The commissioner is going to provide us with police protection. We have been given permission to visit the refinery."

That's all we need to hear. Our equipment is ready to go. We quickly grab our backpacks, camera bags and vessels for the storing of water samples, and jump into our rickety car. We bump down a trail that does not deserve the term "road". Our goal today is the refinery of Thar Jath, where we will really need police protection. Our plan is to take samples of water directly on the refinery's premises. We believe that the wastes stemming from the refinery are seeping into the groundwater of such villages as Rier. The refinery's security forces could well be opposed to our taking of samples from this controversial site. The "police officers" sitting in our car are two young guys, who have just turned 20. Both are wearing colorful shirts, and each has an AK-47 Kalashnikov—a Russian automatic rifle—draped over his shoulder. We have for many years criticized Sudan's lack of civil structures ever since the bloody civil war came to end. We are being accompanied today by police officers. They represent the government and personify its legitimate monopoly on force. For us, this constitutes—at the very least—a small sign of hope, an initial step forward.

We get out of the car and start hiking. We have all of our equipment on us. One of the objectives of our aircraft-borne inspection of the region was to precisely determine the location of the pools filled with produced water. We were successful. This now enables us to efficaciously make our way through the bush and high grass, and to get to one of the two large evaporation ponds. A hike of 20 minutes brings us to a fence fortified by barbed wire. The two large-sized evaporation ponds are behind it.

It is just before noon. The persons accompanying us lead us to a gate, upon which a couple of staff are conducting welding work. A quick exchange of words between the police officers and the workers, and we are suddenly on the premises of the oil company. Things start happening fast. We work together to open the vessels, which we then fill with the water found near the ponds' banks. We quickly log the date and time of the sample, record the GPS data, put everything away, and then head quickly out. Our speed comes from our have trained this procedure. We need three minutes to fill a set of samples. This is comprised of 8 bottles.

Having the police to get you through the door is an opportunity that may never come again. We take advantage of the opportunity by gathering samples of the water in one of the retention ponds. It is located in the immediate vicinity of the CPF. Our orientation guides us perfectly. It takes us only a few minutes to reach the pond. Our airborne exploration proves to have been the perfect preparation. A fence is now standing in the way of our getting the sample so desired. No one is around to open the gate. "Access only by authorized personnel" is the message on a sign. We are in a hurry. One of the young men from the village of Rier recognizes the situation as providing him with a way of getting a water sample. Moving quickly, the young beanpole grabs a set of samples, and, while being watched by our police friends, rolls himself under the entry gate. He then strolls unperturbed to the pond, where he collects a full-scale sample of water for us. This brings the total number of sets of samples taken of the water from the produced water basis of the CPF to three. This should yield—at the very least a good quantity of data.

We have commissioned a certified scientific laboratory in Kenya with the analysis of the samples of water. The analysis strongly indicates that there is a direct connection between the waste water released from the refinery and the contaminants proved by us to be found in the well water. To be noted: the refinery is just one of many sources of contaminants. It is highly probable that the 97 oil wells in Thar Jath also contaminate the groundwater.

It is the morning of April 25th. We are about to leave the village of Rier. We are in time to see tanker trucks arrive to fill plastic containers with water. This forms part of the potable water supply program being undertaken by the oil industry in Thar Jath. We take a sample of this. The water stems from a facility that uses chlorine to produced water from the Nile. We visit the facility's managers. They promise us that the potable water is produced in accordance with "recognized guidelines". We pose the question of what kind of treatment is used—such as filtering, reverse osmosis or something similar? None of these, report the managers. The only thing done to the water is adding chlorine to it. The results of the testing of the sample indicate that this so-called "drinking water" has considerably-sized residues of chlorine compounds.

We head toward Koch (photographs on the right), in order to find the luridly green pit. We did record the pit's GPS data while on our reconnaissance flight. We were not, however, completely directly above the pit when securing this data. Will we be able to find the pit containing the drilling fluids notwithstanding this? A small road splits off from the main one to Koch. Our GPS device tells us that the waypoint that we established while in the airplane is but a few hundred meters away. We are gripped by "hunting fever". Everyone in the car quiets down upon our turning on to a small road. This excitement is followed by a mood of disappointment. The road ends 100 meters on. It is in the middle of nowhere. We are getting ready to turn around. We then suddenly realize that the end of the road is in a clearing in the thick brush. Is the pond perhaps in there? The only thing we can see is a wall of mounded earth some two meters high. We quickly jump out of our car and climb carefully up the wall. It encircles a pit full of drilling fluids. We yell "hello" to indicate that we have reached our objective. The coordinates are N 8° 38' 8" and E 29° 58' 49.9". We want to forestall our young interpreter's clambering down the steep, unsecured wall, but he beats us to the punch. He rushes down to the wa-

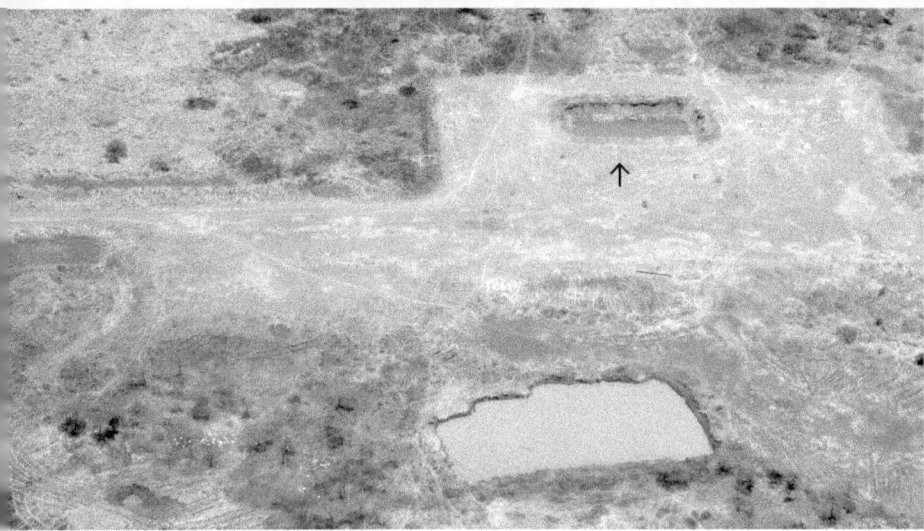

The abandoned pit containing drilling fluids is found in Koch. It was discovered during a reconnaissance flight (bird's eye view). The liquid contained in this pit is so contaminated with noxious pollutants that Sign of Hope refers to this pond as the "poisonous pit of Koch".

ter, grabbing a couple of water sample bottles along the way. He then fills them with the drilling fluids using water in the pit. It takes him quite a bit of effort and a couple of slips and slides that nearly give us heart attacks, but he is soon standing in front of us, the filled bottles in his hands. We want to chide him for his youthful recklessness, but we can't really manage to do so.

*

Some 3,000 readers of "Hoffnungszeichen" ("Sign of Hope"), our monthly magazine, stage at the beginning of June an unusual protest. They dispatch postcards that we created to Omar Hassan al-Bashir, the president of Sudan. They call for the protection of ground and surface waters in the country's oil fields, and for an improvement in the supply of potable water to the people involved. We send on June 30th another letter to the WNPOC. We do not get a response.

*

Our next expedition to Southern Sudan takes place in November 2009. Its purpose is to investigate the wells in the northern part of the region—in the vicinity of Nhialdiu, Bentiu and Guit. The trip is also to lead to the analysis of the drilling fluids issuing from the test drilling sites in the oil fields of Mala and Thar Jath. Our objective is the determination of the extent of the contamination of potable water in the northern reaches. This expedition is also being preceded by a reconnaissance flight. This will enable us to to identify and thus later quickly re-find as many mud pits containing drilling fluids and abandoned drilling sites as possible. Accompanying us on the trip is once more a team from "AFP". A freelance journalist is also part of our team. He writes for the "Frankfurter Rundschau" (a Frankfurt-based daily newspaper) and other media. We are on another low-altitude flight over the CPF. We make this time a curious discovery. We have heard that a large-sized facility for the treatment of produced water is to be built. Our flight enables us to establish that this facility is gigantic. It occupies an area some four times greater than that of the CPF itself. Our "birds-eye" view permits us to see that black foil has been placed upon several of the ponds of the facility, which is still under construction. The photographs taken from the plane seem to show that the foils' surfaces are already ripped. This observation provides us with a strong reason for taking a close, ground-side look at this.

On November 9th, we visit a hospital in Bentiu. Bentiu is the capital of Unity State. The hospital has 120 beds and was built by the oil companies, which then transferred ownership of it to the Sudanese government, we are informed. At the facility, we meet with its medical director, its director of finances and administration, and with patients. The physicians tell us that the most common ailments are malaria and diarrhea. The hospital has 3 to 10 patients a day. The victims of diarrhea are generally children. Patients suffering from such serious ailments as yellow fever or kidney disturbances are flown by the WNPOC to Khartoum. The hospital in Bentiu does not charge patients for treatment. As the patients tell us, they do themselves have to pay for their medications.

The physicians tell us that most of the patients come from Koch and Rier, and thus from the immediate vicinity of the CPF and its related production facilities. The two hospital staff members have been informed of the salinity of the potable water, and are aware of the problems arising from the drilling fluids at the drilling sites. They are also conscious of the grave danger posed by the contaminants to the groundwater.

The staff members report an overall increase in the number of persons falling sick. Even more pronounced has been, they say, the losses suffered in the herds of cattle. The number of dead cattle has been rising constantly and significantly.

Our next stop is the ministry of health, where Klaus Stieglitz delivers several copies of the reports compiled from the results of the samples of water that we took. He also presents the work of Sign of Hope in Unity State. We brief the director of health in the region, on the results of our analysis. We have taken more than 50 samples of water in Thar Jath and environs. We report on the composition of the chemicals in the produced water released from the refinery and in the large number of noxious substances-containing ponds found at each oil drilling site. We emphasize that these chemicals and salts—plus such poisons as boron, barium, nickel, cadmium and iron—are on their ways into the upper layer of drinking water. High concentrations of salts and of poisonous lead have already made their way into many wells. The non-contaminated waters of the region do not contain such salts and lead. As we point out, the results of the analyses of the water wells in Rier, Pakur, Bouw and many other villages constitute proof of this.

Dr. Hella Rüskamp, the German hydro-geologist, is accompanying us on this expedition to the oil fields. Dr. Rüskamp elucidates for the director of health in the region the scientific causes and effects of these matters. She details the overwhelming proof of misdeeds. Her elucidation goes on until deep in the night. Her elucidation covers "ion balances", "the chemistry of water" and the comparability of this and that sample. The director of health confirms the existence of another report, about which we have already been informed by people living in our area of investigation. The report states that a number of people have died from consuming a "white powder". Three of these victims were reported to be children who died in 2008. It should be noted that nobody has gathered all the facts of the matter. Nor has anyone scientifically investigated the causes. We are especially interested in population figures, as obtaining these will enable our determining how many people are affected at all by problems with drinking water. We ask for and get the figures. The director states that the areas most seriously affected by contamination are Koch and Guit, followed by Rubkona.

He sounds somewhat resigned as he summarizes the results of our intensive talk: "We learn each week of new outbreaks of acute diarrhea. There is nothing that we can do about them. We would probably today be better off had oil not been found in our ground. I thank you in the name of the suffering people here for your efforts."

*

The European Coalition for Oil in Sudan (ECOS) is based in the Netherlands. On November 11th, the Coalition sends a draft of its report on the involvement of oil companies in violations of the human rights of the people living in Sudan's Block 5A. The report goes to former members of the Lundin Oil-led consortium, and to the governments of the countries in which these companies operate. The research conducted by European NGOs has revealed a large number of violations. Sweden's Lundin Oil, Malaysia's Petronas and Austria's Österreichische Mineralölverwaltung (OMV) are being called upon to respond to these. Lundin Oil disputes the charges, and provides responses to their individual points. Lundin CCs its response to Petronas and OMV, both of which had held shares in the consortium. Neither responds.[29]

*

We proceed upon our expedition to Southern Sudan. Our plan is take more samples from the drill fluids found in the abandoned pit near Koch. The pit creates a noxious smell. During our last visit to it, we lived in perpetual fear of falling in while taking a sample. To traverse the steep embankment, Klaus Stieglitz acquired suitable equipment from a store for mountaineering gear in Germany. Since Stieglitz is not a climber, he has had to be instructed in the use of hooks, ropes and eyelets. He has practiced Abseiling in his home's staircase.

Klaus Stieglitz is compiling a diary of this trip. His entry for November 12th is later published in the monthly magazine issued by Sign of Hope. This article, in turn, provides the organization's many supporters with a detailed look at what its teams actually do in the field:

I practiced at home each and everything that I would need to do with the climbing gear. I got very familiar with its employment. It's now time to put this new expertise to use. I am standing at the poisonous pit of Koch, from whose water we took a sample a half a year previously. I snap the last of the karabiner. I start descending. My objective is to reach the surface of the water. My backpack contains the bottles for the samples, rubber gloves and a mouth protection mask. I reach the muddy bank of the pond. I look for a safe place to stand, and find a rusty pipe. I quickly fill the bottles. I take a final look at the surface of this little lake. I know how much poison is contained in this body of water, since we have already taken samples of its water. Notwithstanding my wearing a mask over my mouth, I can still smell the water. It reeks of mold, lack of life, death and poisons. I am overcome by a feeling of helplessness. This is because I am not able to stop the poisonous water that I am looking at from making its way—drop by drop—into the ground. I want to put an end to this seepage, but I can't. Unfortunately.

I perform an initial quick test on the banks of the pond. Its only findings are that the water exceeds the ranges measured by this device of analysis. What this means: the pond is still extremely gravely contaminated. The poisons have already been incorporated into the upper aquifer. They will find their way into the potable water of many thousands of people, some 300,000 of which live in the immediate vicinity—some 50 kms x 80 kms in size—of the oil fields of Thar Jath and Mala.

The people suffering most from the contamination of the environment caused by the oil industry are the people living in Rier. They have to contend with the contamination stemming from the more than 30 oil wells already drilled, and from the immense pollution issuing from the refinery in Thar Jath, where produced water laden with salts and heavy metals is disposed of in inappropriate ways. We have taken a number of samples proving the presence of these substances in the wells in Rier.

Sign of Hope wants to drill a deep well. It will enable us to tap another aquifer, which probably still contains clean water. Our objective in doing so is enabling people to be accorded their right to clean drinking water, a right stripped by the oil industry.

We arrive on November 13th at WNPOC Base Camp, where we confer with the staff member responsible for its Community Development Program. This program comprises the provision of medical treatment, the handling of its logistics, the pursuit of development activities for women and for the young, and the conducting of a health enhancement outreach. The program also maintains a container in Rier. It dispenses medications and enables the treatment of minor health problems. Rier's residents tell us that this container is occasionally staffed by a medical practitioner.

We run into the Apostolic Administrator of the Diocese of Malakal just before our departure from Southern Sudan. The

Southern Sudanese received in 2006 his doctorate from Universita Urbana in Rome. This is the papal university.[30] We conduct a very deep talk. The Catholic priest then addresses a few words to the "AFP" journalists: "I see nothing coming out of the oil. In the north, where the oil is going and the refineries are, there is an economic boom. But the production areas which should have benefited first have no services, no development. There is nothing and on the contrary, things have got worse. Oil could have been a blessing for Southern Sudan had it been used properly, first for the development of the area where petrol is produced, and then the rest of the country, but it's exactly the contrary that is happening."[31]

*

Sign of Hope publishes on November 16th a press release. It is simultaneously released in Nairobi and Singen, Germany. It informs the public about the organization's trip to Southern Sudan, and makes it aware of the problems of contaminated water.

Hoffnungszeichen | Sign of Hope e.V. is an organization dedicated to preserving human rights and providing development assistance. The organization recently undertook a six-day trip to the oil fields of Thar Jath and Mala in Southern Sudan. This provided the organization with further scientifically-based proof of the contamination of the region's groundwater by oil companies. Klaus Stieglitz is vice chairman of Hoffnungszeichen e.V. Stieglitz presented this finding, and elucidated how the study producing it was compiled. He also presented the details of the organization's trip to the oil fields. "The exploration of oil in the fields of Thar Jath and Mala joins with the production of such at the Central Processing Facility (CPF) in constituting a grave peril to the region's people, their animals and their environment.

We had previously carried out a detailed and scientific analysis of the various samples of water taken from oil facilities and drinking water wells. We recently conducted quick tests. They delivered information substantiating our previous findings. According to these, the produced water stemming from the CPF is a proven source of contamination. Another source of pollution is constituted by the chemicals used in the process of drilling for oil."

These two sources of contamination have already reached the layers containing potable water. Dr. Hella Rüskamp is a German hydro-geologist. She is part of the Sign of Hope's team. Dr. Rüskamp explains: "The chemism of the water in the samples (meaning their characteristic chemical composition) taken at the CPF is the same as of that of the water found in the wells located in the villages in the vicinity of the facility. The composition of the water of mud pits containing drilling fluids evinces practically the same hydro-chemical composition as that of the samples that we took in the villages. The water at the drilling pits also shows an extremely high concentration of salts and of such elements as cyanide, chrome, lead, nickel, cadmium, boron, strontium, barium and arsenic. The first quick tests were made at another drilling pit confirm our previously-compiled findings. According to them, the pollutants have already reached the first layer of potable water. I have found high concentrations of salts in such potable water wells as those in Rier, Buow, Pakur and Guit. Also found in several samples of potable water were lead and chrome. By way of contrast, the natural bodies of water have an entirely different water chemism. Natural bodies of water evince virtually no heavy metals. They also have a substantially different distribution of minerals.

The contamination stemming from the mud pits at drilling sites and the CPF has already made its way into the potable water layers. The most alarming findings came from the samples made of the water in the wells at the village of Rier. This village is located in the immediate vicinity of the oil processing facility, and where both sources of contamination of water are found. They are compounding each other in the area."

The contamination has a serious and highly negative impact upon the daily lives of the local people. The residents of the village of Rier are no longer able to use their wells. In the large number of villages located near the oil production and processing facilities, the local residents complain about their water's saltiness. People drinking this water are in danger of suffering a lasting dehydration ensuing from diarrhea. A failure to treat this causes the sufferer to die. The concentration of heavy metals in these bodies of water will give rise to further negative ramifications upon the health of the some 300,000 people living in the region affected. This region comprises some 4,000 square kilometers. Sign of Hope's team also found unsealed pipes at two abandoned bore holes. The pipes are thus conveying oil to the surface.

Klaus Stieglitz is Sign of Hope's vice chairman. He urges the regime in Khartoum and the WNPOC oil consortium to expeditiously take remedial action: "Thar Jath is experiencing a human tragedy. The people living in several of the villages in which we took samples of water are no longer capable of drinking the water from their wells. This means that they do not have access to clean water. We are particularly calling upon the WNPOC consortium to dispose of the produced water in appropriate ways. This will put an end to the arising of any further danger from the contamination of the drinking water. In addition, we are also asking WNPOC to immediately begin with the remediation of the oil drilling pits and of the strongly-polluted water they hold. We are also calling upon the consortium to ensure that neither humans nor animals have access to these bodies of water. The oil companies are charged with immediately taking the actions necessitated to *avoid an environmental catastrophe encompassing the world's largest swamplands.*

Sudan's government is called upon to promptly implement the measures required to set up a state system capable of monitoring and supervising the quality of potable water. Sudan's oil fields can not be allowed to remain a legal no man's land, one that is being left unsupervised by the regime in Khartoum for purposes of fostering the oil business. Sudan has formulated standards that apply to drinking water. These now have to be effectively implemented. Our appeal to Sudan's government encompasses its ensuring that the oil companies operating in Southern Sudan comprehensively and unconditionally institute measures that protect the environment, with this particularly applying to the shielding of surface and groundwater from contamination by noxious chemicals. Based in Khartoum, Sudan's government has recruited oil companies for operation in the country. To ensure the health of the population, the government has to greatly improve the quality of drinking water. It also has to prevent an environmental catastrophe."

"Voice of America" and the "BBC" report on the same day on the intolerable conditions prevailing in the region. Their reports are based on our findings.[32/33]

*

It is also on November 16th that Dieter Zetsche, Daimler's CEO, announces Mercedes' takeover of the Brawn GP Formula One racing team. For the first time since 1955, a Mercedes team will be competing in the Formula 1, which is the major leagues of automobile racing. This will commence in the 2010 season.

*

A large number of international media join in reporting on our findings in Southern Sudan. "The Guardian" issues on November 19th a series of photographs of the situation.[34] "TAZ" is a German daily. It runs on November 22nd an article on this environmental scandal.[35] In the article, Petronas is described as being the leading member of the consortium coming in for such strong criticism.

*

The WNPOC's initial response comes on November 24th. It is occasioned by a query lodged with it by the Business & Human Rights Resource Center. This international observation organization is headquartered in New York and London. In its query, the Center made reference to the report broadcast by the "Voice of America", and asked the WNPOC to comment on it.[36] The WNPOC categorically denies the charges made by Sign of Hope. [Translator's note: the following English shows great deficiencies. In the interest of the accurate quoting of it, no corrections have been undertaken.]

WNPOC categorically denies and resents recent accusations by Sign Of Hope (SOH) alleging that WNPOC's operations have caused water contamination as they are baseless and unjustified. Further WNPOC conducts its operations in close cooperation and under the auspices of the Ministry of Energy and Mining (MEM). It has been WNPOC's policy to always adhere to international HSE (Health, Safety and Environment) standard in carrying out its operations and strictly emphasise on zero pollutant and discharge, in sensitive ecological areas, such as the Sudd Swamps. This policy is fortified by the certification of WNPOC HSE's adherence under the ISO 14001 (for Environmental Management System).

The EIA [Energy Information Administration] *carried out for Block 5A reflected that the underground water in the Sudd Pond has a naturally high salinity. Soil analysis proves that the nature of the soil, in the area, has negligible permeability, thus virtually eliminating vertical and horizontal migration. The alleged elevated concentrations of the "contaminants", reported by SOH* [Sign of Hope], *do not bear any resemblance to our Produced Water samples.*

Mindful that the natural characteristics of the water around that area is saline which is reflected in our EIA Report WNPOC, as part of Community Development, built a water treatment for the local communities. With regards to the mud pits, all of them are back filled and covered according to international standards and practices.

As a responsible operator, WNPOC continuously conducts tests and monitors the quality and properties of the Produced Water from our operations. In addition WNPOC conducts regular internal audits, gives full co-operation and is transparent to the Government of Unity and Government of Southern Sudan whenever they require information or conduct visits. In addition the oil industry operation in Sudan including WNPOC, had been audited by a Norwegian Directorate For Nature Management. WNPOC has also been informed that an international and reputable consultancy company (a third party) is being appointed by the MEM to conduct a fact finding study, in relation to SOH's allegations. In short WNPOC has always strictly complied with all the environmental regulations, procedures, and international best practices in carrying out its operations.[37]

*

Sign of Hope countered on November 27th the consortium's attack by issuing a further press release.

The German human rights organization Sign of Hope hails the initial statement from the WNPOC consortium on the contamination of drinking water in the WNPOC's area of operation. The following constitutes Sign of Hope's response to the WNPOC's statement.

Singen/Germany—Sign of Hope's chairman, Reimund Reubelt, is welcoming the fact that WNPOC (White Nile Petroleum Operating Company Ltd, Khartoum) is now publicly addressing the issue of contamination of drinking water sources in part of Unity state, Southern Sudan: "We appreciate the fact that WNPOC finally has decided to address the public concerning the contamination of drinking water in its area of operation. After having seen the first analysis of water samples in early 2008 we have repeatedly and continuously addressed WNPOC to come into a dialogue about this issue with no reaction from their side so far. That is why we are welcoming this first reaction from WNPOC. Nevertheless the WNPOC press statement which was circulated on November 25, 2009 still requires a response from our side:

In its statement WNPOC is labelling our findings as 'baseless and unjustified', which is not true from our point of view. In order to assess the sources of contamination of the near-surface aquifer and of surface water we have taken more than 50 water samples in the vicinity of the oilfields of Thar Jath and Mala. Those samples were scientifically analysed by an internationally accredited laboratory, based on the WHO drinking water standard. Samples of possible contamination sources also underwent scientific analysis. By drawing the results of the analysis, we were being assisted by Dr. Hella Rüskamp, a Senior German hydro-geologist. In order to assess the potential danger and in order to localize the contamination of drinking water, we have taken many samples at drinking water wells in literally all major human settlements in the region. Moreover we have taken numerous samples at sur-

face water bodies. We did so before and after rainy season in order to examine a possible natural salinity by evaporation."

Taking that into account Dr. Hella Rüskamp is stating: "There is no significant difference in results of the water samples when we compare the samples taken before and after rainy season. That means there is no reason to believe that the salinity is of geogenic origin. We were able to characterize a natural distribution of minerals which we found at surface water bodies and at non-contaminated drinking water wells in that region. The mineral distribution in naturally occurring waters is dominated by bicarbonate (HCO_3), sodium, magnesium and calcium. The portion of chloride is considerably low in naturally occurring waters.

In contrast to that water, wells that show a high degree of salinity have a completely different mineral distribution. These samples are dominated by sodium-chloride with a low portion of bicarbonate. In the contaminated water wells salts come along with considerable concentrations of heavy metals like lead and chromium.

Samples of produced water flowing off the Central Processing Facility (CPF) and samples of mudpits showed a literally identical mineral distribution as contaminated water wells did. That means that there is clear evidence for a direct correlation between disposed waters and the contaminated water of the upper aquifer. The ponds for the produced water nearby the CPF are not sealed with plastic sheets so that a permanent infiltration of salts and other contaminants will diffuse into the water aquifers and the concentration of contaminants will steadily increase there."

Rüskamp is concluding the results: "Drinking water wells that are contaminated with salts are located in areas with unpolluted surface water bodies and with bio-environmentally intact plants. From a hydro-geological and from a geological perspective there is no considerable origin of geogenic salinity in this area.

A major source of contamination are the mud pits at the more than 30 oil-boreholes. In order to keep the salts and the chemicals of the drilling process from seeping into the ground the mud pits should be fully lined with plastic sheets. We have inspected several abandoned oil boreholes. We have seen several abandoned bore-holes where there was obviously no plastic lining at all. We have taken liquid-samples of mud pits of two of those boreholes. The drilling fluids contained extremely high concentrations of salts, pre-dominantly potassium chloride (TDS: 47,200 mg/l; electrical conductivity: 78,800 μS/cm). That means that the drilling fluids in these mud pits have not been removed after cessation of the drilling process as WNPOC was pointing out. The drilling fluids also contained high concentrations of contaminants like boron, lead, barium, strontium, nickel, cadmium, chromium and iron. Heavy metals like chromium and lead could already be found in considerable concentrations in contaminated water wells. These heavy metals could not be found in naturally occurring waters in that area.

Even after rainy season the water levels in the mud pits have fallen significantly which gives evidence that there is no naturally occurring barrier layer of fine sediments. On the contrary: There is an obvious infiltration of the contaminated drilling fluid into the upper aquifer."

Klaus Stieglitz, Sign of Hope's vice-chairman, who led four fact-finding missions to the area, adds: *"WNPOC is claiming that all mud pits are 'backfilled and covered'. When I was travelling through that region this month I could spot from the air several abandoned boreholes which were obviously not backfilled and covered. Together with my team I inspected on the ground two of those locations where the drilling fluid re-mained in unfilled mud pits. Those mud pits can be found at N 9°6'44,7"; E 30°7'19,1" and N 8°38'8"; E 29°58'49,9". There is open access to these* mud pits which are a danger for human beings and cattle. Moreover these mud pits were obviously not lined with plastic sheets."

Concerning the so called "bioremediation plant" close to the CPF, Stieglitz says: "When I was visiting the area in April this year I appreciated the construction of this plant as a positive step taken by WNPOC. When I returned this month I had to see that large parts of the plastic sheets were completely torn up and pulled into pieces. This remediation plant will not work without a proper plastic lining."

Reubelt is concluding Sign of Hope's position: "We are very willing to enter into a dialogue with WNPOC that aims at ending the contamination of drinking water as this would be of help for the suffering local population.

Besides that, WNPOC's argumentation could not convince us. After having studied the consortium's statement we still have good reason to believe that the water quality for the local population would be better by far if WNPOC had disposed waste water properly. We are wondering why WNPOC does not spend a single word on the issue of heavy metals in its statement. In naturally occurring waters there are literally no heavy metals. On the other hand we have found considerable concentrations of heavy metals like lead and chromium in the contaminated water wells. These heavy metals can also be found in the drilling fluids of the mud pits. Can there be more obvious evidence? Instead of hiding behind certifications and well-sounding policies WNPOC would have been well-advised to give answers to these questions.

According to our findings both produced water flowing off the CPF in Thar Jath and waters found in drilling pits at oil wells are major sources of contamination. To that end we urge WNPOC to make sure that the newly erected remediation plant will work properly. The torn-in-pieces plastic sheets have to be replaced by *an in-tact plastic sheet lining. If this is not the case this remediation plant is not more than window dressing.*

Moreover we repeat our previous recommendation directed towards WNPOC to immediately rehabilitate the highly contaminated water in the oil well drilling pits and make sure that neither human beings nor livestock can have access to these waters. Whereas our organization has shown concrete and substantiated results of analysis to the public, WNPOC has only produced claims which have not been substantiated so far.

In that context we ask WNPOC to make their environmental impact reports public and include analysis lines that show the chemical composition of produced water before treatment and after treatment in the remediation plant. WNPOC claimed that all mud pits were back filled and covered according to international standards and practices. We must doubt this. That is why we finally ask WNPOC to publish a documentation in which the consortium is describing if and how it has removed drilling fluids from the mud pits and if and in which way these fluid have been disposed. This would be a more constructive approach than superficially refuting our findings. It is not our aim to blame certain companies for their environmental misbehaviour. It is our aim to stop the pollution-input in order to prevent an ecological catastrophe. WNPOC's 'zero-pollution-policy' is a good idea. WNPOC should start to implement it."

No response followed. WNPOC does not release the EIA report for perusal. Nor does the consortium prove how the report, which is being kept secret by top management, and which supposedly confirms the environmental compatibility of the conditions of oil production in Thar Jath, differs from the one compiled by the Norwegian Directorate for Nature.

*

In its edition of December 14, 2009, "Handelsblatt" issues an exclusive report stating that Mercedes' participation in the Brawn Formula 1 racing team has gotten it involved in a cheating scandal.[38] The acquisition of a stake in the team made Mercedes a party to a contract of sponsoring concluded with Henkel, a Germany-manufacturer of detergents.[39] Henkel committed itself in July 2009 to sponsor Brawn's Formula 1 team starting in 2010. The three-year contract foresaw a donation of € 30 million.[40] The contract was signed for the Henkel group by its head of sponsoring activities.[41] At the time of conclusion of the agreement, Henkel's staff member had been engaged for a long time in fraudulent activities. These involved the trading in counterfeit receivables to be paid by the company. These were written on Henkel letterhead that had been stolen.[42] The staff member earned millions. These stemmed from factoring companies.[43] On October 19th, he turned himself in.[44] It turned out that there were suspicious circumstances associated with the contract of sponsoring. Henkel's managing board states that it was not aware of its commitment to support Formula 1. It therefore declares its contract with Mercedes to be null and void.[45] "Handelsblatt" learns from well-informed sources in Mercedes that the company is insisting upon the fulfillment of the contract.[46]

*

On December 17th, the analysis of the samples of water collected by us in November 2009 has been completed by a scientific laboratory. We find several values unsettling. A sample taken by our organization on November 11, 2009 of water from a well in Rier is proved by the laboratory to have 0.58 mg of lead per liter. The analysis of a sample collected on November 13, 2009 of water from a well in the town of Koch shows a level of lead contamination of 0.59 mg per liter. The World Health Organization has set the guideline value of 0.01 mg per liter of potable water.[47] This means that the water in Rier and in Koch exceeds this ceiling 58-fold and 59-fold respectively. An analysis of the drilling fluids contained in a pit near Koch reveals that this liquid, which was collected on November 12, 2009, had 2.06 mg of lead per liter.

*

On December 21st, Mercedes' Grand Prix team announces the conclusion of a long-term contract with Petronas, the Malaysian oil and gas company.[48] Starting in 2010, Petronas is to be the main sponsor of Mercedes' racing team. Petronas' name will be affixed to it.[49] The team will thus commence its first season in Formula 1 under the name "Mercedes GP Petronas Formula 1 team".[50] This agreement means that the Silver Arrows and their drivers' clothing will sport from now on the easily-recognizable Petronas logo.[51]

Daimler's press release goes on to state that this is the basis for a new partnership. It will be between Mercedes-Benz, which has a long and successful history in automobile racing, and Petronas, which plans on being a long-term player in the field. This partnership will pave the way for the forging of an even more extensive working relationship between the two companies, states the release.[52] As the release puts it, by entering into a strategic partnership and business relationship with Mercedes-Benz, Petronas, an oil and gas company, will be provided with a way of expanding its operations—with this especially applying to the after-sales market for lubricants—on a sustained basis.[53]

In an article published on the same day, Germany's "Frankfurter Allgemeine Zeitung" daily newspaper reports that Petronas will be spending more money during the term of its long-term contract than Henkel's head of marketing had promised to enable the comeback of the Silver Arrows.[54] The article's author notes that Petronas could afford to do so.[55] Daimler has disclosed Petronas' key indicators in its press release. Owned by the Malaysian government, Petronas had sales of $US 77 billion in financial year of 2008/2009, and a profit of $US 15.3 billion.[56] The McLaren and Lotus Formula 1 racing teams had also tried—in vain in their cases—to secure funding from the Malaysian company,[57] as had the Sauber team. The latter had been, along with BMW (prior to its withdrawal from the Formula 1). a long-term partner of Petronas.[58]

*

On December 23rd, in a teleconference with journalists, Mercedes confirms the truth of the rumors that have long been flying around:[59] Germany's Michael Schumacher, who has won the world championship seven times, will return to the Formula 1 for the 2010 season, and thus three years after having ended his career in the competition.[60] Schumacher, one of the great legends of automobile racing, will drive one of the cars forming the Mercedes GP Petronas Formula 1 team, along with Nico Rosberg. He is also a German. The country's racing fans are ecstatic. The real Silver Arrows are finally back[61].

Yesteryear's Formula 1 heroes—
Juan Manuel Fangio talking to
other drivers

2010

Enter Daimler

On January 25th, the new Mercedes Petronas (Petroliam Nasional Berhad) GP team is officially presented to the general public. Venue for such is the Mercedes Museum in Stuttgart.[1] The
throng of media is so large that not all of the journalists find
a place to sit. TV stations start their live coverage of the event
prior to the official beginning, so as not to miss a single thing.
Six hundred people attend the event in person.[2] "This presentation of our team represents a new and certainly the most important chapter in the more than 100-year history of Mercedes
and racing," states Norbert Haug, the head of Mercedes racing
team.[3] Dieter Zetsche, Daimler's CEO intones: "We are putting
the final touches on Germany's national Formula 1 team." He
adds: "We are entitled to be a little bit proud of our country".[4]
Virtually all of the media in Germany report these statements.
The parties involved have set their sights on a single objective: winning the world championship.[5] The team's drivers are
Michael Schumacher and Nico Rosberg. They wear the team's
new racing uniform, upon which—breast-high—the name of
the team's new main sponsor—"Petronas"—is emblazoned in
large letters. The sides of the race cars, which bear the new de-
sign, also display the name.

★

We are enthusiastic viewers of Formula 1. And we are impressed by the revival of the Silver Arrows, which are truly a racing legend. Our grandparents and parents have described the thrill arising from such names as Caracciola, Rosemeyer, Fangio and Stirling Moss. We ourselves watched Niki Lauda, Ayrton Senna and his ilk. The hype unleashed by Michael Schumacher's winning of the world championship had the same effect for Formula 1 that the victory achieved by Boris Becker at Wimbledon had on tennis and the staging of the FIFA World Cup in Germany had on football: the sport has become part of the country's collective narrative. Mercedes' recruiting of such a widely-liked person for its team is thus very clever. But does that apply to its forging of a partnership with a company such as Petronas? Mercedes likes to advertise its environmental friendliness and its support of sustainability. Perhaps we should simply ask Daimler how it views our findings, which detail Petronas' responsibility for the contamination of the environment in Southern Sudan.

*

On February 5th, the article "The victims of the boom" is published in "Frankfurter Rundschau". It reports on Sign of Hope's trip to Sudan in November 2009.

*

On February 15, 2010, the Bündnis 90/Die Grünen party lodges a parliamentary query in the Bundestag.[6] The formulation of the query was managed by the office of Kerstin Müller, an MP. We met with one of Müller's staff members in Berlin. At the meeting, we gave him an in-depth briefing on the environmental pollution of Thar Jath, and on what we discovered about it. The party then commissions the conducting of further research on the situation. They use the results to put together an impressive picture. They also show why such a country should not be forced all by itself to wage war on environmental pollution. The party's account of what is going on in Southern Sudan incorporates the fears of international observers, who perceive the ongoing destruction of the environment in such places as Thar Jath's giving rise to an ever-greater destabilization of Southern Sudan. This is because armed conflicts frequently ensue from strife on such environment-related issues as access to clean water and good grazing areas. Such observers are concerned about the imminence of an "environmental war" in Southern Sudan, which, like the one in the Niger delta, could lead to crimes against humanity.[7] The query asks Germany's government to answer 15 questions. Doing such will establish whether or not the government will dedicate itself to improving the situation in Southern Sudan (described in the query), and, if so, how it will go about doing such. A thrust of the party's query is rapidly bringing about an expeditious intervention in Thar Jath, which is the venue of the scientific proof compiled for the contamination of water being perpetrated by the oil industry.

*

Germany's government responds on March 2nd to the parliamentary query.[8] Its answer shows that the government is aware of the findings of the investigation of the drinking water carried out via a commission from Sign of Hope.[9] The government shares, by and large, the views of the party. In key differences, the government rejects the idea of launching national or international-level efforts for Unity state in general or for Thar Jath in particular. The government's position is that the problems affecting Southern Sudan can be solved only by creating and implementing a concept encompassing all of Sudan and forming part of Germany's development work as a whole. The government gives a positive answer to the question of whether or not a further independent investigation would be an efficacious way of assessing the real scope of contamination.[10] While doing such, the government puts the investigations conducted by Sign of Hope in its place. It cites the counter-arguments offered by oil companies. These especially include the tests of water listed by the White Nile Petroleum Operating Company (WNPOC) and showing low levels of pollution. The government also mentions the "independent assessments" performed by the Norwegian Directorate for Nature Management, by Sudan's Ministry for Energy and Minerals and by other institutions of on-site potable water supply.[11]

*

The government fails to respond to one of our main points of criticism, which is that we have not gotten to take a look in the appraisals claimed to exist. Has the WNPOC actually carried out these investigations? If so, do they say what WNPOC claims they do? Our data is available for all to see. It was and can be verified by scientific methods. The accountability of our work also applies to the testimony provided by the local population affected. There is a positive side to the government's response. It confirms its taking the topic of water supply in Sudan very seriously. The government also announces that it will pursue this objective, which is a component of its development work. We know what this means. It might take some time for something to happen. We have to find other ways—concrete measures—of expeditiously helping the people living in Unity.

*

We get in touch on March 11, 2010 with Daimler AG. Motivation for doing such comes from the statements made by this corporate group as to the protection of the environment's being a key objective. Daimler is one of the founding members of Kofi Annan's Global Compact,[12] and, as such, has incorporated all of the principles formulated by this international business initiative into its own code of conduct. These principles include the protection of the environment. Entailed in this is the verification of business partners' also adhering to the rules that Daimler has imposed on itself by being part of the Global Compact.[13] We are sure that this paragon of ethical actions will give a fair hearing to our case. We thus write a letter to Daimler's CEO.

Dear Dr. Zetsche,

We followed with great interest the media's reports on the presentation on January 25th of the Mercedes GP Petronas Formula 1 team.

As you no doubt know, your partner Petronas is actively pursuing in Southern Sudan the production of crude oil. Sign of Hope is an organization devoted to protecting human rights and rendering assistance. Our partners in Southern Sudan asked us at the end of 2007 to investigate the drinking water there. This is because they had received reports that a number of people there have taken sick, even died, after consuming the water in wells located near the sites of oil drilling and extraction. Assisted by a German hydro-geologist, we have made several trips to the region. During them, we have collected more than 50 samples of water. The scientific analysis of the samples of water revealed that the upper potable water aquifer is contaminated by wastes stemming from oil production. We are permitting ourselves to enclose in this letter the two statements made to the Human Rights Council of the United Nations. These statements summarize our position.

The region in Southern Sudan is called "Thar Jath". It is here that the White Nile Petroleum Operating Company is active. The WN-POC is a consortium, in which Petronas holds a 68.9% stake. We have already made several attempts to directly contact the WN-POC. They were not successful. The reports that we have issued to the public have been covered by "CNN", the "BBC", the "Voice Of America", "dpa", "AFP" and many others. The WNPOC responded to this by issuing a public statement. It does not want to talk to us on a one-on-one basis. We are enclosing a selection of clippings in this letter.

We are well aware of the importance that your company places upon environmental protection, innovation and security. This emboldens us to voice our wish to enter a dialogue with you in your role as the partner in Germany of Petronas. We would request your elucidation of your position in this matter.

We are of course ready to meet with you. Please feel free to contact us should you need further information.

Best regards from Singen

We send on the very same day a letter to Michael Schumacher. It is identical to the one sent to Daimler—except for one thing. We tell Michael that we have often experienced the following when traveling through the most remote areas of Africa. When we introduce ourselves as being German, the local residents very often respond by addressing us as "Michael Schumacher". His successes as a race car driver have served as a bridge to the people in Africa. This is not a bit of flattery. The respect and interest accorded to this man is scarcely to be believed.

*

The first race of this year's Formula 1 is on the track at Manama, Bahrain. It is held on March 14th. Michael Schumacher's return to racing after a break of three years is being closely followed. This is not surprising. From Kerpen, Germany, Schumacher has won, after all, seven world championships. This makes him a legend among drivers. The return begins acceptably. Michael Schumacher starts out the race—his 250th in the Grand Prix—from seventh place. He betters that to sixth by the end of the race. This earns him eight points in the ranking of the drivers.[14] Formula 1 experts see that Mercedes' race cars do not yet have the chops to seriously compete with the technically-perfected vehicles operated by Red Bull, Ferrari and McLaren. Schumacher is also very satisfied with his result. The subsequent races will show what still needs to be achieved by technology. Something that everybody is already aware of: Nico Rosberg, the other Mercedes driver, is currently the better one of the two. He finishes the race in Bahrain precisely one place ahead of Schumacher. The test runs have already revealed that Rosberg is a faster driver than Schumacher. The former won every training session in which Schumacher, holder of all records involving the Formula 1 championships, also competed. Mercedes race team views the results achieved by Schumacher and Rosberg as being a major success.[15]

*

It is the beginning of March and African Water is once more heading to Africa. After a long internal discussion, Sign of Hope has decided to dare to drill a deep water well. To that end, we have commissioned African Water with doing such. Its mission will last three months. Its success is uncertain.

*

On March 22nd, the USA's Department of Justice charges Germany's Daimler AG with corruption. The charges arise from years of investigations. They have convinced the Department that Daimler used bribery to secure lucrative orders during the period 1998–2008. According to the indictment, Daimler has breached US laws on corruption in 22 countries.[16]

*

At the hearing on April 1st, Daimler and the USA's Department of Justice agree on a settlement. It spares the company a long and drawn out trial. To achieve this, Daimler renders comprehensive admissions of guilt, and commits itself to satisfying a large number of stipulations and to paying a penalty of nearly $US 185 million. The documents published by the Department reveal that it took months of work to prepare the settlement.[17] Daimler's willingness to participate and to make comprehensive concessions to the Department were motivated by the company's wish to avoid the fate of Siemens. Its bribery trial in the USA cost the group a total of more than € 1 billion.[18] To avoid that fate, Daimler, one of Germany's showcase companies, prefers to be listed for a period of several years as a convicted offender serving a sentence on probation. This sentence is subject to the strict supervision by the USA's Securities Exchange Commission and Department of Justice.[19]

*

The third race in the Formula 1 one season is the Grand Prix of Malaysia. Petronas has been since 1999 the main sponsor of the race. After having finished second in the qualifying session, Nico Rosberg really steps on the gas for the race. He starts the race, which is held on April 3, 2010, from the first row. After having recorded strong times during the training rounds, Michael Schumacher experiences problems with his tires during the qualifying session. He overcomes a miserable start to snare

Sign of Hope commissioned the drilling of six deep wells, and thus proved that it is possible to find clean drinking water, with this even applying to the oil field of Thar Jath. You just have to drill deep enough.

Above | Children playing at the deep well in Rier. A solar-powered pump transports the water into an elevated tank. This yields the pressure needed to send the water out of the taps at the outlet.

Below | Deep well in Rier

eighth place at the starting gun. The loss of a wheel nut causes him to leave the race in its tenth round. Rosberg finishes the race in third place, with makes him part of the victory celebration. The Mercedes team is getting a bit giddy from its successes.[20]

*

African Water commences on April 7th the drilling of the first of the solar-powered deep water well commissioned by us. The well is in Bouw. The hydro-geologist commissioned by us has conducted an analysis of the geological formation in our area of investigation. It has convinced her that a further groundwater reservoir has to lie well below the upper aquifer. Proof of her analysis comes only in the form of the water shooting out of the hole drilled.

The team drilling the well is comprised of Kenyans, and include a master and an assistant driller, a mechanic and an electrician. The team is backed up by a German master driller and by Hella Rüskamp, our geologist. Auxiliary work is handled by local residents, as they have been teached.

The drilling of these wells requires the employment of special-purpose devices. One of them is Salzgitter's Multidrill RB 225. It is sent by ship from Germany to Kenya, and then trucked on nerve-wracking roads to the region. The fact that the upper potable water aquifer is contaminated by chlorides, sulphates and heavy metals means that the drilling has to ensure that no "short circuit" ensues between the upper aquifer and the one thought to exist much deeper down. To achieve this, a fluid finder is deployed. It takes samples of the second, lower aquifer.

The drilling finds water more than 200 meters below the surface. Analyses reveal that it is fossil in nature, and that is suitable for drinking, with no limitations on this. The investigation shows that the aquifer is not supplemented by an influx of ground water. This means that its quantity is finite. The investigation does, however, find that this reservoir is large-sized in nature. The amount of water that can be pumped up suffices to make it worthwhile to create a deep well. This will soon provide the population of Bouw with access to clean water. The well-drilling crew is ecstatic. Is this the way to solve the problems shared by other communities in the region?

The construction of a well costs some €200,000. Such a well suffices to supply some 3,000 people with water. We are not financially capable of drilling deep wells capable of providing water for all of the people affected in the region. But we now have a way of showing how this crisis is to be solved. Other parties are going to have to defray the costs of drilling the requisite wells. These are the parties causing the contamination. The only problem is that they are not yet ready to live up to their responsibilities.

*

We get a response to our letter to Dieter Zetsche, Daimler's CEO. A company staff member calls us up. He has been commissioned by Zetsche with the commencing of a dialogue with us. We find the fact that we have yet to receive a response in writing to be somewhat curious. But the staff member charged with dealing with us is obviously interested in what we have to say. Several friendly telephone calls are followed by Daimler's first written response—an E-mail with his contact information.

We now officially know that one of Daimler's senior managers has been charged with the responsibility for our concern. And we also know that this manager handles CSR (corporate social responsibility), and that this, in turn, is part of the

External Affairs and Public Policy area. This means that we are talking to the right person in the organization, one who is very prominent in it. We view "Corporate Social Responsibility" as being the societal conscience of Daimler AG. We are looking forward to working with the company.

Something is finally happening!

*

We receive on April 30th an answer from Michael Schumacher. Written on his personal letterhead, his letter states that he is aware of our being in contact with Dr. Zetsche, and that this topic is being handled by the company's CSR department. For that reason, he "would want to ask us to pursue this matter with it." We had not expected to receive such a friendly response from him. The letter indicates that either he or his office did launch an inquiry at Daimler's headquarters, so as to find out what our concern is about. The fact that he went to such procedure is highly appreciated.

*

The highly promising telephone calls with the manager who is responsible for us at Daimler causes Sign of Hope's team to confer at our organization's headquarters in Singen, Germany. Our goal is to decide what we want to achieve with Daimler's assistance. We agree that the most important thing to be attained is to get a look at the documents about which the WNPOC claims that they do exist and they do prove how well and honestly the consortium operates in Thar Jath. We regard these claims as being adventurous. They also prevent official bodies from undertaking all requisite measures.

On May 20th, we send a letter containing these points to Daimler. In the letter, we request access to the documentation of the procedures employed by Petronas/the WNPOC when disposing of produced water and of other wastes ensuing from the production of oil. A second step would be our verification of their properly implementing the procedures documented. Doing this, in turn, necessitates the conducting of field work. Can Daimler get this done? In our letter, we propose a date for a personal meeting. The date is in the immediate future.

This gives rise to a further round of telephone calls with Daimler AG, which is headquartered in the Untertürkheim borough of Stuttgart. In the calls, we learn that Daimler views itself as being the intermediary of communication between Sign of Hope and Petronas. Daimler wishes to set forth its dialogue with us. The company tells us that it has learned of the WNPOC's plans to hire a Norwegian consultant. This, in turn, will chronicle its findings on the WNPOC's environmental performance.

*

The European Coalition on Oil in Sudan (ECOS) publishes in June its final report on the comprehensive research it has conducted on the participation by non-Sudanese companies in crimes perpetuated against the population of Sudan.[21] The report is entitled: "Unpaid debt. The Legacy of Lundin, Petronas and OMV in Block 5A, Sudan 1997–2003". It raises telling accusations—and provides well-substantiated proof of such. Objects of the report's criticisms are the oil companies and, as well, the governments of the countries in which the members of the Lundin consortium are headquartered. Due to the requirements that they have entered into—on the prevention of violations of human rights—they should not have made any investments in a country gripped in civil war.[22] These countries are Sweden, Austria and Malaysia, and they are called upon to launch investigations that will identify and bring the guilty to answer in a court of law.[23] The report is taken up all throughout the world, generating articles in the "Washington Post" and the "New York Times" and other influential media, and unleashing a wide-ranging public debate in Scandinavia. Sweden's state attorneys commence what will become a comprehensive investigation. The governments of Malaysia and Austria do not, however, respond to the criticisms. Nor do their countries' oil companies—Petronas and OMV—answer them. The area of concession covered in the ECOS report is Block 5A, and is thus the same one in which Sign of Hope has proven the existence of an alarming damaging of the environment. Petronas Caligari, a 100% subsidiary of Petronas, which itself is owned by the government of Malaysia, was originally the "junior" partner of the Lundin-operated Sudanese oil consortium. As such, the former also was involved in the latter's misdeeds. Since Petronas Caligari's acquisition of the stakes held by Lundin itself and by OMV in 2003 and 2004, Petronas Caligari now owns 67.875% of the renamed consortium, which is now called the White Nile Petroleum Operating Company (WNPOC). The ECOS report presents a wealth of facts. They prove that Petronas Caligari has obviously been responsible for many more abuses than the ones substantiated by us. The public debates on the Sudan always refer to the consortium as being the "Lundin" one,[24] thus causing Petronas and OMV to be kept entirely out of the public eye. The Scandinavian public[25] remains highly interested in cases of involvement by European companies. The accusations levied against Petronas and OMV are, conversely, scarcely covered in their home countries' media.

*

On June 21st, Sweden's state attorneys announce that they have commenced an inquiry. Its purpose is to investigate the accusations raised by the report issued by ECOS against Lundin Oil. This inquiry is confined to the Swedish parties possibly involved.[26]

*

On July 20th, we—Reimund Reubelt and Klaus Stieglitz, the two members of Sign of Hope's executive board—make the two hour trip from Singen to Stuttgart's Untertürkheim borough. We are to pay a visit to Daimler's headquarters. After having passed through several security checks, we are received by our contact at Daimler. The room in which our meeting is held with him is decorated in a high-end, high-tech, low-key style.

As is our wont at such meetings, we have brought a large amount of informatory materials with us. We start by providing an overview of Sign of Hope and what we want to achieve today. We start by making it clear that we are not there to secure donations from Daimler for our organization. We then hand our contact a comprehensive preliminary report. It contains all of the facts gathered by us. We also present photographs taken in Southern Sudan, elucidate the methods employed when taking samples of water, detail the sources of contamination identified by us, delineate the ramifications upon humans of the contamination of the environment by Petronas, and report that our findings are being looked at by Germany's Bundestag and by the UN's Human Rights Council. We also inform our contact at Daimler of the great interest shown by the media in our work. Our mentioning of this interest elicits what we perceive to be a twitch in this manager's face. His response is to state that Daimler views Sign of Hope as an organization striving to achieve an improvement in the lives of the people in Sudan. The manager says that it is much more efficacious to talk with each other than trying to out-scream another. Those engaging in "name-bashing" do get public attention. According to him, this does not, however, result in any progress. That is also our opinion and approach. The manager concludes our meeting by making commitments that sound binding. They involve getting in touch with the top echelons of Petronas. These commitments also express Daimler's dismay at having learned of the charges levied by our organization on the conduct of one of Mercedes' sponsors. We leave Daimler headquarters with the good feeling of having found an advocate and ally.

*

We speak with Daimler at the end of July. Our talk is about the independent appraisal that has just been commissioned. Daimler offers to ensure that our study of Petronas' actions is delivered to the party compiling the appraisal. Now our campaign is getting somewhere! We have found the lever that, now pressed, will move Petronas to finally respond.

*

Meeting on July 28th, the UN's General Assembly passes a resolution expressly recognizing the right to water and sanitary facilities as being a human right.[27] No country votes against the resolution. There are, however, 41 abstentions, with these including the USA, the UK and Austria. Malaysia, Sudan and 120 other countries vote in favor of the resolution.[28] The General Assembly recognizes the right to consume impeccably clean potable water and to use sanitary facilities to be a human right that is indispensable for the full enjoyment of life and to the realization of human rights.[29] The UN also calls upon countries and international organizations to provide funding—to be deployed via their international assistance and development programs—enabling the expansion of the requisite capacities and the transferring of promising technologies. These parties are to especially dedicate themselves to stepping up their efforts to improve access for all to impeccable potable water and to sanitary facilities.[30]

*

Responding to an initiative jointly launched by Spain and Germany, the UN's Human Rights Council approves on September 30th a resolution setting up a legal framework for the guaranteeing of the right to water and to sanitary facilities.[31] The human right to water thus becomes a component of international law.[32] This represents the decisive step towards the establishment of the human right to water as a legally enforceable one. It is now up to the world's countries. They have to promulgate the corresponding bodies of laws.

*

Sign of Hope's next trip to Sudan is to be to the oil fields in the Blocks 1, 2 and 7 concession areas. These are located further north in Unity state. This new focus is occasioned by the fact that we have extensively researched and documented the contamination of the environment in Thar Jath, and by reports that the Greater Nile Petroleum Operating Company (GNPOC) is a dirtier operator than even the WNPOC. Our preparations for our trip entail our informing on October 15th the government of the state of Unity of our pending arrival and of our plans. We enclose in our letter the findings of our investigation of Thar Jath (Block 5A).

*

We receive on October 22, 2010 a "Dear Hoffnungszeichen" E-mail from Lieutenant General Taban Deng Gai, the governor of Unity State. In it, the governor personally thanks us for the material that we sent to his government. He has obviously taken the time to peruse it, and thus has not contented himself with passing it on to his government. In his E-mail, the governor informs us that environmental contamination perpetrated by the oil industry is an important issue in his state. He welcomes our work. He says: "I wish to encourage your mission in this important field in our oil producing region and you have my full support in your mission."

The governor wishes to meet us during our trip to his state. He also names his minister for the environment and natural reserves as our contact. The support from the government of the state of Unity that we so hoped for is now being provided. It will open doors that had been previously shut to us.

*

Sign of Hope's team travels to Southern Sudan on November 8th. We are being accompanied by three "AFP" journalists. This trip is to investigate the effects of the contaminants released by the oil industry upon the upper aquifer found north of the city of Bentiu. We also have to conduct an inspection of the newly built deep water well in Rier. This trip will also take us to Duong, where we will visit the clinic operated by our staff members.

We travel on November 9th from Nairobi to Bentiu. We meet on November 10th with William Garjang Gieng, the Minister for Environment and Natural Resources of the state of Unity. This is followed by a meeting with Taban Deng Gai, the state's governor. He states that he is very interested in the objectives of our trip. The governor offers his proactive support for our research. To that end, he assigns William Garjang Gieng to accompany us upon our investigation.

This means our having gotten a ministerial "retinue" for our subsequent travels. In addition to the minister himself, the retinue is comprised of four Sudan People's Liberation Army soldiers, each armed with an AK-47 assault rifle and each displaying the posture of a bodyguard ready and willing to attack at any time. The soldiers emanate such a feel of authority that we get access to areas hitherto off limits to us. This martial retinue causes watchmen to zealously fling open plants' gates. The minister is an interesting person. He is nearly two meters tall, and weighs some 70 kilos. One of his forearms has been permanently stiffened by an injury suffered in the war. Freedom fighters are highly respected in Southern Sudan, with this especially applying to those bearing visible proof—wounds—of their efforts. Another impressive thing about William Garjang Gieng is that he retains his black suit and tie during the entire "field trip". Although we are more lightly dressed—in polo shirts and trekking pants—we are bathed in sweat the entire time. "Clothes make the person." If this maxim still applies anywhere in the world, then it is in Southern Sudan.

We manage to visit on November 10th the FPF ("field processing facility") of Unity. While we are doing such, we brief the highly-interested minister of our approach and of the findings that it has produced. Although smaller than Thar Jath's CPF, the FPF produces similar emissions. The presence of the minister enables us to get past the security personnel and to be admitted to the premises. We then conduct an extended inspection of the facility. We are even able to take photographs of the command center located within the building. We gain important insights into production and operating processes. We are allowed to take—undisturbed—samples from the liquids in the pits.

Our talks with the minister reveal that his ministry is not equipped to conduct investigations such as the one that we are doing. The ministry does not even have any devices capable of performing even the simple tests that we have been conducting ever since launching our search for the causes of the contamination. The conductivity of water has a lot to say about its level of contamination. Additionally a determination of the water's pH helps establish its quality. This lack of equipment means that Unity's Ministry of Environment is not capable of checking a possible case of contamination by going to a place to take a sample of its water—and by performing a quick test informing it whether or not the water is palatable. This, in turn, would enable the ministry to institute protective or remedial measures.

We proceed during November 11th–13th upon our investigation of the oil fields. Accompanied by William Garjang Gieng, we travel from village to village. We inspect the facility and take further samples. The contamination of the Unity, Al Nar and Toma South oil fields is dramatic and obvious. The investigation of the produced water management system in the Unity oilfield produced shocking results. It is not the case that no rules have been formulated for the disposal of produced water. What we see at this site is virtually a mockery of such. Large-sized pools filled with oil are situated in the vicinity of the processing facility. That wouldn't be so bad if the pools' bottoms and sides had been covered by plastic lining, as required by regulations. This plastic covering would prevent the contaminants from seeping into the ground, from which they feed into the groundwater. The bottoms of these "oil lakes" have not, however, been covered with lining. What we are told is a "produced water treatment system" appears to us as nothing more than a collection of simple seepage pits.

In November 2010, we were joined by the minister of the environment of the state of Unity in inspecting the oil facility in Al Nar, where we found 1,000 liter tanks, many of them leaking the oil endangering the ground water.

We next inspect oil drilling rigs. Used to dispose of the drilling fluids, the pits are located next to the rigs. These pits too are not covered with plastic lining, meaning that the drilling fluids—which is customarily contaminated with a large number of chemicals—can seep unhindered into the ground. The Toma South and Al Nar processing facilities also have "oil lakes" that lack these linings. The produced water is obviously also disposed of here by letting it drip into the ground. Situated next to these environmental horrors are tanks whose capacities are 1,000 liters each. These are leaky. Their contents are slowly entering the ground and thus contaminating it. A photographer working for "AFP" is accompanying us. He takes photographs that document all these abuses. It is these photographs that make their ways around the world. What we witness in Southern Sudan is not a possible peril. It is, rather, an environmental catastrophe. It's high time that something be done about it.

The oil fields that we and William Garjang Gieng visit belong to the Block 1 concession area. The holder of the concession is the consortium Greater Nile Petroleum Operating Company (GNPOC). Of its shares, 40% is owned by China National Petroleum Corporation (CNPC), whose proprietor is China's government; 30% by Petronas, which is owned by the government of Malaysia; 25%, by the Oil and National Gas Corporation Limited (ONGC) Videsh, 80% of whose equity belongs to the government of India; and 5% by the government of Sudan's Sudapet (Sudan National Petroleum Corporation).[33]

While on our trip, we seek out the people who live in these oil fields. We get to know a 30 year-old living in Marial-Guit. We ask her how the water tastes. She grabs her throat. "It hurts here when I drink this salty water. The taste of this water closes your throat, it is too salty." The young mother is standing next to the well in Marial-Guit. She is worried about her four children and their drinking water. "Drinking the water from the well causes our stomachs to rumble. We villagers have a lot of cases of diarrhea," says the young woman. The water in the well at Marial is not only unpalatable. There is also too little of it. "The well is soon going not to have any more water in it. When there's no more, I am going to have to get water from the swamp for my children," says the tall woman.

Anyone drinking the water from the well in Marial is going to get sick. The diarrhea plaguing the village stems from the great concentration of salt in the well water. We perform a quick test of the water in the well. It reveals that this concentration comes to 7 grams per liter of water. That is a record—a very saddening one. This concentration causes the water's drinker to experience within a few minutes diarrhea. This effect is well known to anyone who has cleansed his or her intestines by ingesting Glauber's salt. This ingestion is standard practice in Germany for those wishing to go on a cleansing fast. In Sudan, this diarrhea can be life-threatening. This is because hot weather causes the body of the person experiencing watery diarrhea to quickly dehydrate. Should the loss of liquids not be remedied by the immediate provision of clean water, the person's life is in acute danger.

On November 13th, we say goodbye to William Garjang Gieng. Our goodbye present to him is a water analysis device. We also record for him the ceilings placed by the World Health Organization, which refers to the values capable of being determined by the device as being "measurable parameters". Will our gifts and efforts result in the state of Unity's first drinking water regulation? The minister profusely expresses his thanks.

Our bush clinic is located in Duong. This is also in the state of Unity. To reach it, we have, however, to take a plane, so as to traverse the swamps. We are eagerly awaited in Nyal. It is a good feeling to see our colleagues again. Sign of Hope's medical treatment facility—its first—is located on the edge of a swamp. This clinic is headed by its clinical officer. The personnel in charge of medical treatment are from Kenya and Uganda. Like the rest of the staff members here, the personnel show the utmost in selflessness and in the ability to withstand hardship when providing care. Their patients are afflicted by malaria, and by bronchial and kidney ailments. The personnel help mothers give birth. They also get people suffering from malnutrition—many of them children—back on their feet. Our talks with our colleagues last well into the night. Topics are how to improve the provision of supplies and how to handle personal concerns. These are related by the clinic's staff members to Klaus Stieglitz.

*

We stage a press conference in Nairobi on November 16th. The "dpa" news agency distributes in Germany the findings of our research.[34] According to it, the oil companies are endangering the lives and health of 550,000 people.[35]

*

The race on November 14th in Abu Dhabi brings the Formula 1 season to an end. The winner of the previous year's event, Sebastian Vettel wins once more the race, and, the world championship for the year. This is a huge surprise. Vettel is only 23 years old. This makes him the youngest Formula 1 champion of all time. The Mercedes team has not lived up to expectations. During the season, its drivers recorded only three top (first to third places) finishes. All three are wracked up by Nico Rosberg. He ranks 7th among the drivers, Schumacher 9th. Mercedes itself finishes fourth in the rankings of best automobile constructors.

*

We brief Daimler on December 1, 2010 on the results of our investigation of the oil fields in the Bentiu area. In order to augment our written remarks, we send along the film broadcast by "AFP". We will dispatch a comprehensive collection of photographs documenting our findings. What we saw during our trip has made us angry. And we convey this wrath to Daimler.

"It is hard to find words capable of describing what we saw [...] What we proved is going on in Thar Jath through the undertak-

ing of comparative analyses is to be seen by the naked eye in the Unity oil field, which is north of Bentiu. Please permit us to declare that we are so ashamed by and angry at the practices pursued by your partner Petronas that we would have preferred to make sure that the journalists prominently cited the names 'Petronas' and 'Daimler AG' in their reports. We would have loved to have asked the journalists to conduct further research involving contacting both companies. We didn't do that. This is because wrath is a bad counselor, as everyone knows, and because we were still involved in a dialogue. To which it must be said that we have the impression that the findings produced by our last visit to Sudan have changed the basis of the discussion between our organization and your company. We believe we should stop conducting this discussion on the level of the exchanging of expertise. We believe that we need to speak to each other on the basis of these photographs, which require absolutely no elucidation. [...]

Please spare us—and yourselves—any wearisome forging of contacts with any presidents of Sudan-based oil companies. We wish to concentrate ourselves on employing our bilateral relationship to learn how Daimler AG itself views the actions taken by Petronas, its partner, and to discover which concrete steps you will derive from this view."

*

We promptly receive an answer. Daimler writes us on December 2nd that these photographs enable their understanding of our position on the WNPOC/GNPOC. The company now wishes to find ways of better asserting its influence. No answer, however, is forthcoming to our questions as to Daimler's relationship with Petronas.

*

The WNPOC does in fact respond. On December 30th, we receive a fax from its president. The fax states that in reference to the various communications, he is "pleased to inform that we have finally managed to obtain all required clearances from the Partners and Authorities". This is why the WNPOC can now enter into a dialogue with us. This will enable the two parties to exchange information on the WNPOC's operations and to discuss such matters.

To be especially striven for is an elucidation by the WNPOC of the measures that it has instituted to safeguard health, safety and environment. The president also states that we will be shown the various processes and tracking/monitoring mechanisms employed by the WNPOC when pursuing its oil-related activities. These, in turn, handle the problems and topics found and addressed by our organization. The consortium has also assented to the organizing of a visit by Sign of Hope to its production facilities. This will be part of "our engagement with your organization."

Daimler's efforts have really paid off. What we didn't manage to do—despite many years of efforts—is going to happen. We are to finally get a look at the procedures. It is perhaps thanks to the horrifying photographs taken in Sudan that Daimler's managers now realize what's really at stake in the "case", which is how they refer to the environmental catastrophe in Sudan when discussing it with us.

United Nations Global Compact

The Ten Principles of the UN Global Compact

Human Rights   Principle 1: Businesses should support and respect the protection of internationally proclaimed human rights; and

Principle 2: make sure that they are not complicit in human rights abuses.

Labour   Principle 3: Businesses should uphold the freedom of association and the effective recognition of the right to collective bargaining;

Principle 4: the elimination of all forms of forced and compulsory labour;

Principle 5: the effective abolition of child labour; and

Principle 6: the elimination of discrimination in respect of employment and occupation.

Environment   Principle 7: Businesses should support a precautionary approach to environmental challenges;

Principle 8: undertake initiatives to promote greater environmental responsibility; and

Principle 9: encourage the development and diffusion of environmentally friendly technologies.

Anti-Corruption   Principle 10: Businesses should work against corruption in all its forms, including extortion and bribery.

https://www.unglobalcompact.org/what-is-gc/mission/principles

2011

Fact-checking

It is January 9ᵗʰ and George Clooney is in Juba. The Hollywood
star is in town to witness the voting on the referendum stipulated in the peace agreement of 2005. It is to enable the people of Southern Sudan to decide whether or not the region is to
become a country, and to thus gain its independence from Sudan.[1] Since the turn of the millennium, Clooney has been one
of the activists who has been disseminating information on
the crimes committed by the Bashir regime in Sudan.[2] He has
been since 2005 the most prominent supporter of this seces-
sion. He has accordingly served as the movement's advocate
to the USA's Congress and in the UN's Security Council. He
has spoken out for independence at a meeting with President
Obama, and at a large number of public events.[3] As Clooney
watches, 98.8% of the voters come out in favor of independence.[4]
He is especially impressed by a 90-year old woman. This is the
first time in her life that she has voted. To get to the polls, she
had to walk miles to "vote for freedom", as Clooney later puts it.[5]

★

On January 11ᵗʰ, Sign of Hope writes to the Greater Nile Petroleum Operating Company (GNPOC). This associate of the White
Nile Petroleum Operating Company (WNPOC) is responsible
for the conditions at the Unity oil field. Adhering to the ap-

proach that we took with Daimler, we describe the findings of our investigations. We courteously request the GNPOC's detailing of its point of view as to these—dreadful—conditions. We inquire as to how the GNPOC's handles the treatment of produced water and other chemicals-laden working materials. We also request the consortium's provision of an overview as to how it helps ensure that the local residents get clean water. Daimler gets a copy of the letter.

The latter answers us on the very same day. They are gratified by the response supplied by the WNPOC, which has thus fulfilled a demand placed by Daimler. Things are thus moving ahead. And Daimler will strive to maintain the pressure. Notwithstanding this, the company fails to answer our carefully-formulated questions. Nor does Daimler mention the GNPOC.

*

In January 2011, Daimler becomes the first manufacturer of automobiles to join the LEAD group of the Global Compact. Germany's business community is well represented in this. Also members since 2011 are BASF SE, Bayer AG and Deutsche Telekom AG. "The LEAD Group pursues the aim of setting standards for anchoring sustainability within a company. Its participants have undertaken to implement the "Blueprint for Corporate Sustainability Leadership", a comprehensive "road map" incorporating 50 or so specific measures," states Daimler's portrait, which goes on to declare: "As part of the UN Global Compact, Daimler is also committed on an ongoing basis to the principles of integrity and business ethics. The internal policies of the company, particularly its New Integrity Code, are based on the principles of the Global Compact and are in conformity with Daimler's corporate values."

Daimler was one of the first companies to sign the UN Global Compact. As such, Daimler committed itself in 2000 to adhering to the ten principles formulated by the Compact. The companies participating in the Compact also pledge to ensure that the principles' implementation encompasses their advocation of the thrusts of the work of the United Nations, and their facilitation of the attainment of its globe-spanning objectives. By being a participant in LEAD, Daimler also commits itself to promoting the spreading and other companies' joining of the Global Compact.

*

On January 20, 2011, we write to the WNPOC. We convey our willingness to enter into a dialogue. Our letter also contains a listing of all the information to which we would like to have access. We request the WNPOC's provision of a documentation of its environmental management system and of that on the treatment of produced water and of drilling fluids. We request, further, the gaining of access to the report compiled by the Norwegian Directorate for Nature Management, and to a documentation of the so-called "bioremediation plant". We emphasize that a precondition for the conducting of this bilateral dialogue is our receipt on a prior basis of the information requested from the WNPOC. This is to be accompanied by their response to our questions.

*

Announced on January 23ʳᵈ is Daimler's setting up of a division of "Compliance and Integrity". The head of this newly-created division is to be a member of Daimler's managing board.[6] This position is to be occupied by Christine Hohmann-Dennhardt. She thus becomes the first woman on the board. An attorney by profession, Hohmann-Dennhardt is currently a justice on Germany's Bundesverfassungsgericht (Supreme Court). Daimler's goal in creating the division and the position is to combat corruption within the company.[7]

Hohmann-Dennhardt stems from an SPD (Germany's Social Democratic Party) background. Her career included a stint as the municipality of Frankfurt's officer of social affairs and a tenure as the state of Hesse's minister of justice. The state's governor at the time was also a member of the SPD—Hans Eichel.[8] It was the SPD that proposed her being appointed to the bench of the Bundesverfassungsgericht. During her time on the high court, Hohmann-Dennhardt worked to revise family law. According to Frankfurt's "Frankfurter Allgemeine Zeitung" ("FAZ") daily, she played a decisive role in ensuring the survival of the family-related policies enacted by Germany's federal administration at the time, which was an SPD-Green coalition. A key component of this was the according of legal equality to same-sex couples.[9] Another milestone of these policies was the decision—which was supported by Hohmann-Dennhardt—to recognize legal equality in another area—that of the entitlement to support held by an unmarried parent who is raising her or his child alone and vis-à-vis the other parent. This entitlement now has the same status as that accruing to a parent who was married.[10] Hohmann-Dennhardt also formed part of a dissent that made national headlines. She and another justice (Renate Jäger) rejected the majority opinion that the government's widespread use of electronic eavesdropping—"Großer Lauschangriff"—is constitutional. Hohmann-Dennhardt completely rejected that deployment.[11]

The "FAZ" found it amazing that Daimler "is recruiting such a lefty to its managing board". The newspaper added: "Hohmann-Dennhardt is, however, clever and knows how to get her way. And having a former Supreme Court justice on it is, of course, highly prestigious for any such body."[12]

*

We learn on February 2nd that Daimler is trying to convince its Malaysian business partners to get the GNPOC, their associate company, involved in the dialogue with Sign of Hope. Are things finally moving forward?

*

Rebecca Hamilton's article appears in the February 12th edition of the "Washington Post". It reports on the need to regulate Southern Sudan's oil industry. As Hamilton puts it, this regulation constitutes one of the greatest challenges facing the new government of South Sudan.[13] Experts would consider it questionable that the presence of oil in one of the world's poorest regions would benefit the people living there. When researching her article, Hamilton interviewed William Garjang Gieng, who had accompanied us during our last trip in the region. He confirmed that the greatest problem facing the region is the contamination of its water. He told Hamilton that he traveled to Khartoum shortly after being appointed to his position. The purpose of his trip was to confer with the consortia headquartered there on the disposal of produced water. The consortia promised to improve the system, but refused to commit themselves to a schedule for doing such.[14] "Communication is always very nice, but implementation is a difficult thing" is Gieng's experience.[15] Responding to a query placed by the "Washington Post", a spokesperson for the GNPOC—the consortium operating in the Unity oil fields—announces that there are now plans to remove the oil and to remediate the site within two years.[16] The consortium is very committed to implementing the highest standards and to minimize environmental damage—or, in cases in which its should occur, to fully alleviate it.[17] The consortium is already doing a lot for the communities in the region.[18]

Rebecca Hamilton then finds out what this assistance looks like. She visits the village of Kilo 30. Its residents report that the GNPOC has sold them used oil barrels for 15 dollars per piece. These barrels are then filled with fresh and clean water on a periodic basis. The only problem is that the tanker trucks containing the water sometimes fail to show up. This forces the residents to once more consume the contaminated water.[19] William Garjang Gieng conveys to the "Post", which is one of the world's most famous newspapers, the fact known to all of the region's people who are directly affected by the oil industry's pollution: "Oil can stop at any time, but the soil, the water—this needs to last forever."[20]

*

In a press release dated February 15th, Daimler confirms the setting up of its new division of "Integrity and Legal Affairs" and that Dr. Hohmann-Dennhardt will run it. She will be the first woman on the company's management board. Her position makes her responsible for the company's world-spanning compliance and legal organization. This encompasses business ethics and the sustainable embedding of the principles of integrity and compliance in all of the operations of the company.[21] Hohmann-Dennhardt's main job will be serving as an intermediary between Daimler and the USA's justice and tax authorities. These, in turn, have been charged with monitoring the company's business activities. Daimler's corruption scandals have put it on probation in the country. One expectation placed upon Hohmann-Dennhardt is her going toe-to-toe with Louis Freeh, the former head of the FBI.[22] Freeh had been appointed an outside monitor of the company's operations. As such, he roams freely throughout the company. This has already given rise to several incidences of strife.[23] Daimler is facing an increasing number of cases in which the excessive amount of caution insisted upon the Compliance division has caused a transaction to be called off—although this was in fact eligible for authorization.[24] Befitting her status as a famous legal expert, Hohmann-Dennhardt is expected to go to bat for Daimler's internal procedures in cases in which the USA's monitors plan on interfering in them—and on revamping decision-making processes.

*

A possible date for our next meeting with the WNPOC rapidly turns out to be April 7th. We recognize the opportunities that it offers, and reiterate the conditions that we insist upon being adhered to from the very inceptions of this dialogue. We want to be supplied with a comprehensive range of process documentation—and to get access to the report compiled by the Norwegian Directorate for Nature Management. A seemingly endless number of faxes and E-mails are exchanged between the WNPOC and Sign of Hope. Daimler pushes the WNPOC in this area. Daimler emphasizes that Sign of Hope has already substantially reduced its demands for the provision of documents prior to the arranging of this meeting. As Daimler insists, the WNPOC is now required to provide a sign of its willingness to launch a constructive dialogue. This is to be, at the very least, the WNPOC's supplying of the report compiled by the Norwegian Directorate for Nature Management. This report is referred to on the WNPOC's Website. Daimler even goes so far as to issue an ultimatum. This report is to be transferred to

Sign of Hope by March 17th. The WNPOC is also to use the forthcoming meeting to subsequently supply to our organization the process documentation that has yet to be provided to it.

*

On March 22nd, we do receive from the WNPOC the report issued by the Norwegian Directorate for Nature Management. We can't believe our eyes. The press release sent by the WNPOC at the end of November 2009 had labeled our criticisms as being fully unfounded and unsubstantiated. The WNPOC supports its claim by stating it had been audited by the Norwegian Directorate for Nature Management. "In short WNPOC has always strictly complied with all the environmental regulations, procedures, and international best practices in carrying out its operations."[25] As shown in an answer of Germany's government, in 2010, this "verification" by the Norwegian Directorate for Nature Management was cited to the government, which was processing a parliamentary inquiry placed by the country's Greens environmental party. This inquiry was made to assess the truth of charges raised.[26]

The reason for our amazement was the following. It had taken the exerting of considerable pressure by Daimler to get the WNPOC to furnish this study, which now turns out to be that of the Norwegian Directorate for Nature Management. It also emerges that the study, which had been compiled in 2009, did in fact explicitly and comprehensively list many of the countless risks and unresolved waste disposal problems caused by the exploration and production of oil in Southern Sudan. The report urgently called for the making of further full-ranging studies and the undertaking of the measures required to protect the environment.[27] It would not suffice to commission a further study showing that these demands had been fulfilled.

Daimler asks us to assess the report. We are glad to do so. The company asks us to deliver our assessment in English. We accept, knowing that this could be because it might be relayed to Petronas (Petroliam Nasional Berhard). As Daimler thus also gets to read, the risks and their possible consequences for the environment discovered by us were described in this large-scale study, and were thus known as early as 2009. The perusal of the study causes us to expand our list of questions to include the 30 points raised by the Norwegians. These points address the problems most urgently needing solution.

*

We meet on April 7th for the first time with representatives of the oil consortium. The meeting is planned to go for three days. It is being held in Juba. The representative of the government of Southern Sudan at it is William Garjang Gieng, the Minister of Environment. The meeting on April 8th is preceded by a dinner held on the evening before. It is supposed to break the ice.

The dinner begins with Minister William Garjang Gieng's giving a brief introduction. Bacho Pilong, the president of the WNPOC, then presents an overview of the consortia operating in Southern Sudan. This includes their rates of production. According to Pilong, the largest of the 19 oil companies active in the region is Petrodar (250,000 barrels a day), followed by the GNPOC (140,000 barrels a day) Petroenergy (20,000 to 40,000 barrels a day), and the WNPOC. The latter produces 18,000–19,000 barrels a day from its Block 5A, 5B and 8 areas of concession.

We ask Pilong whether or not he can also speak for the GNPOC. He says no. Pilong goes on to emphasize that the WNPOC has provided $US 14 million in funding to development projects. His presentation concludes with his informing us that Norconsult, a Norwegian consultant, has been commissioned with the conducting of a study. It will soon evaluate the charges levied by us. The study's findings won't be available until July. Hadn't the WNPOC already informed Daimler last May of the hiring of consultants from Norway?

When giving our presentation, we emphasize that our analysis will start by considering the questions raised by the report compiled by the Norwegian Directorate for Nature Management. We do not waste any time at all mentioning the absurdity of the claim originally advanced by the consortium that this report constitutes proof of the harmlessness of the WNPOC's conditions of production—as obviously intimated by the WNPOC to the government of Germany. Rather than doing that, our presentation shows that the tests undertaken by us complement the findings of the Norwegians. They had warned, after all, of the risks facing the upper aquifer and of the damaging of health associated with this. Their study had called for the conducting of further, more detailed ones. Sign of Hope had compiled in 2010 such a study. It proved that these risks had already become a reality.

Our next step is to elucidate to the meeting's participants the 30 recommendations contained in the Norwegians' report. Since two years have elapsed since its issuance, these recommendations may well be regarded as a kind of litmus test for the attainment of quantifiable progress. It is for this reason, we emphasize, that the assessment of whether or not the recommendations listed have already been implemented is of decisive importance. These recommendations cover the effects of the production of oil. We have identified the produced water and drilling fluids as being the main sources of contamination. To compile this assessment, we require access to the written documentation of the consortium's waste management

Leaks constitute a great danger to upper aquifer. The photographs on the top and on the left are of the oil processing facility in Thar Jath in February 2015. Right below: spills from oil tanks forming part of the facility in Al Nar, which is north of Bentiu, photos taken in November 2010.

procedures. International standards commit the WNPOC to doing such. The WNPOC promises to provide us with this access. This documentation is of course available, it says.

A concern raised by the Norwegians' report is the efficaciousness of the bioremediation plants for the treatment of produced water. We share this concern, we note. The Norwegian experts had cast compelling doubts as to the ability of such systems to break down poisons. The experts had called for the undertaking of an independent study. This is because they assumed that these poisons were agglomerating themselves, and damaging the environment in the process. We ask if this study has by now been conducted. The Norwegian experts had also urgently demanded the compilation—as soon as possible —of an Environmental Impact Assessment, an Social Impact Assessment, and of a full-scale Strategic Environmental Assessment. We raise the question: has any of these studies been carried out? The WNPOC says no. The WNPOC's president does state that Norconsult will now consider these issues. We want to know why actually the customary procedure of re-injecting the produced water is not being employed by the consortium. "It could damage the oil reservoir" is the WNPOC's response.

This exchange is followed by the presentation given by Dr. Hella Rüskamp, the hydro-geologist. It details the scientific approach taken in the compiling of our study. She starts by telling the participants what caused us to pursue such a project: well water with a salty taste, an ever-greater number of health problems and complaints about the increasing number of livestock deaths in the vicinity of CPF.

Hella Rüskamp then provides an overview of the geological conditions in the region, and an elucidation of the directives upon which our work is based. She continues by presenting to the meeting's participants the key features of the sam-

Residents in the region put thorn
bushes on water wells that have
been shut down.

ples of the water taken from the region. The ionic balances reveal two different kinds of water. Comparable are the surface water and well water kinds, with the latter referring to wells delivering water of potable quality. We designate this set of water "Type 1". "Type 2" is characteristic for well water featuring a high concentration of salts, of water in the retention ponds holding drilling fluids, and of the produced water issuing from the CPF.

"Water Type 1" is a hydrogen carbonate type showing a dominance of calcium/magnesium/sodium. It is found in surface water bodies and in wells providing potable water. "Water Type 2" is a chloride type. Its dominance is that of sulphate/sodium. It is found in well water showing a high degree of electrical conductivity, produced water and pits containing drilling fluids.

The following parameters exceed the permissible values set by potable water directives: sodium, chloride, sulphates, nitrates, lead, chrome, iron, manganese, selenium, aluminum, fluoride, ammonia, boron and PACs (polycyclic aromatic hydrocarbons).

In addition to the above breaches of the potable water rules mentioned above, the samples of drilling fluids and of those taken by from ponds forming the bioremediation system of produced water treatment contain nickel, arsenic, cadmium, barium, strontium, benzene, tuluene and aliphatic hydrocarbons (chains-formed hydrocarbons).

Type 1 is naturally-occurring water. Type 2 is a completely different kind. It is a type of contaminated water found in the polluted upper aquifer. Showing a comparable ionic balance, Type 2 is to be identified in the produced water flowing from the CPF and in drilling mud pits created to hold the drilling fluids. In some of these samples, sodium chloride accounts for more than 80% of mineral concentrations in them. The comparison of the two types of water proves that there is a direct connection between the introduction into the water circulatory cycle of the contaminants produced at the CPF and via the mud pits and the finding of contaminated water at the handpumps.

This contamination has rendered the water from the wells in Duar, Rier, Bouw, Pakur, Guit and Marial undrinkable for human beings and animals. Local residents are forced therefore to rely on swamp water to drink, in cases in which lakes are in their vicinity. Several villages are supplied by tanker trucks. Recycled metal or plastic containers serve as reservoirs for such water. Due to pollution with fecal bacteria the water quality is unacceptable. The only way of sensibly supplying the population living in the oil fields with clean drinking water is to drill wells deep enough to tap the groundwater reservoir lying far below the surface.

The WNPOC's delegation raises the question: how can the water found in a number of groundwater wells have a concentration of salts that is greater than that of produced water? Hella Rüskamp provides the explanation. As the hydro-geologist explains, there are 79 pits containing drilling fluids that have not been sealed. This should have been done to prevent the infiltration of contaminants into the ground. These pits are to be regarded as being a main source of the contamination. The concentration of oil wells in the vicinity of the CPF is much higher than that of the entire project area as a whole, and these wells' unsecured mud pits significantly compound the contamination. Also contributing to the salination of the potable water and of the entire wetlands region—the Sudd constitutes one of the world's largest swamplands—has been the disposal of produced water. This is due to the water's evaporating in the produced water ponds. This causes, in turn, the agglomeration of minerals. The influx of further produced water laden with salts into the ponds furthers this process of accumulation of noxious items.

The WNPOC casts doubt on the relationship between the production of oil and the contamination of water in such further, remote communities as Nhialdiu, Duar, Pakur and others. The consortium claims in fact the converse. The fact that contamination is also found at such remote sites proves that the contamination can't have anything to do with the production of oil, they say. In response, Hella Rüskamp shows the three zones of contamination that she has identified as existing, and elucidates how they are affected by the direction of the flow of groundwater. In this region, the groundwater flows from the southwest to the northeast, and thus towards the Nile and the Bhar-el-Ghazal river, which is on the northernmost edge of the area of investigation. This flow is why all sites south and west of the area of exploration evince lower concentrations of salts and heavy metals.

We notice that the subsequent presentations by the WNPOC and of the operators of produced water facilities specify varying amounts of the produced water incurring on a daily basis—with this ranging between 15,000 and 25,000 barrels. According to the WNPOC, this water contains 2,232 mg of dissolved solids per liter. This is along the lines of the results of our tests. This figure enables the extrapolation of the amount of salts requiring disposal.

We pose the question: is it true that from the time of commissioning of the CPF in 2006 and until the putting into operation of the bioremediation facility at the end of 2010 the produced water was released into the ambient environment? The consortium does not dispute this implicit fact. The operator of the new bioremediation facility is asked whether or not it can remove minerals and heavy metals. The operators says that it can not do this. This lack of dispute causes us to present the following calculations to the other participants at the meeting. Let's assume that the figure of 15,000 barrels of produced water a day is correct. That means in turn five tons of salts a day. This translates into 1,900 tons a year. Since salt is incapable of being evaporated or absorbed in the bioremediation plant, we then pose the question of where the thousands of tons of salt generated between 2006–2010 are to be found, if not in the upper groundwater? The other participants can't answer the question. We also quite naturally want to know what happens to the salts accumulating in the bioremediation facility. The answer: there is not yet a plan to deal with them.

The WNPOC intensively insists upon the truth of its claim that high levels of salts were also found in previous years. These "findings" were made during the drilling of the wells found in the current oil fields. These high levels of salts made the water unpalatable. The consortium states that samples made in 1968 and 1982 had up to 1,280 mg TDS (total dissolved solids) in them. The results of our analyses show in some cases values that exceed this figure five-fold. This difference thus also constitutes proof of how the oil industry is causing the water to change.

The characteristics of the ground give rise to disputes. The WNPOC advocates the point of view that the soil found in the project area are virtually impermeable. This is why it is not to be expected that pollutants would be able to make their ways from the surface into the groundwater aquifer. This point is refuted by Dr. Rüskamp, who cites the proven physical and chemical processes taking place in the pore water and the seepage trial runs she herself conducted. Dr. Rüskamp states: "One evening, I poured water into one of the dry mud pits at a site where we were about to drill for drinking water. My purpose was to expedite our commencing of drilling on the following morning. But as it dawned, the 25 m³ of water were gone." Deep dry cracks provide all-encompassing access to the ground aquifer located near the surface. As has been proven, this aquifer is refilled, albeit slowly. Dr. Rüskamp raises a further point. There is no such thing as impermeable soils, with this especially holding true of swamplands featuring unhardened sediments.

*

On April 8th, we are flown by a corporate helicopter to the oil fields, where our first stop is an oil rig. We are briefed on how the drilling process is conducted. We are able to inspect a pit containing drilling fluids. This pit has been covered by foils—it is a showpiece. To be noted is that the foils have a thickness of only about half a millimeter. They aren't very tear- and wear-resistant. A large number of small-sized defects in them are perceivable by the naked eye. Nearly two meters of the border is defective. This enables the wind to get under the foils. We take photographs documenting all of this.

Our next stop is the produced water treatment facility. It is not capable of neutralizing salts and heavy metals. To carry out this kind of remediation processing, the system also has to be completely covered with foils that are absolutely waterproof. This fact is confirmed by the operator. Visual inspection is the only way that the quality of being waterproof is verified. The fact that there is a huge variety of outside influences capable of causing damage makes the system's efficacy seem even more questionable.

The sight of two decommissioned skimming ponds raises further concerns. "Skimming" describes the process of using a kind of scraper to mechanically remove the residue oil from the surface of the produced water. We get to inspect the ponds.

Neither has been sealed. Even more disturbing is the fact that their surfaces and edges are still covered by oil. In a counter-productive and unfortunate move, the WNPOC refuses to allow us to take samples of the water found in the facility during our visit there.

At the end of our encounter, we agree to exchange the information stipulated upon by May 12th. The president of the WNPOC voices in no uncertain terms his view on how bad he finds our having gone public with our information.

*

Daimler and Petronas announce on April 29th the expansion of their working relationship in the area of car racing.[28] The 2011 edition of Germany's DTM touring car season will start on May 1st. The venue for the first race in the season will be the track in Hockenheim. This race will be Petronas' first as a sponsor of Mercedes-Benz's DTM team.[29] All of the nine drivers in the team will now wear racing overalls and helmets spotting Petronas' logo, which will also be emblazoned on the team's race cars.[30] Mercedes-Benz maintains, in addition, two Formula 3 partner teams. Their vehicles will also display the Petronas look.[31] Mercedes is gratified by the product development efforts supplied on a continuing basis by its partner Petronas, as this fosters its vehicles' abilities to successfully compete.[32] Petronas views the expansion of its partnership with Mercedes as constituting an important step "towards the attainment of its business objectives of strengthening on a worldwide basis its business field supplying lubricants, and, as well, its technical participations." [33]

*

The following months see a large-volume of communication among Sign of Hope, Daimler and the parties responsible for the WNPOC. We compile a comprehensive overview of the contents of the talks in Juba, and relay this to the meeting's participants. We brief William Garjang Gieng, the state of Unity's Minister of Environment, on the key activities. Notwithstanding all this, we do not receive the process documentation agreed upon.

*

At the end of May, we get in touch with Germany's GIZ Agency for International Development. The fact that our projects in Bouw and Rier—involving the drilling and building of deep wells—went so successfully encourages us to strive to ensure the constructing of further ones as quickly as possible. We lack the financial means to do such. But we possess a quantity of knowhow sufficient to launch at a large-sized project at GIZ.

Our first meetings with GIZ cover the various programs of support available. We learn that Germany's government has allocated € 13 million for the improvement of the supply of water in Southern Sudan. At these talks, "public private partnerships" (PPPs) are brought to our attention. In such arrangements, the government enters into a contract with a private company. This sets up a relationship that apportions responsibilities between the two in the way best suited to achieve the objectives established to foster the common good. PPPs are used to structure development assistance projects. The private company invests proprietary funds, and receives such from the German government. That would be an elegant approach for the WNPOC to take. This approach would also nicely solve the problems faced by the people of Southern Sudan. This is a way of bringing together two financial powerhouses in order to do good deeds. Have we finally in fact found the lever capable of getting things going for the people in Southern Sudan?

*

At the beginning of June, we speak on the telephone with our contact at the WNPOC about such a PPP. He seems interested. This causes us to send him on June 7th an initial, still very vague presentation of the form that such a PPP might take. Our proposal foresees a project capable of reaching two objectives. The project will provide the financing for measures designed to properly dispose of the produced water by removing the salts and heavy metals from it. Funding will also go to activities supplying the population with clean drinking water. These activities comprise especially the building of deep wells. Of key importance is the WNPOC's furnishing of proprietary funds to such a project.

Prior to our conducting in-depth talks with official bodies in Germany on the setting up of such a PPP, the WNPOC has to commit itself to making such investments.

*

We receive on June 27th a response from the WNPOC as to our proposal. The consortium seems to be quite impressed with it. The WNPOC declares its fundamental willingness to contribute proprietary funds to a project in which Germany's government is involved. The consortium is also prepared to supply its own stock of expertise. The WNPOC rejects, however, our proposal for the treating of produced water. The consortium emphasizes that it does not want to do anything conveying the message that it has not adhered to the extant of code of laws applying to the disposal of such. The water produced in the CPF of Thar Jath is being treated in a proper way. The objective of such treatment processes is not to yield drinking water, and drinking water alone, they say. The consortium knows that we hold another view. This because we are aware of the fact that the Sudd and the organisms living it in are used to ingesting a natural amount of minerals, and not the one found in produced water. This is ten times higher. Notwithstanding this, the consortium would be interested in the PPP proposed by us. This is because the building of deep wells would be a good fit with the WNPOC's on-site community development projects. The WNPOC would be prepared to render the technical expertise requisite for this aspect of the project. The WNPOC informs us that it has tentatively selected a company—Darcy Engineering—to lead manage this.

*

We consider this to be a major step forward. The next one is to bring together GIZ and the WNPOC. We view our role to be the facilitator of the process of launching a project initiated by Germany's government and featuring input from the WNPOC. The first thing for us to do is to put the two parties in direct touch. Once achieved, we will step back from the project, for which we will serve as an observer and consultant. We let the WNPOC know that we consider such a project to have the potential of substantially improving the lives of the people of the state of Unity. We would still love to have the issue of produced water treatment included in this project. We will contact GIZ about this. We will have to see what this project actually turns out to look like.

*

On July 9th, Southern Sudan moves from being partially autonomous to becoming the fully-autonomous Republic of South Sudan.

*

We hold on July 11th the first in-depth talks with GIZ about the PPP to be created by the German government and by the WNPOC. The talks are held in Sign of Hope's offices. After they are over, we are able to inform the WNPOC that the staff member responsible for processing the matter seems to be highly interested. He will not be in his office until August 8th, but will, upon return, formulate approaches as to what the next requisite steps towards the setting up of such a working relationship could look like.

*

On July 27th, Daimler inquires as to the status of the negotiations between the German government and the WNPOC. We exchange information on the telephone about this.

*

On July 28th, Hella Rüskamp reports having found clean drinking water in the deep well just drilled in Marial-Guit. This represents the third one to have been drilled by us and our partner.

*

The UK's "Daily Mail" publishes on September 17th a story on the shooting of a Mercedes commercial in Los Angeles.[34] The article is full of photographs. The commercial is to be exclusively broadcast in China. In it, George Clooney showcases the exciting features of the new E-class of Mercedes. The British tabloid finds that the Hollywood star and Mercedes make a pretty couple. Both look best in silver.[35]

*

On October 28th, the WNPOC recalls itself to our mind. Its management informs us that it is still very interested in the PPP. It wants to know whether or not the official bodies responsible for the matter have launched the appropriate actions. We are able to promptly tell the consortium that a meeting with GIZ will take place in the week to come. And that we assumed our meeting with GIZ would be followed by its compiling of a draft plan of the project, and that it would directly send that to Petronas.

*

On November 1st, we receive from the WNPOC a three-page summary of the report compiled by the Norwegian experts. The consortium's release informs us that Norconsult was commissioned by the Khartoum-based General Directorate of Environment and Safety (GDES) and the government-owned Sudanese Petroleum Corporation (SPC), to conduct an environmental audit of the WNPOC.

The summary of this environment audit was written by the WNPOC. It reads like a press release. It states that the audit was necessitated by—despite the WNPOC's strictest possible adherence to HSE (Health, Safety and Environment) methods and despite its generous financial support of local communities—the consortium's being exposed to the accusations levied by these communities and by such NGOs as Sign of Hope. These, in turn, had claimed that WNPOC's activities had led to the contamination of the drinking water available in a large number of villages located in the Thar Jath vicinity. These charges had drawn the attention of the world's public.

The summary states further that Norconsult's experts had proved that impacts on environment from WNPOC operating activities inside Thar Jath are assessed as minor, while impacts outside of Thar Jath are assessed as negligible. In various venues, the release of the produced water treated could have led to an increasing of the concentration of salts on the ground's surface. This poses only a very low danger to the groundwater, as the aquifer in question lies under thick, impermeable layers of clay.

The release also states that the environment located in the vicinity of the produced water ponds has been moderately encumbered. The areas outside this region show negligible amounts of contamination. The potential for an accumulation of poisons is minimal. A number of the metals proved to be in the water had been shown to be strongly present in samples of tissue. These concentrations, though higher, were still below the ceiling set for such items. This is the level at which they would damage sensitive predators.

For the regions outside Thar Jath, the impact of the production of oil upon humans and animal is negligible in scope. Contaminated water was not found by the Norwegian experts.

These, in turn, have suggested the expedited compilation of environmental impact audit. Another recommendation: the formulation and implementation of an environmental monitoring program. Norconsult has also called for the undertaking of technical improvements precluding the realization of potential perils. Sign of Hope has not been briefed on how the Norconsult study was set up. We have also not been provided with the points upon which its conclusions are based. We therefore can not issue a conclusive evaluation of it. We are capable of refuting one of the audit's premises. The ground in the Sudd is not impermeable.

While transmitting the results to us, the WNPOC informs us that it is willing to set forth the productive talks with us. The consortium reiterates its interest in participating in the GIZ project. We are amazed at the WNPOC's failure to provide the study to the general public.

*

A workshop is held on November 3rd at GIZ's offices, which are located in the Frankfurt suburb of Eschborn. The workshop is charged with formulating a basic concept for projects and then plans for their implementation. We present our project for the drilling of deep wells at this workshop. We also have the opportunity to discuss once more the initiative that we have planned for Petronas. GIZ has compiled a five-page draft. It takes into account the precondition of Petronas' involvement not being regarded as a confession of guilt, but, rather, as an expression of its commitment to CSR (corporate social responsibility). The key thing for Sign of Hope is not to secure any confessions, but ensuring that the people in South Sudan get assistance.

*

Daimler launches in November its "Integrity in dialogue" initiative. It is intended to unleash months of intensive discussion, with this encompassing all of the company's levels of hierarchy, its divisions and its sites of operation, on the meaning of "integrity" and its application at Daimler.[36] The question to be considered is which values are to guide Daimler's actions —both within company and in its dealings with business partners and clients?[37]

*

The last race of this year's Formula 1 takes place on November 27th in Brazil. It was a disappointing year for the Mercedes team. Neither Michael Schumacher nor Nico Rosberg were among the competitors for the title. Neither of them finished among the top three in the races held this year. In the final rankings of the drivers, Rosberg finishes 7th and Schumacher 8th, both far behind Sebastian Vettel, who has once more won the world championship, and his closest competitors. The only consolation for the Mercedes team is its victory in the rankings of the most successful engines. This win is due to two other teams' having equipped their cars with Mercedes engines.

Sign of Hope views the reeds-based bioremediation facility at Thar Jath as being one of the main sources of contamination of the upper aquifer. Even if this facility would function properly, it still would not be capable of breaking down salts or heavy metals. Required for the facility to function properly is having a layer of foils that is undamaged and thus impermeable. A photograph taken in November 2009 gives rise to the assumption that the layer of impermeable foil was deliberately destroyed prior to the filling of the facility with produced water.

2012

An elegant solution

Ever since the gaining of independence in July 2011, South Sudan and Sudan have been arguing about the fees levied by the latter for the transporting of the oil produced in the former country, which accounts for three quarters of the two-country total. But, since the young country lacks access to an ocean, South Sudan is dependent upon the pipeline running through Sudan to Port Sudan and its oil terminals. This dependency causes Sudan to levy high fees.

The conflict over the division of oil revenues escalates in January. Sudan confiscates the oil from the south. It refuses to let tankers loaded with oil from the south leave the harbor of Port Sudan.[1] The justification for such is South Sudan's alleged failure to meet its payment obligations.

On January 29th, Stephen Dieu Dau, South Sudan's Minister of Petroleum, tells the media that South Sudan is halting its production of oil, which is said to already have been reduced by 90%. This means that South Sudan has lost practically all sources of income. Sudan is also suffering huge losses of revenues. The two countries' economies are nearly completely dependent upon the income from the oil business.

*

In spring, at the end of its financial year, Petronas (Petroliam Nasional Berhad) publishes its Sustainability Report for 2011.[2] In the report[3] , Sudan and South Sudan receive an entire page. Petronas is a business that takes a neutral, non-political stance in any market in which it operates, states the report.[4] And the company welcomes a peaceful transition, one benefiting the people and fostering social and economic progress in both countries.[5]

Petronas has expanded its business in South Sudan by opening an administrative office in Juba. Its activities in Sudan are being pursued.[6] Petronas' business in the two countries is on course for further growth.[7] In addition to producing oil, Petronas operates 83 gas stations in Sudan. This network is to be expanded.[8] As of this writing, Petronas is the second largest supplier in this market, holding a 17% share. Petronas is in fact also the number one provider of aviation-use kerosene.[9]

The highest priority is accorded in all areas to assuring the health and safety of personnel. "Sustainability issues encompassing environmental and socioeconomic concerns influence our business at all our areas of operations," states the report.[10] "We endeavour to minimise the risk and impact of our operations on the environment through careful planning and monitoring of our activities,"[11] the report continues. "For example, the water quality at our bioremediation projects at WNPOC and GNPOC sites are regularly tested to ensure the levels of heavy metals and trace elements in soil and plant samples are within normal levels of international oil and gas industry standards. In addition, WNPOC has conducted an Environmental Fact Finding Study at its bioremediation site for the benefit of the environment and surrounding communities."[12]

Sign of Hope would appreciate getting an opportunity to see these tests and studies. The only study cited by the WNPOC publicly as proof of proprietary protection of the environment is the one compiled by the Norwegian Directorate for Nature Management. This study does not confirm the harmlessness and environmental friendliness of Sudan's oil production and waste disposal methods. Rather, the study attests to—via the publishing of a long list of issues requiring clarification—the uncertainties associated with the methods. Sign of Hope's study of water quality has already answered several of this list's questions. We have also proved that these methods and the ways in which they are applied by South Sudan's oil industry are extremely dangerous and damaging.

The Norconsult study is never mentioned by name. Nor has it been placed on-line or been made accessible in any other way.

*

At the beginning of March, the White Nile Petroleum Operating Company (WNPOC) consortium is rechristened the SUDD Petroleum Operating Company Limited (SPOC). This move does not change the consortium's ownership structure. The renamed company is registered on March 7th in Mauritius.

*

On March 16th, George Clooney is joined by other activists and by politicians and clergy in being taken into custody for a short period of time. All had been participating in a demonstration held in Washington.[13] The demonstration was staged in front of Sudan's embassy. Its cause was to protest the violations of human rights and the war crimes committed by the country's government. The protesters refused to voluntarily end the demonstration, notwithstanding demands by the police to do so.[14] George Clooney pays a fine for "civil disobedience" and is then released.[15]

*

On March 24th, Germany's GIZ agency for international development relays an in-depth proposal to Petronas. It foresees a bilateral project enabling the building of deep wells. The project's language shows a great degree of diplomacy. This is to take into account the sensibilities of Petronas. We approve of this. We view the project as constituting a great opportunity to improve the lives of the people in Unity in sustainable and meaningful ways. It's now up to the two partners, who will be conducting the negotiations on the project. Should the project be implemented, Sign of Hope will serve as a consultant and controller. The only thing now to be done is to wait and see.

*

On April 15th, Nico Rosberg wins the Grand Prix of China in Shanghai.[16] This is the first victory recorded by a Mercedes driver in the Formula 1 since the 1955 season.[17] Journalists calculate that this makes it precisely 20671 days since the last victory, which was gained by Juan Manuel Fangio in Italy.[18] Mercedes' team speaks of the writing of a new chapter in the history of the Silver Arrows.[19] The race was nearly even more successful for the team. Michael Schumacher was doing very well during the race when an error committed by a mechanic forced him to leave it.[20]

*

At the end of April, Klaus Stieglitz is contacted by a professor working for the University of Petersburg. This professor, a graduate of Oxford, is organizing a vocational training seminar for Petronas. Stieglitz is invited to discuss via Skype with members of Petronas' Corporate Social Responsibility (CSR) department in Malaysia. The topic of the discussion: the relationship between businesses and NGOs. Stieglitz plans on taking part in the discussion. The establishment of the contents of such causes Petronas to raise the demand that Klaus Stieglitz is not to mention Sudan. He then decides not to participate.

*

In June, the government of Sudan officially informs that of South Sudan that all agreements involving the exporting of the latter's oil via the former's territory have been suspended. This entails the latter's halting all transports of oil via the former's territory within two months. The government of South Sudan accepts this ban. It orders oil consortia to have completely shut down their pumping of oil by no later than August 7th.

*

At the end of July, George Clooney shoots a further Mercedes commercial. Venue is Italy's Lago d'Iseo. A crowd is in attendance.[21]

*

Sign of Hope learns in August that GIZ—repeated queries notwithstanding—has not heard from Petronas about the proposed project. We suggest GIZ's contacting Daimler. We are subsequently informed that Petronas has obviously responded.

*

On September 27[th,], under the auspices of the Union of African States, Sudan and South Sudan sign an agreement in Addis Ababa revamping the apportionment of oil revenues. This doesn't suffice to relaunch the oil production in South Sudan. The border between the two countries also has to be agreed upon. Further negotiations are required.[22]

*

On September 28th, Mercedes announces that its three-year contract with Michael Schumacher will not be extended upon expiry. The Silver Arrows racing team also informs the world that the UK's Lewis Hamilton, who won the world championship in 2008, will be Schumacher's replacement.[23]

*

Christine Hohmann-Dennhardt has initiated Daimler's promulgation of an Integrity Code. This takes place on November 1st. The directive's formulation has required months of corporate-wide dialogues.[24] It accounts for employees' repeatedly uttered wishes for transparent and comprehensible rules on how to behave properly.[25] The directive reiterates Daimler's commitment to its global responsibilities. The company is a founding member of the Global Compact. As such, Daimler pledged in 2000 to engage in business activities fostering the protection of human rights and of the environment; the respecting of fair labor practices; and the combating of corruption.[26] Daimler also views its responsibilities as encompassing its dedicating itself to ensuring that its business partners and customers adhere to the operating principles of the Global Compact.[27] These primarily include the worldwide countering of corruption, the remediation of societal relationships suffering under it, and the enabling of fair competition.[28]

To convey Daimler's corporate values to its business partners, Daimler promulgated its "Ethical Business. Our Shared Responsibility" guidebook.[29] Daimler states: "Going beyond pure adherence to the rules, Daimler strives to establish an ethical corporate culture in which employees act in accordance with shared values. We expect such conduct from all our employees as well as from our business partners. This includes contractual partners such as joint venture partners, authorized dealers, general distributors, suppliers and body builders, as well as sales, marketing and sponsorship partners."[30]

The brochure continues: "Furthermore, Daimler expects its business partners to abide by all applicable regulations and laws."[31] "Since ignorance is no excuse, each individual is personally responsible for becoming informed about the relevant regulations",[32] it states. "If national or international laws or industry standards cover the same topics, the more stringent provisions always apply",[33] the guideline demands. The booklet also states: "For Daimler, ethical principles are not optional, but serve to guide our conduct. We subscribe to the view that no business deal can ever justify putting our company's reputation at risk. We expect the same of our partners."[34]

This precisely-formulated code of corporate ethics imparts in us the feeling of having found the perfect partner for our attempts to assert the interests of the people of South Sudan. Daimler is obviously doing more than preaching responsible behavior. The corporation is enforcing it, with this comprising its business partners.

*

On November 25th, the last race of the Formula 1 season is run in Brazil. The season started well for the Silver Arrows. It couldn't, however, follow up after the summer break on its success in China. The season was for Mercedes the worst since its having rejoined the circuit. In the ranking of the drivers, Rosberg plunges to 9th place, Schumacher falls to 13th.

*

December 10th is the UN's Human Rights Day. On it, a two-day meeting starts in Stuttgart. Daimler has arranged it. It is between Sign of Hope and the SPOC. In addition to their delegations, the meeting is attended by experts from Norconsult and from African Water. South Sudan's Petroleum Ministry was supposed to send representatives. This was called off at the latest minute due, obviously, to problems securing visas.

Daimler's representative kicks off the meeting by stating that the company's view its role as being an intermediary between Petronas and Sign of Hope. This is because Daimler is not involved on the operative side.

Emi Suhardi is the SPOC's president. He starts by providing an overview of all the consortia that are active in South Sudan. He then goes on to give a detailed look at the SPOC. Suhardi emphasizes that the SPOC strives for excellence in the HSE (Health, Safety and Environment) area. He proffers two certificates. They were issued by Moody International, and they attest to Block 5B's observation of internationally applicable environmental standards.[35] He concludes his presentation by elucidating his consortium's Community Development Programme, which has received nearly $US 46 million in funding from the SPOC.

Next up is a presentation of the independent appraisal compiled by Norconsult, a consultancy based in Norway. Norconsult was commissioned with the gathering of samples, and with their analysis and assessment. Purpose of this investigation is the compilation of an evaluation of the ramifications of the WNPOC's activities upon the environment and their possible imperiling of the health of humans and animals. According to Norconsult's experts, they concentrated this investigation upon two possible sources of contamination—the treatment of produced water issuing from the Central Processing Facility (CPF) in Thar Jath and the pits containing drilling fluids.

We receive, once more, a detailed elucidation of the CPF's remediation system, which is said to have been in operation since 2009. Norconsult states that, prior to this, the produced water was disposed of by channeling it into a system of interconnected pits. The reason why the bottom of the pits were not sealed through the placement of coverings was that much of the earth underneath was classified as being impermeable. The earth's geo-physical conditions were regarded as constituting adequate protection against its and the groundwater being contaminated.

Listed as being possible causes of contamination were the produced water, the pits containing drilling fluids and leaks in the drilling and processing operations. Norconsult collected samples of water, of earth and of tissues within the CPF and its vicinity. These had revealed that the danger to people and animals located outside the CPF is negligible. According to Norconsult the quality of water is questionable when one considers the customary standards for potable water. This water has values near the ceiling on palatability for humans and animals. Samples taken of surface waters situated in the vicinity of the CPF and of water from village wells did not yield proof of an impact from the oil industry. A low level of danger exists within the CPF.

Norconsult's expert did not find any contamination of the surface waters and of the groundwater ensuing from the operations of the CPF. The exceeding of ceilings also registered by Norconsult was explained to be caused by natural processes or other factors. The waste water in the remediation facilities do contain large amounts of salts—but not of other materials in concentrations exceeding permissible limits. The disposal of salts-containing waste water in neighboring woods results in an increase in the amount of salts found in the earth in these areas alone.

The main point of entry of the produced water and other contaminants-laden liquids from the surface into the subsoil is via morphological structures and naturally-incurring gradients. The risk that corporate operations lead to the contamination of the ground water is said to be very low. This is confirmed by the fact that the layers in which this water permeates are under a thick shield of clay.

The samples gathered of the tissues of animals living in and from the ponds of the bioremediation facilities are said not to revealed any exceeding of guideline limits. Several metals discovered have the potential to be accumulated via the food chain. The samples indicate, however, that the only one actually doing such is selenium. None of the concentrations of metals found in fish tissues is expected to cause effects in the animals eating them. All told, the taking of samples was restricted to the area within the CPF, with the exception of one taken during a field trip of a pit containing drilling fluids.

Norconsult's experts recommend the conducting of an environmental compatibility audit and the no-delay setting up of an supervision system. Also required are improvements in the equipment used to preclude the emission and dispersion of noxious items. This potential to cause damage has to be conclusively excluded. To depict what needs to be done, the Norconsult staff members show photographs of containers out of which chemicals are overflowing, of defective fences and of oil-covered retention ponds. As the experts point out, the danger of noxious items' getting into the environment is larger during the rainy season.

The results of the analysis seem valid to us. Completely unconvincing are, however, the conclusions that the imperiling is low within the CPF and, further, negligible outside it. The formulation of these conclusions is obviated by the way in which the study was designed. It never planned to investigate all possible sources of contamination. All of the samples investigated by Norconsult were made in the water treatment ponds comprising the bioremediation facility, which was commissioned only in 2009. A mere one sample was taken from a pit containing drilling fluids. To come up with an authoritative assessment of the risk, the study's scope should have included the covering and measurement of all sources of contamination.

There are a total of five main sources of contamination, in addition to those ensuing from defective containers, pipes and similar equipment. The produced water currently requiring treatment and disposal is joined by the residues of that released into the environment in previous years. The latter has never been disputed by the SPOC. The same applies to drilling fluids. The fifth source of pollutants is the leaking of such liquids into the ground water aquifer during the drilling process itself. At the presentation, we point that out to the other participants at the meeting. They then confirm that Norconsult investigated solely the current state of the treatment of produced water. The study thus provides insights—at most—into the consequences of one source of contamination under today's conditions. This does not really advance the research into the real causes, we tell the others.

There is a consensus among the participants that bioremediation facilities are not capable of breaking down salts, metals, heavy metals or radionuclides. To convey the amounts of residues remaining on site, we use the production figures provided to us to compile a rough estimate of such. Norconsult's water samples—taken from the outlets of the bioremediation facility—yield values that extrapolate to some 700 tons of salt a year. This has been deposited in the "wooded area"—the swamplands lying immediately adjacent to the facility.

Norconsult collected samples at the point of the feeding in of the produced water into the produced water treatment process. We use the resultant values to calculate the amount of some 7,200 tons of salt to be disposed of every year. This, in turn, means that the location of the remaining 6,500 tons a year to be disposed of is unknown. The best outcome would be the salts' having been deposited on the bottom of the sealed remediation ponds, from which they would have been removed and disposed of in appropriate ways. International rules demand the furnishing of a documentation of such, which we have never received.

We use photographs from November 2011 to prove that the bioremedation ponds in Thar Jath lack a waterproofing meeting the standards set by corporate rules. The photographs that we took of an empty pond reveal that the foils lining the bank are in fact intact—and that those on the pond's bottom show a high degree of damaging. This has been caused by caterpillar tractors—as shown by the tracks. A drainage capable of returning contaminants-containing liquids emanating through leaks into the cycle of disposal does not exist. This in turn means that—in the worst case—should the waterproofing not function—6,500 tons of salts would be making their ways each year during seepages into the upper aquifer.

We notice something else. The figures supplied to us enable our calculation of the amount of water produced in the facility. A comparison between the amounts taken up and released every day—and the factoring in of the volume evaporated—yields a huge difference. This loss is not to be explained by the produced water treatment methods presented to us, assuming their diligent and professional application. In a nutshell: the fate of 862,800 liters of produced water a day is unknown. We tend to favor the assumption that these 862,800 liters seep from the bioremedation facility into the ground ever day. That is the only way we can account for this difference. This, in turn,

Above | Drinking water is carried in buckets and cannisters. People waiting at a drinking water dispensing outlet in Rier.

Below | the dung dropped by cows being watered at the wells can contaminate the upper aquifer. Sign of Hope has launched workshops on the protection of water. At them, the people are taught to keep their livestock away from the wells.

would constitute direct proof that the produced water treatment system leaks.

Norconsult's study is based on, in a further point of criticism, highly questionable premises. The claim that the ground water permeable layer is protected against water infiltrating from above by a thick and impermeable layer of clay is not accurate. All of the samples taken during drilling in the area under question display porosities to be classified according to the applicable DIN norms as being "weakly permeable", and not at all as "impermeable". Such a classification does not exist in DIN, and that is because it is impossible. The scientifically-proved mean of the amount of fresh water feeding into the upper ground water aquifer during the three months-long rainy season amounts to 20–100 mm a year, as compared to the average annual precipitation of 1,200 mm. Also to be taken into account are soil conditions, which show a great degree of variation. During the dry season, the "black cotton soil" typical of the region develops deep cracks, through which surface water can seep into layers lying deep down.

The infiltration of produced water into the upper aquifer is clearly revealed by analyses of the water's chemistry. African Water comprehensively investigated this for Sign of Hope. The organization's findings are now being detailed once more—with the Norwegian experts in attendance.

The ground water found in the upper aquifer has natural characteristics leading to its being classified as contemporary era-created, hydrogen carbonate-dominated water. The chemical composition of the water found in the upper aquifer under the oil field has a completely different "look". This water has a chemical composition found only in the drilling fluids and produced water tested. This constitutes clear proof of contamination through the oil industry.

We had sent our study to Norconsult. Their experts now tell us at this meeting that they had not been aware of the differences proved. While dispatching the study, we had also furnished a map pinpointing our venues of samples-taking. We no longer have any reason to wonder why Norconsult never repeated this sampling at those areas. The Norwegians state that the transmission of our documents within their company was obviously a victim of a communications problem.

We ask the SPOC's CEO if the recommendations contained in Norconsult's study have been implemented. He says no, despite the fact that sixteen months have elapsed since the completion of the study. SPOC rejects our criticism by pointing out that all environmental protection measures have to be approved by South Sudan's authorities. We refute this contention. South Sudan's Petroleum Act of 2012 contains the generally-applicable principles of the "polluter pays".[36] The Act also comprises an entire catalog of rules facilitating the protection of the environment and requiring oil companies to institute internationally-recognized best practices.[37] Another factor requiring considering is the principle of "polluters pay". This has applied throughout the world since its being promulgated in the United Nation's environmental summit in Rio in 1992.[38] All these stipulations compel the polluter to respond immediately in cases of serious incidents—in this case, of contamination.

We draw the SPOC's president's attention to his statement—contained in a press release issued at the end of 2009—that the WNPOC/SPOC has always pursued—in accordance with the internationally-applicable HSE standards—a strict "zero pollutant and discharge" policy in such ecologically-sensitive areas as the Sudd. The president refuses to recognize any self-contradiction. He explains that this only applies to the exploration of resources.

We insist once more on getting a look at the documents that we have striven to secure so many times. We are told that the authorities of South Sudan have to approve each release of such documents. This unfortunately impairs the communication. At the end of the meeting, we ask if Norconsult's study corresponds at all to one of the investigations recommended by the Trondheim Report of 2009 as being needed to be immediately performed. Both the SPOC and Norconsult declare that this is not the case.

It remains unclear how the Norwegian experts could conclude that the imperiling of health within the CPF is low—and negligible outside it, with this "mystery" especially applying to the endangering of people living outside Thar Jath. Norconsult itself noted in its study that its objective was not to cover all potential sources of contamination found with the WNPOC oil fields. The experts reported having taken only a few samples in Mala—and having conducted no further field work there or in any other WNPOC area outside of Thar Jath.

The study's findings are thus not based on its actual research. Nor is the study's approach internally coherent. Its ultimate conclusions are simply not at all substantiated.

*

At the end of 2012, we reach the following agreement with the SPOC. It will provide us with the documents requested by us. This has always been a matter of basic agreement, the consortium reiterates. It courteously requests our excusing the exceptional slowness of communication. This was caused by the complicated process of consultation with South Sudan's officials and with the companies involved. We should not delude ourselves into believing that the conditions of operation in South Sudan are the same as those in Europe or in the USA, in which oil companies have a greater freedom of operation.

Our main thrust is providing on-site practical assistance. This is being pursued by the GIZ project. We do not want to do anything to endanger the project. We decide to refrain from exerting any further pressure, and to await the delivery of the documents promised to us. We receive no feedback from the Ministry itself. It in turn is being kept abreast of developments. This is being accomplished through exchanges of information.

*

→ Sidebar: Norconsult, human rights and the independence of auditors

It's worth taking a closer look at Norconsult. The company is renowned. Polls of Norwegian students on their favorite employers in the country place Norconsult near the top of these rankings. The students prize the consultant's positive working environment—and the prospects of having an international career through it. Norconsult operates highly successfully in a large number of countries.

This Norwegian corporate role model has, however, often been the object of criticism. This has been levied by human rights activists, who have noticed that Norconsult's appraisals have failed to observe human rights. In December, 1997, the Society for Threatened Peoples issued a scathing critique of Norconsult and their fellow Norwegians' Norwegian Agency for Development Cooperation (NORAD). The Society claimed the duo had issued fallacious reports on their having taken into account the concerns of the indigenous people when compiling a feasibility study for the construction of a dam to be located in northern Namibia. This case has gone down into history as the "Epupa debate".[39]

A German ethnologist had been commissioned by Norconsult with the contacting of representatives of the Himba, the tribe directly affected by the project. The Himba live in the region in which the dam was to be built. The ethnologist was clearly and unmistakably told by the tribe that it rejected both of the locations suggested for the dam, and, as well, any discussion about possible indemnification, reported the Society.[40] The Himba were not ready to yield the land in which their ancestors had lived.

The construction of the dam would mean the end of the archaic lifestyle and culture of the Himba, pastoralists living in the valleys of the Kunune, which is located in the lands forming the border between Angola and Nambia, noted the project's critics.[41] As the human rights experts pointed out, notwithstanding this, Norconsult had claimed that the Himba had consented to the launching of negotiations on the amount of indemnification to be paid to them[42]—and thus to their being resettled. This was definitely wrong.

The government of Namibia planned to reach a decision on the project in February 1998. This raised the peril of a fait accompli's being executed—against the express will of the people directly affected by the project and causing the breaching of their compulsory rights to participate.[43] Sweden's development assistance arm had already withdrawn from the project.[44] The only party still pursuing the dam project was NORAD, which was boosted by the appraisal issued by Norconsult. Questions as to the economic feasibility of the dam had caused the World Bank, the European Union, Dresdner Bank and many other parties to decide to not participate in the project, reports the Society for Threatened Peoples.[45]

Norconsult's project head had told journalists months prior to the publishing of the feasibility study that the consultant was expecting to reap follow-up contracts. These would be yielded through its work on the dam project.[46] This constitutes a clear

conflict of interest, states Morton Rønning, the Norwegian journalist: "Does anybody believe that this wish for new contracts
will not influence the company's own so called independent studies of the consequences?"[47] National and international-level protests caused the construction of the dam to be halted.[48]

The publicly-conveyed criticism obviously failed to teach
Norconsult anything. An official mediation pursued in 2015 in
Norway considered Norconsult's contraventions of Organization
for Economic Cooperation and Development (OECD) directives.
These arose from its appraisal of dam projects in Malaysia. The
consultants from Norway were hired to compile a study of the
feasibility of building dams located in the rain forest of the Malaysian island of Borneo. Norconsult failed to enlist the involvement
of the population indigenous to the region when putting together
its study. Norconsult's staff had, in fact, gone so far as to refuse to
speak with representatives of the parties opposing the dam projects, who had made the trip to Norway for that purpose.[49]

The mediation established clearly that consultants are also
required to observe the OECD's directives on multinational transactions. This especially applies to the protection of human rights.
The compilation of feasibility studies requires the securing of the
participation of the population involved. Also compulsory is the
taking into account and consideration of the rights of indigenous
people that accrue to them in such endeavors. Also coming in for
criticism was Norconsult's acting as a consultant for the controversial project, and that it had concluded further agreements with
the commissioning party prior to submitting its appraisal. Another critical point: Norconsult's maintaining of the view that it
had to keep these matters confidential.[50]

The mediation concluded in August. Norconsult committed
itself to disclosing its proprietary stakes in companies, and to expand its corporate directives to encompass the stipulations fore-

seen by international rules on the maintenance of the diligence requisite to engage in such transactions. A key pledge rendered by Norconsult: to secure participation by the citizens affected. Such critical observers as the Switzerland-based Bruno Manser Fonds, which fights for the interests of the residents indigenous to Borneo's rain forests, regard the agreement reached by the official mediator with Norconsult as being an admission of its having failed to conduct the requisite examination of human rights when entering into business relationships with the Malaysian company that commissioned the building of the dams.[51]

Norconsult insists that it has verified the adherence to rules by its Malaysia-based commissioning party—Sarawak Energy Berhad (SEB). This adherence is said to be a product of SEB's having signed the Hydropower Sustainability Protocol.[52] This reasoning causes critics to shake their heads.[53] International environment experts have been questioning for many years the efficaciousness of such self-commitments. This is because they are formulated by the large-sized energy companies themselves, and because they contain no compulsory enforcement mechanism.[54]

Via Norpower, its Malaysia-based subsidiary, Norconsult participates in the dam projects. These have been for many years the objects of widespread debates in the public arena. This has been due to the projects' failures to take into account the interests of the population involved, and to corruption and to construction deficiencies. The corruption controversy is centered around Sarawak Energy Berhad, which is headed by CEO Torstein Dale Sjotveit, a Norwegian.[55] This debate is being waged not only in Malaysia, but, rather, also in the countries in which companies that want (or wanted) to participate in these projects are headquartered. Criticisms voiced in Australian media caused a company from there to withdraw from the dam projects.[56]

The Murum dam has already been completed. In a violation of OECD rules, Norconsult compiled the expertise for this structure, which evinces dramatic construction errors. This fact was conveyed in 2014 to the general public by a whistle blower, who leaked the findings of Norconsult's secret investigation.[57] The setting forth of protests led in November 2015 to the canceling of the construction of the Baram dam.[58]

The fact that Norconsult is expanding its business in Malaysia joins with the above-mentioned developments in casting doubt on the independence of the consultant's audits. A further factor speaking for dependency is that the appraisal commissioned by the South Sudan Petroleum Ministry was paid for by the operators of the oil consortium.[59] Petronas owns a majority share in the consortium's equity. Petronas is also leading the development of Malaysia's energy sector, with this particularly applying to Sarawak.[60] The company is thus a promising source of further commissions. Norconsult's track record shows that the consultant's greed for such commissions has clouded its objectivity of focus. This doesn't have to be premeditated. As stated by the Norwegian journalist Morten Rønning. "Believing is seeing!"

Riek Machar (left) and Salva Kiir commemorate in Juba John Garang, the rebel leader who was killed in a helicopter crash in 2005.

2013

The country recognizes the danger

On April 20th, Nico Rosberg—in a surprising success—wins the second pole position of his Formula 1 career. It is at the Grand Prix of Bahrain. Notwithstanding this success, his team does not hold great expectations for the race itself. It turns out that they are right. Rosberg is passed repeatedly during the race, which he finishes in ninth place. The Silver Arrows have trouble getting the best-performing tires.

★

On April 30th, the last of the three well-building projects undertaken by Sign of Hope in Rubway, Kuach and Nhyaldiu—each supported by Germany's BMZ Ministry of Economic Cooperation and Development—is concluded. The wells are then commissioned. With the help of these deep wells roughly 13,000 people can be supplied with potable water on a daily basis. Each of these wells can provide 10,000 liters of fresh water per day. This means that each person has 2.3 liters available now. The aggregated costs of these three wells amounted to € 463,000. The German Ministry for Economic Cooperation and Development (BMZ) has contributed € 200,000 to this project. It is one of the most impressive experiences for us to see the joy in the faces of the people who we could assist with these wells. We are repeatedly asked whether it is our task to alleviate the damages caused by the oil industry. Our answer is: It is the nature of humanitarian aid to assist exactly there where human beings suffer. This is irrespective of what or of who has caused their suffering. In the same way Klaus Stieglitz builds his mandate on a quote of Hildegard von Bingen: "Care for life, wherever you find it."

*

The Grand Prix of Spain is held on May 12th. Nico Rosberg starts it from, once more, the pole position, with Lewis Hamilton in second place. Daimler boss Dieter Zetsche is at the race. "I'm the lucky charm," he tells the TV cameras.[1] But not for Mercedes' two drivers. Rosberg finishes sixth, with Hamilton a dismal twelfth. Same problem as previously. The Silver Arrows' tires fail to give them the proper traction—this time as early as after five rounds have been completed, with this lack's being visible to the naked eye.[2] "Der Spiegel" describes the race as being a further embarrassment, and reports rumors of Mercedes' competitors' having started to make fun of it.[3]

*

The Grand Prix of Monaco is run on May 27th. Nico Rosberg begins the race, as he had in the past, from the pole position. This time, he leads the race from the opening gun to the crossing of the finishing line. This is set to be a triumphal moment in Rosberg's career. Precisely 30 years previously—in 1983—his father, Keke, won the very same renowned race. Keke was racing in those days for the Williams team. Nico's triumph is marred by accusations levied by competing teams. Mercedes is said to have conducted secret and impermissible test drives prior to the race.[4] To test the tires manufactured by Pirelli, Mercedes undertook a drive lasting three days and covering 1000 kilometers. The tires used were those also employed by Mercedes' race cars.[5] The problem with that: the rules forbid such tests.[6] Pirelli argues that an agreement with FIA (Fédération Internationale de l'Automobile—the world association of racing)—stipulates that the company is allowed to test its tires for each car. The extent of this test: one thousand kilometers of driving.[7] FIA has, however, predicated the permissibility of such tests on all teams having the opportunity to conduct them.[8] Mercedes' competitors cry "distortions of competition", "illegal advantage" and "fraud".[9] A racing insider tells the "Spiegel" that Mercedes probably also used the tests in question to try out special aerodynamic components. These were then subsequently incorporated into the race cars prior to the race in Monaco.[10] Niki Lauda, head of the supervisory board of Mercedes' Formula 1 team, responds to the charges by stating that FIA had approved the test drives.[11] Announced in June is that Mercedes will have to answer to a tribunal convened by FIA. This court reaches at the end of June the verdict—after a hearing lasting several hours—that Mercedes and Pirelli are to receive a warning.[12] A further slap on the wrist is Mercedes AMG Petronas' Formula 1 team's not being permitted to participate in the forthcoming Young Driver Test.[13] The incident leads to no other consequences.

*

Responding to an initiative from George Clooney, Nespresso announced in July[14] that it would join the USA's TechnoServe assistance program in launching a project in South Sudan designed to revive the country's coffee sector.[15] The region's long tradition of coffee cultivation had been interrupted by the decades-long civil war. South Sudan is considered to be one of the birthplaces of coffee. Its climate is ideally suited for the growing of high-quality coffee. It is one of the few areas in the world in which coffee still grows wild.[16] This long-term project is to be carried out with the country's government, and is designed to make it less dependent upon oil.[17]

*

On September 17th, the Juba-based Committee for Land, Agriculture, Natural Resources and the Environment of the Parliament of South Sudan submits a report on the impact of the oil industry in Unity and in the Upper Nile, and how oil companies have been handling these effects.[18] According to this report, the production of oil has resulted in the poisoning of significant numbers of livestock, and has exposed vegetation and human beings to great perils to their health. To provide an example of this: in the period 2000–2008, contaminated water devastated some 100 hectares of forests in the area of Paloich. This water had been released without ever having been treated in any way. The ensuing salination is also very negatively affecting the soil. The Committee demands of the country's parliament the prompt enactment of an environmental law. The Committee also calls for the promulgation of an act especially addressing the relationship between oil and the environment. Oil companies are to be required to dispose of produced water and spilled oil in proper and appropriate ways, and to thus ensure that humans and animals are not exposed to any endangering. A final demand is the commissioning by the country's Ministry of Environment of experts capable of conducting a comprehensive societal and ecological audit of the regions affected.[19]

The report leads to a three-hour, hotly-fought debate in Parliament.[20] This process concludes with the Committee and the country's Ministries of Petroleum and of the Environment committing themselves to jointly submitting this environ-

Above | Located in Nyal, Sign of Hope's bush clinic is a main source of medical treatment for the residents in the region.

Below | A staff member at the hospital in Rumbek explains the importance of hygiene.

mental audit to Parliament within three months. The objective of this is to rapidly institute measures protecting people, animals and the environment from experiencing further negative effects emanating from the production of oil.[21]

*

At the end of September our clinic in Nyal is operative since 100 days. The clinic is a huge sign of hope. This is not only since many seeking help receive basic medical treatment there on a daily basis. But this is also since the clinic helps us bridge the ever growing tensions between the ethnic groups of the Nuer and the Dinka. Our hospital in Rumbek is located in the area of Dinka people. Our clinic in Nyal is situated in the area of Nuer people.

Nyal is located particularly remote in the southern part of Unity State. During the rainy season the dirt roads are flooded. There is no longer any way of getting through by lorries. The health center has to be supplied by air on a temporal basis. This is as long as the bumpy runway is not inundated. The Sign of Hope-staff members conduct protective vaccinations. They help with deliveries and treat ailments such as malaria, respiratory and diarrheal diseases and skin problems. In special feeding schemes people who suffer from hunger are nourished. Moreover employees of the organization conduct small surgical interventions.

Each morning, when the clinic opens its doors, sick people arrive and patients receive medical examination and treatment. People here look for a spot in the shade in front of the outpatient care rooms. Here simple benches serve as seating. A staff member who originates from Nyal himself makes use of the waiting time. He teaches patients and their relatives about hygiene. He explains why it is so important to wash one's hands and how people can impede the transmitting of inflectional diseases. With regard to medical aid Sign of Hope talks to the few other organizations on-site and help each other where possible. Our organization and the government of Unity State have agreed on a Memorandum of Understanding. Here our obligations to provide medical aid are stipulated as well as the services of support the Ministry of Health of Unity State renders to our clinic.

*

At the end of September, further details of the report issued by the Committee for Land, Agriculture, Natural Resources and the Environment become known. The regions affected are said to be experiencing large numbers of miscarriages, of premature births and of malformed children.[22] Many women have been rendered infertile.[23] The Minister of Petroleum confirms the information presented in the report, with this especially applying to malformations.[24] There was incident in Paloich, in which a mother gave birth to a child lacking eyes, a nose and genitals.[25] The Ministry of Petroleum commissions the compiling of a medical audit, so as to find out the real causes.[26]

*

Published on October 15th is the United States Agency for International Development's (USAID) concluding report on the activities of the Economic Governance Project in South Sudan, which was commissioned to implement the HSE (Health, Safety and Environment) Management System—in accordance with the Petroleum Act of 2012.[27] South Sudan's Ministry of Petroleum places the report on its Website. The study conducted by this American organization finds a large number of alarming aspects in the documentation of the production and other

Abandoned oil well at Thar Jath. Gunfire is the probable cause of the leaks in this oil well. The ammunition found in the immediate vicinity of the well indicates that a tank was stationed here during the fights for this oil field (photo taken in February 2015).

operations undertaken by the country's three consortia—the Sudd Petroleum Operating Company (SPOC), the Greater Pioneer Operating Company (GPOC) and the Dar Petroleum Operating Company (DPOC). Provided by the consortia themselves, these documents covered the ramifications upon health, security and the environment of their activities.[28]

According to the study, a large number of these documents lacked the details required to properly report on production procedures and processes forming part of them.[29] The documents contained numerous examples of pledges to adhere to corporate philosophies' being—inadequately—substituted for the provision of proof showing that the requisite operations yield security and that they are capable of being documented. The upshot of all this: in a number of cases it was not possible to establish whether or not the requisite management systems had at all been implemented at the consortia's various sites of oil production.[30]

According to the American experts, the documents contain no information explicitly designating the persons responsible for the pursuing of the remediation of decommissioned production sites and of other projects that been concluded.[31] The experts stated that there were reasons to believe that several of the oil firms maintained quality assurance programs that rely upon the limited objectivity shown by internal auditors of such.[32] The experts discovered documentation of risk control procedures that are not capable of reaching out to communities or to other outside parties facing environmental perils.[33] The American experts also noticed that the scope of the oil companies' security management systems is restricted to proprietary staff members, and that, accordingly, such systems limitedly—or not at all—encompass the health and security the people living or farming in the vicinity of the facilities.[34]

This focus on the security of own workforces has the implication that there are very few plans for dealing with potential ramifications upon or imperiling of the environment by both normal operations or through accidents of such.[35] Processes of risk assessment and management were said not to encompass subcontractors, thus obviating any—requisite—supervision of such.[36] The Americans also cited indication of crises' leading to misinterpretation of the code of rules.[37]

As a general rule, inspections and case studies had established a significant discrepancy between the documentation of operations and the reality of such.[38] This lack of correspondence gives rise to the conclusion that the implementation of a well-functioning HSE management system has been a failure.[39] The exclusion from consideration of the endangering of local residents and of the protection of the environment have been nearly completely lost from consideration, stated the American experts.[40] These gaps have negatively influenced the fulfillment of security and environmental standards.[41]

To solve the problem, the USAID's expert held seminars attended by staff members working for the country's Petroleum and Environment Ministries and for the National Oil and Gas Commission of South Sudan.[42] A large number of representatives—from a wide variety of departments of the government of South Sudan—had expressed their concerns as to the security of oil production facilities and as to their ramifications upon the environment. The seminar was well attended. Its participants were briefed on the applicable codes of laws and how they are to be interpreted in daily work.[43] One problem became apparent. Officials often still do not know what the internationally-valid rules are. This lack of knowledge causes these people to be unaware of their ways of exerting pressure. South Sudan lacks procedural rules that standardize such interventions.

A further seminar covered the ways and means of convincing oil companies to live up to their obligations.[44] The experts see the most important problem as stemming from the dual role occupied by the Ministry of Petroleum, which is both the promoter of oil production and the defender of human beings and of the environment. It is well known that such conflicts of interest lead to the reaching of decisions not respecting the interests of human beings and the environment. This structure of responsibility is not capable of regulating the oil industry in a way leading to a credible protection of the environment.[45]

*

On October 22nd, Geoffrey York, political correspondent for Canada's "The Globe and Mail", reports that one of the largest foreign investors in Canada's energy sector has broken the embargo on the delivery of weapons imposed by the United Nations on Sudan due to the Darfur conflict. The report names Petronas (Petroliam Nasional Berhad). Owned by the Malaysian government, this company has just announced plans to invest $US 36 billion in British Columbia. The article states that human rights and weapons trade experts have found that Petronas has supplied the kerosene fueling Sudan's bombers and ground war-waging aircraft. These, in turn, have flown missions in Darfur.[46] These charges are backed up with photographs taken in 2011 and 2012. They show Petronas tank trucks' filling the military jets stationed in the Nyala airport.[47] The UN's experts confirm that this constitutes a breaching of the embargo.[48] Petronas does not respond to the charges posed by this Canadian journalist. The company does, however, confirm the truth of the charge. This confirmation is made to the Swiss "Small Arms Survey" organization. Petronas has an excuse to offer. The airport in question is actually for civilian use.[49] The company couldn't do anything about the military's having assumed control over it.[50]

The General Secretary of the Canadian chapter of Amnesty International strictly rejects this stance. There are no conceivable grounds justifying such a breach of the embargo. Nor is there any way to excuse this.[51] Petronas' response unsettles him, the General Secretary states.[52] This presents the situation as being the company's serving civilians at the airport, which is occasionally taken over the military. This downplaying of responsibility does not represent an appropriate fulfillment of diligence responsibilities.[53] The representative of Amnesty International calls upon the Canadian government to more closely scrutinize the human rights track records of such companies as Petronas when considering the approval of transactions encompassing non-Canadian companies.[54] Other Canadian media start covering this topic.[55] Calls are voiced to reconsider the $US 36 billion deal.

Responding to the numerous reports in the media, Petronas publishes on October 25th a press release presenting an explanation as to why it has delivered kerosene to Sudan's air force.[56] According to the release, Petronas' subsidiary Petronas Marketing Sudan Limited (PMSL)—which operates in Sudan and which is the object of criticism—has supported since 2007 the joint mission being undertaken by UNAMID (African Union/United Nations Hybrid Operation in Darfur) by providing it with kerosene.[57] The contract with UNAMID was extended in 2013 by a further five years.[58] Petronas is thus directly enabling UNAMID's rendering of humanitarian assistance.[59] The statement issued by the Malaysian company says that it wants to emphasize that the reason for its presence at Nyala airport, which is a civilian-use one, is to be of service to UNAMID and to airlines, be they from Sudan or abroad.

The company alleges that the control over the services provided at the airport of Nyala is occasionally taken over by Sudanese officials, with these especially including the Civilian Aviation Authority. In such cases, PMSL—as is the case for the other providers of on-site services—is required to observe the locally-applicable stipulations, with these including the directives issued by Sudan's Civil Aviation Authority (CAA).[60] Such a directive could contain the instructions to supply the Sudanese air force with kerosene.[61] The only alternative would be to completely shut down this business. This would also, however, mean not being able to supply UNAMID and other parties.[62] Petronas considers the contract to deliver supplies to UNAMID to constitute sufficient proof of its support of humanitarian assistance in Sudan. The Malaysian company rejects the intimation that the situation gives rises to a questionable human rights track record.[63] PMSL observes local and internationally-applicable laws and will continue to do such.[64]

The General Secretary of Amnesty International Canada rejects this position. The fact that support is being provided to UNAMID does not constitute a reason to excuse or justify the breaking of the embargo.[65] Petronas has to ensure that its transactions do not lead to any possible breaking of the embargo.[66]

A former member of the UN's Panel of Experts also publicly refutes the stance taken by Petronas.[67] The provision of support to an international peace mission does not justify the provision of banned auxiliary military supplies. This would be analogous to someone's excusing the delivery of weapons to the Darfur rebel groups by pointing out that these weapons are also being supplied to the peacekeeping troops.[68]

*

A Kenyan radio station reports on October 28th that the Chairman of the Parliamentary Special Committee on Land, Agriculture, Natural Resources and the Environment in South Sudan has criticized the country's Petroleum Ministry. Occasion for the statement is the presentation of the report at a workshop hosted by the Institute for the Development of a Civil Society.[69] The Chairman is cited as saying that the Ministry is now trying to do something about the pollution of the environment by the oil industry.[70] But this doesn't change the fact that the oil ministry is the causer of the contamination.[71] The Ministry is after all there to make sure that oil is produced, as this earns money for the government.[72] It is also a positive thing that the Ministry is now taking on the protection of the environment. Its main job remains, this notwithstanding, fostering the oil business.[73] The Deputy Minister of Petroleum is taking part in the workshop. She admits to the oil industry's causing of damages and environmental problems.[74] While doing such, she pledges that the Ministry will join the parties involved in working hard to come up with ways of reducing environmental risks.[75] The broadcaster reports that the Minister of Petroleum has come out in favor of the resettlement of the people living in the areas involved.[76]

★

At the beginning of November, official institutions in the state of Unity announce that they will start treating severely oil companies that pollute the environment.[77] The institutions state that nearly all oil wells in Unity had been damaged during the rainy season, which lasts from April to November. The ensuing leaks from the oil wells are now posing a threat to the people living near them's health and livelihoods.[78] The oil companies operating in Unity are said to have warned the residents against dwelling close to the oil rigs. For their own security, the residents are not to drink any water taken from bodies of water located in the vicinity of the oil wells.[79] Founded using support from the Norwegian People's Aid, a working circle comprised of South Sudanese journalists takes on the job of raising the consciousness of local residents about this danger.[80]

The measures undertaken by the government of Unity comprise the imposition of stipulations upon the oil industry, which is now required to designate areas as being dangerous, and to build facilities providing clean drinking water, medical treatment and education.[81] The government of Unity also encourages local workers employed by the oil companies to found proprietary unions, and to ensure that information on accidents is more rapidly communicated to communities in the region.[82]

*

The 2013 Formula 1 season comes to an end on November 24th, with the staging in Sao Paulo of the Brazilian Grand Prix. The season has proven Mercedes' most successful since its return to Formula 1. Mercedes' drivers won three races, and finished in the top three six times. The drivers also did well in other races. These successes cause Lewis Hamilton to place fourth among the Formula 1 drivers, with Nico Rosberg finishing sixth. In the rankings of the teams, Mercedes finishes an excellent second, behind Red Bull and ahead—barely—of Ferrari.

*

A brutal power struggle breaks out in South Sudan on December 17th. It is between South Sudan's President, Salva Kiir, and Riek Machar Teny, who had been Kiir's Vice-President prior to being thrown out. Machar is backed by an army of his own.

It now battles South Sudan's military. Both sides show the utmost in brutality when waging war. They show absolutely no consideration to civilians. This power struggle is primarily about gaining control over the country's oil. South Sudan's oil fields become the main targets of the rebels.

As war breaks out, acting on a commission from Sign of Hope, African Water's team is undertaking the drilling of two further deep wells. The holes drilled are sealed. South Sudan's military helps the teams get evacuated out of this war zone.

*

Battles are launched on December 19th in the state of Unity. On the first day of warfare, eleven people are killed in the Thar Jath oil field.[83] A week later, South Sudan's government admits that the rebels have brought the oil field of Thar Jath under their control.[84] The oil producing facilities have been damaged.

Life is hard for the people in South Sudan—even for the ones living far away from the oil fields. The people living in the cattle camps are open-minded and hospitable. They are ready to share the little that they have.

2014

Fighting for oil

The Grand Prix of Australia is the first race of the 2014 Formula 1 season. It takes place on March 16th on Melbourne's Albert Park Circuit. Lewis Hamilton has the pole position. Two places behind is Nico Rosberg. He in turn zooms out to the front of the pack at the start of the race—and never looks back. Hamilton is hampered from the very start by the misfiring of his motor, which forces him to leave the race early on. Rosberg's victory is the 100th achieved by a Silver Arrow in a world championship race.

*

Sign of Hope and representatives from Germany's GIZ agency for international development meet on March 25th in Konstanz. The objective of the meeting is to discuss the future of the two groups' working relationship. Germany's Foreign Ministry has issued travel warnings for South Sudan. This has caused the evacuation of GIZ' s staff from the country. One reason why GIZ wants to pursue the working relationship with Sign of Hope is our maintaining of local personnel in South Sudan.

We learn during the meeting with GIZ's representatives that the organization—via its GIZ International Services arm—has called off its talks with Petronas (Petroliam Nasional Berhad) on the project of building wells. This was due to Petronas' refusal to participate in these. It had purportedly learned that the only companies eligible to enter into such partnerships with Germany's government are those based in Germany.

*

The 2014 Petronas Malaysia Grand Prix takes place on March 30th on the country's Sepang International Circuit. It is the second race of this year's Formula 1 season. Hamilton is the fastest driver in the first free practice session; Rosberg in the second and third ones. Hamilton achieves the top speeds at the subsequent qualifying session. This gives him the pole position. Rosberg starts the race, once more, two places behind him. Hamilton wins the race, with Rosberg coming in second. This is the first top two finish by a Mercedes team since 1955's Grand Prix of Italy. Rosberg tops the rankings of the Formula 1 drivers. Hot on his heels is Hamilton.

*

On May 24th, Mercedes and Petronas announce the long-term setting forth of their partnership. Venue for the announcement is Monaco.[1] We are striving for "a decade of partnership"[2] state the two. "We are proud to be the partner of Mercedes-Benz, the manufacturer of the best automobiles in the world. This partnership covers race courses and forms part of our strategic network of corporate alliances," adds Tan Sri Dato' Shamsul Azhar Abbas, Petronas' president.[3] "The working relationship between Mercedes-Benz and Petronas is to be extended from the race track to the world's streets. This will be a key thrust of this strategic network of corporate alliances," he continues.[4] Trade journals comment that its sponsorship of Mercedes seems to be paying off for Petronas.[5] Toto Wolff, Executive Director of the Mercedes team, tells the media that Petronas has become the most famous energy company in the Formula 1 since 2010 and its joining the team.[6] "We have worked together as a unit. Our world-class partnership has given rise to fluid technology solutions that have yielded provable competitive advantages. These have driven our successes on race tracks in 2014. The final result is a partnership that is bearing fruit on all levels."[7]

*

An article appears in the August edition of "gwf—Wasser/Abwasser". It is entitled "Influence of anthropogenic contaminants on the quality of water in an aquifer in the Sudd, South Sudan". This article presents the scientific study commissioned by Sign of Hope of the potable water in South Sudan.[8] The authors of the article are Hella Rüskamp (African Water), Klaus Stieglitz (Sign of Hope), Christoph Treskatis (professor at the Technical University of Darmstadt) and John Ariki (professor at the University of Juba). Forming part of a peer review process, two independent experts verify the article's premises, methods, analyses and conclusions prior to its being published. The acceptance of the article for publication constitutes the establishment of the scientific accuracy of all of Sign of Hope's findings. The connection between the oil industry and the contamination of ground water has now also been recognized by the academic community as being proven.

*

Sign of Hope's work in South Sudan is being overshadowed by the brutal struggle for power between Salva Kiir, the country's president, and his rival Riek Machar. The number of refugees fleeing to other parts of the country and cared for by our organization strongly increases. Our clinic in Rumbek is capable of operating during the entire year. The security situation is tense in this region—but it is not bad enough to force us to evacuate our non-Sudanese staff. The number of patients treated by us rises dramatically. The combat plaguing large parts of South Sudan makes a number of roads impassable. As a result of this, medications and other supplies have to be flown to the clinics.

Our non-Sudanese staff in Nyal is not capable of working the entire year. This is due to the difficulties prevailing. Notwithstanding this, the vaccination program that we are being joined by UNICEF and WHO in carrying out can be partially pursued. Local personnel staff our facility providing emergency medical care to the people in the region. The ever-larger stream of refugees causes the number of patients forecast to be treated during the year to be set at nearly 60,000.

The lack of security drives many people to flee. They are thus no longer there to cultivate their plots. Extremely heavy rains make roads impassable. Both factors cause the local supply of food to break down. Famine is the result. To mitigate this, we set up an assistance program. It feeds some 11,000 people in various parts of South Sudan. We usually rely on chartered airplanes to convey these supplies. The armed conflicts prohibit this use. Our supplies are flown in by the helicopters of the United Nations Humanitarian Air Service.

*

In November, the scientific article on the connection between the oil industry and the contamination of groundwater is published in English in the "Zentralblatt für Geologie und Paläontologie".[9] We prepare our next trip to South Sudan. Its purpose is to use this article to present the findings of our scientific study to the general public in Juba. One of the objectives of our work to protect human rights has long been to equip the people living in the oil fields with the facts and figures—in this case, contained in a scientific appraisal—that they require to under-

Sent by the oil industry, a tanker truck
brings water to the inhabitants of Rier.
According to Sign of Hope's research,
this water is drawn from the nearby Nile.
The only treatment that it receives is
the admixture of chlorine. According to
the residents, the transports of water
occur irregularly.

stand what is being done to them and to take counteractions. The people should know what is happening to their water. And we want to help them to demand their rights to safe water—in well-substantiated ways.

*

Mercedes' Formula 1 concludes the 2014 season by registering a long list of amazing records. Lewis Hamilton is the world champion, with Nico Rosberg finishing second. Mercedes is the number one constructor of automobiles in the Formula 1. The company has thus finally reached the objectives that it set for itself upon its having returned to the Formula 1. Hamilton and Rosberg won 16 races in 2014. They thus broke McLaren's record of 15, which was set in 1988 by Ayrton Senna and Alain Prost. Mercedes also set a new record for top 2 finishes by a team's drivers. This best mark, too, had been set in 1998 by McLaren.[10] A further all-time high: the Silver Arrow drivers finished in the top three in 2014 more often—31 times—than any other team's drivers in history in one season.[11] The previous record of 29 was established by Ferrari in 2004.[12]

*

At the end of the year, we resolve to visit once more Thar Jath, with this to be done as soon as the security situation permits such. We have received reports of combat having taken place around the abandoned facilities. We have repeatedly perused satellite pictures. These have enabled us to get a fairly good idea of what is happening at the oil fields. Control over them keeps on going back and forth—between the government's army and that of the rebels. Battles are still flaring up from time to time. It's not always easy to answer the question of who controls Thar Jath at the moment. We are well aware of the fact that we will be traveling to an area of crisis, one in which volatility prevails. The people living there need our help more than ever before.

It is possible only to guess at the true extent of the damaging of Thar Jath. We have to assume that the destruction of the produced water treatment facilities and the overflowing of oil have greatly exacerbated the poisoning of the environment. One factor has never been considered by us. It now forces its way into our deliberations. Is building such facilities in areas of crisis—and in which, further, sensitive ecosystems such as the Sudd are found—basically or at all justifiable? This applies especially to the concept of creating above-ground disposal systems.

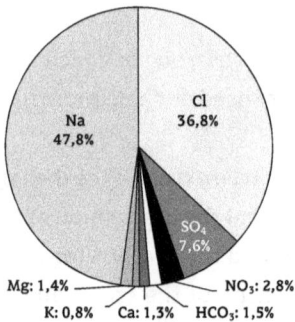

Na 47,8%

Cl 36,8%

SO$_4$ 7,6%

Mg: 1,4%   NO$_3$: 2,8%

K: 0,8%   Ca: 1,3%   HCO$_3$: 1,5%

Electr. conductivity 4300 µS/cm

Produced water

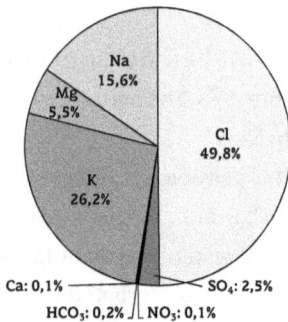

Na 15,6%

Mg 5,5%

Cl 49,8%

K 26,2%

Ca: 0,1%   SO$_4$: 2,5%

HCO$_3$: 0,2%   NO$_3$: 0,1%

Electr. conductivity 78800 µS/cm

Mud pit

Shallow well Rier

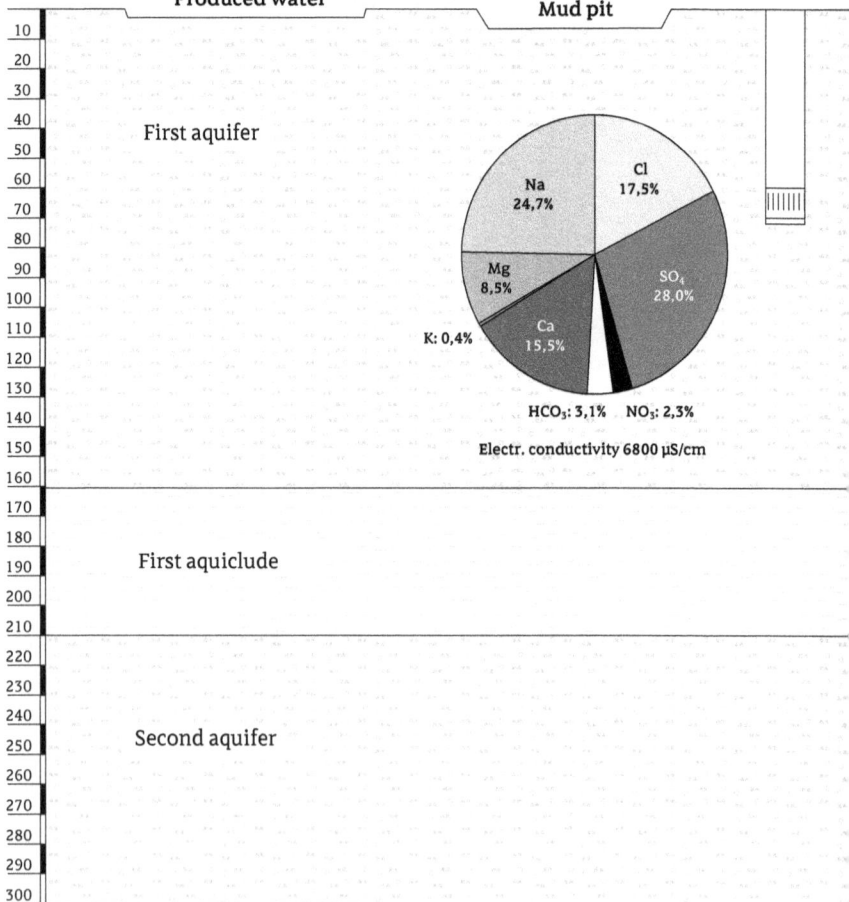

Meters below ground level

10	
20	
30	
40	
50	First aquifer
60	
70	
80	
90	
100	
110	
120	
130	
140	
150	
160	
170	
180	
190	First aquiclude
200	
210	
220	
230	
240	
250	Second aquifer
260	
270	
280	
290	
300	

Na 24,7%

Cl 17,5%

Mg 8,5%

SO$_4$ 28,0%

K: 0,4%

Ca 15,5%

HCO$_3$: 3,1%   NO$_3$: 2,3%

Electr. conductivity 6800 µS/cm

Ion balances of contaminated waters

Cl: 2,3%   SO₄: 0,0%   NO₃: 0,0%

Na 20,8%

Mg 13,8%

K: 2,6%

Ca 12,9%

HCO₃ 47,6%

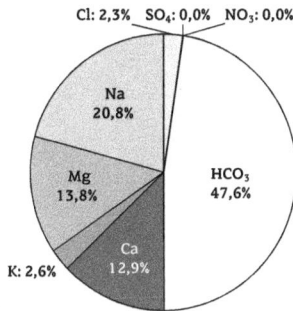

Electr. conductivity 310 µS/cm

Shallow well Leer

Surface water swamps

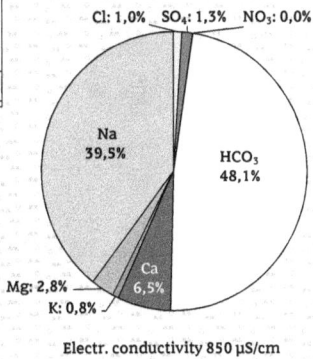

Deep well Bouw

Cl: 1,0%   SO₄: 1,3%   NO₃: 0,0%

Na 39,5%

HCO₃ 48,1%

Mg: 2,8%

K: 0,8%

Ca 6,5%

Electr. conductivity 850 µS/cm

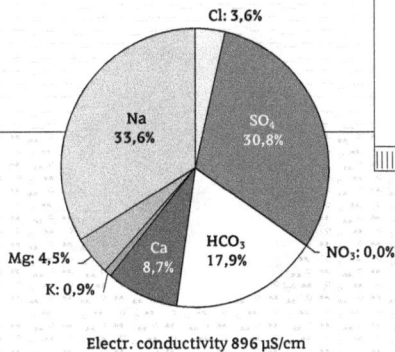

Cl: 3,6%

Na 33,6%

SO₄ 30,8%

Mg: 4,5%

K: 0,9%

Ca 8,7%

HCO₃ 17,9%

NO₃: 0,0%

Electr. conductivity 896 µS/cm

Ion balances of naturally occuring waters

According to the residents of Rier, the tanker trucks don't bring water often enough. When they do finally arrive, groups of waiting people quickly convene. Fights to get the precious liquid frequently break out among the villagers.

2015

The threat

Our contacts on the ground have informed us that it is possible to get to Thar Jath. We decide to give it a try. One main reason for doing such is to prove the oil companies' capability of returning to the region, which would enable them to live up to their responsibilities for the people and the environment. On February 23rd, we travel from Rumbek to Nyal, which is where our bush clinic is located. Our schedule allows us a mere two days there. That is, however, enough time for Klaus Stieglitz to confer with the clinic's staff, to take a look at their work, and to formulate an assessment of the security situation on-site.

*

On the morning prior to our departure to Juba, we visit a nearby cattle camp. These are the main venues of social, cultural and economic life of the semi-nomadic peoples of South Sudan. Every evening, cows and bulls are herded tightly together, and bound to their posts. Their owners live and sleep in the midst of their livestock. These camps have no roofs. The residents' beds are either on the ground, where they sleep under mosquito nets, or on lofts some two meters above it. The animals' dung is used as fuel, causing the odor of burnt items and ashes to waft through the entire camp. The young men living at the camp lead the livestock every early morning out to graze. They return from these pastures every evening.

Everything that the livestock produces is used in the cattle camps. The cattle's milk is drunk, the cows' urine is employed by the residents during their toilettes.

Cows also serve as a currency. A bride's dowry is often denominated in a—large—number of cows. These are then distributed among the bride's relatives. The number of cows belonging to a person is kept as secret as the amount of money one has in a bank account in our parts. The ash of the burnt cow dung serves as mosquito repellent and is known to be anti-inflammatory when applied to people's skin and the hide of livestock.

The local languages have a large number of terms for "cow"—as for the hues of hides. The local residents have a tender and respectful attitude towards their livestock. "Love" songs praise cows' beauty and grace. The men take pride in having a first name taken from an especially strong and magnificent bull.

Livestock rustling is common. In it, the members of one camp can attack that of another, thus provoking the latter to seek revenge upon the former, escalating the spiral of violence in the process. The stronger the weapons, the better your chance of victory. This explains the unfortunate omnipresence of the Kalashnikov AK-47.

*

We fly on February 25th in a one-motor Cessna 208 Caravan from Nyal to Juba, where we conclude our preparations for the press conference to be held on the following day. It serves to enable Sign of Hope to present to the people of South Sudan the results of our study on the contamination of potable water by the oil industry. The press conference is well-attended. It produces a gratifying large echo in the country's media.

The preparations for the press conference to be held in Juba are going much more difficultly than initially expected. This is because of the recent imposition of the requirement that each press conference has to allegedly secure an official approval. To avoid the delays expected to ensue, we simply give our press conference another name, and find another venue. Our event's purpose is to present Sign of Hope's scientific study, which had been published in November 14th in Germany. Our press conference therefore becomes a "colloquium". And where better suited to stage a colloquium than a university's faculty of sciences? Juba has a university, and, thanks to the support rendered by our friends, our colloquium is held at its "American Corner" on February 26th. Why the large number of journalists attended is interested in such an academic event remains our small secret.

Immediately after the press conference, Klaus Stieglitz and Sign of Hope's inner circle of security advisers have a meeting in Juba to discuss whether or not we should dare to fly on the following day to Leer. The purpose of the trip would be to inspect once more the oil fields. We learn that it is possible to fly to Leer. We are still not sure whether or not we will make it all the way to Thar Jath. The security situation remains volatile, but no combat is expected to occur in and around Leer during the next two days. When we get to Leer, we will find out whether we can reach the oil facility, which is nearly 70 kilometers away.

Upon arrival in Leer, our contacts there give us the go-ahead for our trip, and provide us with the passes issued by the local authorities. The people of Leer are in favor of our push, because they know we are striving for their rights.

February 28th, early morning. We travel in two jeeps. We are heading north towards Thar Jath. We have to return by sundown, say the locals. It's dangerous to spend nights outside Leer. That's why we have taken two cars, in case one breaks down. We have no time to make repairs.

Carrying TV and other cameras and equipment, four journalists form part of our party. We reckon it will take three hours to cover the nearly 70 kilometers from Leer to the oil facilities. We have to cross several roadblocks during the trip. They have been set up by the opposition army. We do not experience any major problems while doing so.

We foresaw the facility in Thar Jath's being strictly watched, and that we would have problems therefore gaining access to it—in case that would be possible at all. A completely different and unexpected situation confronts us upon our arrival. The gates stand wide open. The facility has been plundered. No security personnel—no one at all!—is in sight. Countless oil barrels have been strewn around the facility. We see spilled oil making its way into the ground. These are complemented by oil pipes that have been ripped open and by huge puddles full of the substance. The whole facility reeks of oil. This makes it quite hard to breathe.

*

Accompanied by our "retinue" of journalists, we travel from the processing facility in Thar Jath to Rier, which is some 8 kilometers away. The water in the wells in this village is the most highly contaminated. The samples that we took in 2009 showed a conductivity of 6.7 microSiemens/cm. This is extremely and dangerously high. Conductivity is easy to measure, and is a direct indicator of the amount of minerals contained in the water. These minerals are in this context the salts. The test now performed reveals a conductivity—a concentration of salts—of 8.1 microSiemens/cm. WHO has set a ceiling for potable water of a concentration of salts of 2.5 microSiemens/cm.

"AFP's" team interviews a 35-year old woman who has 8 children. To get palatable water, she trudges—two hours there, two hours back—to a small arm of the White Nile. She carries a 20 liter cannister of her head while doing so. "The water in is too salty, the taste is too bad," the woman tells "AFP's" camera. "People drinking it immediately vomit, or get cramps and diarrhea. Children are especially affected." In addition to the salts, the water in Rier contains especially large amounts of lead. A sample taken in Rier has lead amounting to 0.58 mg/l. The ceiling is, however, 0.01 mg/l. The ceiling for this dangerous heavy metal was thus exceeded 58-fold.

The immediate effects of drinking this water are bad. Worse are the long-term of effects of the heavy metals, which are insidious poisons, says the physician who is serving as Sign of Hope's medical consultant in South Sudan. He is traveling with the group of journalists through this area of crisis. Our research causes us to hear rumors of increasing rates of miscarriages and fetal deformities. This applies to both the human beings and the animals in the region. Typical manifestations of poisoning by heavy metals, states the physician. The ingestion of lead can also damage the brain and the neural system, and, as well, give rise to blood diseases.

Another horrifying aspect. The placidity of the water in this remote arm of the White Nile gives residents a false sense of security. This water is home to the parasites responsible for a wide range of the diseases—including bilharzia—plaguing the region. The water also contains the fecal bacteria causing stomach and intestinal ailments, notes the physician.

We encounter during our travels through the contaminated region a large number of members of the opposition army—headed by Riek Marchar—that currently controls it.

We also meet people who are quite aware of and concerned about the water-related programs being experienced by local residents. "What good is oil when we don't have any water to drink?" is a statement that we repeatedly get to hear.

It is not the case that there is no longer any administration in charge of the situation. The problem is that the volatility ensuing from the civil war makes it difficult for administrators to know whom one has to report to—the government or the rebels. We at Sign of Hope are not blind to the fact that both sides are mainly interested in getting their greedy hands on the oil and the good life it promises. During this trip, we are dealing with the rebels. It could well be other side during our next one.

The journalists repeatedly pose the questions: how are these problems to be solved? How can they at least be lessened? How can the demolished oil facilities and the soil that they have contaminated be properly disposed of? There is a simple answer to all these questions, and it is utterly distressing. Hella Rüskamp explains a horrible fact: these damages are irreversible. The contamination of the upper layer of groundwater can not be remediated. The only way to provide residents with palatable water is to drill wells deep enough to tap the second, lower layer. Sign of Hope has proven the existence of this layer. At this moment, the ceasefire is being adhered to by both sides in the civil war. This means that currently it would well be possible to risk drilling several wells, and to do so without worrying about the effects of the war.

★

"Radio Miraya" broadcasts on February 25th an interview with the Commissioner of Pariang County, which forms part of the state of Unity. In it, the Commissioner reports of the death of a large number of livestock.[1] "Radio Miraya" was founded by the United Nations Mission in South Sudan (UNMISS). It is regarded as being the most credible and thus most widely heard radio station in the region.[2] People there believe what "Radio Miraya" broadcasts. Any evaluation of the region's media has to take its biases into account. These are a byproduct of the conflict in the region. The side that has the upper hand gets to distribute its version of events. This kind of reporting has a very limited credibility.

In the interview, the Commissioner announces that 2,500 livestock and a countless number of wild animals have perished. No one knows for sure what's killing them. The Commissioner himself has no such doubts. The animals' deaths are a consequence of the contamination of the environment via the leaks found in the damaged oil wells. He complains that crude oil is still streaming unchecked into the environment, even though the armed conflict to gain control over the oil fields has ended months ago. The previous autumn's floods have been followed by a strikingly apparent increase in illness on the part of people and animals. This is also related to the health problems being experienced by pregnant women and to the increase in the number of deformed fetuses.[3] The Commissioner concludes by demanding that the government take immediate action.[4]

*

"Radio Tamazuj" broadcasts on February 28th a major report. It contains the information presented in the study[5]. This report is then published by the "Citizen". This daily newspaper constitutes the vanguard of—though still rudimentary—well-informed and interested public opinion in South Sudan. "Citizen" publishes a two-page article covering the situation detailed in our study. The newspaper then follows that, three days later, with a cover story. This is a major success. "Citizen" is *the* voice of democracy in South Sudan. It has committed itself to fighting corruption and tyranny.[6]

This means that anybody interested in the subject now has a way of finding out what the oil companies are up to, and how that their misdeeds have caused the problems with drinking water being experienced in the oil fields and surrounding regions. Such people now also have scientific proof of such. John Ariki is a professor at the university of Juba. He is also co-author of our study. He gets up at our colloquium, which is attended by a large number of journalists and students, and summarizes the situation in simple and unmistakably clear words. His gist: it is rather not to be expected that the government of South Sudan will help solve the problem. His words are quoted as follows by South Sudan's media: "The oil companies have a very strong lobby, and they can convince authorities [that the companies] are not the problem, that the problems have been

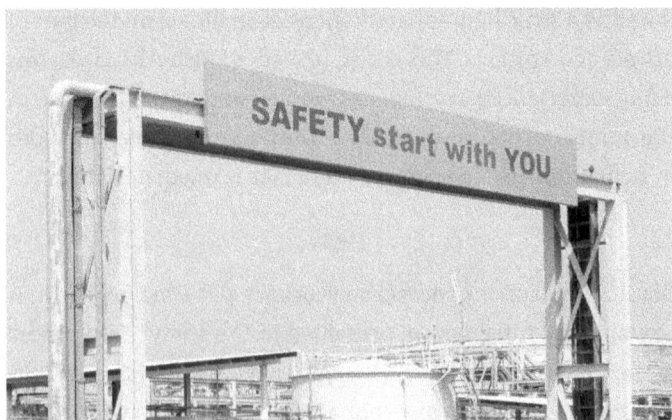

there [before]. The problem lies on the reluctance of the authorities. Even if the community cries no one here will listen to their cry."[7]

"AFP" publishes an article on March 3rd. The article covers our trip to Thar Jath and Rier. In vivid language, the article's author describes the dreadful conditions that he has witnessed there. Especially compelling is his description of the revolting stink of oil hanging over the abandoned facility. This is followed two days later by a report in "Al Jazeera". It contains a wealth of photographs and an in-depth account of the situation. One of the photographs shows Thar Jath's deserted processing facility. The photo shows a gigantic sign. It is fixed above a path that has been completely splattered with oil. The sign advises "Safety start with you". "Al Jazeera" extensively quotes the statements made by the courageous Professor John Ariki at our "colloquium": "Since oil is a source of income [the government] does not want to anger the companies."[8]

"AFP" TV broadcasts at the end of March a program on the problems with water plaguing South Sudan. This represents a key step towards our goal of creating something approaching a public forum in South Sudan. This, in turn, will serve as a conduit for our key messages. We want to make sure that the country's residents are aware of the situation. This, in turn, will equip them to demand the accordance of their human right for clean water.

*

Some five years have elapsed since the launching of our talks with Daimler. It is thus a good time to see what we have achieved. Have we in fact recorded any real successes? Has the supply of water in the region improved for the people living there? In March, Sign of Hope's Reimund Reubelt and Klaus Stieglitz write a letter to Dr. Dieter Zetsche, chairman of Daimler AG's managing board. It asks him to summarize the results ensuing from his company's involvement in the situation.

"Dear Dr. Zetsche,

At the end of 2007, we were contacted by our partners in projects being undertaken in Unity, a state in South Sudan. They reported to us that the quality of water in the region was worsening. Sign of Hope is an organization dedicated to preserving human rights and to providing assistance. We decided to commit ourselves to investigating and improving this situation. The initial analyses of the water gave rise to our hypothesis that the oil companies operating in the region's oil fields of Thar Jath and Unity could be responsible for the contamination of the water.

We spent the next few years conducting comprehensive investigations. These have provided us with the proof of the oil industry's being—via its exploration and pumping operations— the cause of the region's problems with drinking water. These problems are imperiling the health of some 180,000 persons. Petronas sponsors your racing team. Petronas holds stakes in the consortia operating in the Thar Jath and Unity oil field. Petronas owns 67.875% of the equity of the Sudd Petroleum Operating Company (SPOC) (the former White Nile Petroleum Operating Company—WNPOC) consortium; and, as well, 30% of that of the Greater Nile Petroleum Operating Company (GNPOC) consortium. [...]

Our information tells us that Petronas has been since the end of 2009 a main sponsor of Mercedes Benz's Formula 1 race team, which also has incorporated the company's name into its own one. We contacted in March 2010 your company, to brief you on how wastes ensuing from the exploration for and the production of oil are disposed in South Sudan, and on the key role played by Petronas in such misconduct. In May, 2011, Petronas' sponsorship of your company's racing activities was extended to include the team that you maintain in Germany's Touring Car competition.

We wish to start by expressing our thanks to your company's having dedicated itself to resolving the crisis in South Sudan ever since this point of initial contact. This has occurred via your department for Integrity, Law and CSR ('corporate social responsibility'), which is ably and expertly headed by ▆▆▆▆▆▆▆▆. *Your company's dedication led to our organization's being able to meet on April 7–9, 2011, with representatives of the WNPOC in Juba; and from December 10–11, 2012, with teams of senior managers from the SPOC and Norconsult. This meeting took place in Stuttgart.*

In our dealings with your company, we have repeatedly reiterated the objective of our efforts in South Sudan. We want to help the people living in and around the oil fields of Thar Jath and Unity solve the problems that they are facing due to the oil-caused contamination of their water. We have asked your company for assistance in these efforts. The key yardstick to be used in the gauging of the success of the working relationship between Daimler AG and Sign of Hope has always been as far as we are concerned the attainment of a real improvement in the lives of the people living in and around the Thar Jath and Unity oil fields.

Five years have passed since Sign of Hope first contacted Daimler AG. We would therefore like to take this opportunity to request your detailing to us how the people in and around the Thar Jath and Unity oil fields have benefited from the involvement by your company. Has your company produced any substantial and substantiated alleviations in the problems faced by the people living in and around the Thar Jath and Unity oil fields, with this especially applying to their being supplied with clean drinking water?"[9]

*

In April of the year, in a first step, we take samples of the hair of South Sudan's residents, in order to be capable of determining the long-term effects of the contamination of the environment.

*

This time, Daimler responded uncharacteristically quickly. This response did not ensue from Dr. Zetsche's office, but rather from our contact in the Integrity and Legal Affairs division at the company. We are thus hearing from the person with whom we have been in touch for the previous five years. He invites us to a meeting, to be held in Stuttgart.

We meet with him on April 22nd. The venue is Mercedes' offices in Untertürkheim, which is a borough of Stuttgart. We kick off the meeting by presenting the results of our trip to South Sudan in February. We hand him a USB stick. It contains the reports issued by "AFP" and "Al Jazeera". We show him the photographs taken of the processing facility in Thar Jath. The Daimler manager agrees that conditions there are intolerable. He says that, unfortunately, nothing can be done at the moment, since the SPOC is not currently operable. This is due to the civil war. We refute this view. It would be possible to undertake remedial measures on site. We established this fact during our trip. This fact is further substantiated by photographs taken from satellites on an ongoing basis. Remedial measures could be immediately instituted in Thar Jath. Wells could be drilled in its vicinity.

In discussing the quality of water, the Daimler manager refers once more to the Norconsult study, which, as he stated, did not confirm the results of our research. He thus had no other way of substantiating the latter's findings. He has obviously not thoroughly perused either our study or our points of criticism. This lack of thoroughness precludes him from being able to incorporate these findings into the stance that he has taken during our meeting. When all is said and done, the key fact is that Norconsult did confirm the existence of a contamination of water. At the meetings previously held with him (and in the minutes of the meetings in Juba 2011 and Stuttgart 2012), we comprehensively elucidated the false premises contained in the Norconsult study. We also criticized its one-sided focusing on a single (instead of the many) causes of the contamination. This meeting allows virtually for a single conclusion. Obviously Daimler does not accord any substantial importance to its dialogue with Sign of Hope. The manager with whom we are now meeting speaks vaguely of his finding our study "more plausible". All of this does not have the feeling of being an in-depth exchange of substantiated views.

We once more raise the issue of Corporate Social Responsibility (CSR) at this meeting. We ask the manager whether or not Daimler's precepts in this area commit the company to taking appropriate actions. The Daimler manager plays down the issue. Daimler is very moved by the findings compiled by Sign of Hope. But it is capable of assuming responsibility only for its own operations. The only roles open to it vis-à-vis Petronas (Petroliam Nasional Berhad) are for Daimler to act as an intermediary, expediter and facilitator. Daimler has striven to fulfill these roles. To this end, it has brought the SPOC, South Sudan's Ministry of Petroleum and Mining (MPM) and Sign of Hope together to resolve these issues.

We insist that we are not satisfied with that. Five years have to yield real results. Since the working relationship between Sign of Hope and Daimler had not produced any noticeable improvements in the lives of the people of South Sudan, we are now considering going public with this concern. The Daimler manager understands this "to be Daimler's being brought into the matter". There is no way he can approve of that. He does however admit that the outreach from Daimler to Petronas has not gone as well as one had hoped. Notwithstanding this, it is still possible to achieve something, as long as Daimler and Petronas set forth their dialogue. A further problem is MPM's restricting of the flow of information from the SPOC to Sign of Hope. We keep insisting. We ask how Daimler can work at all with Petronas, in view of the former's precepts of operation. These mandate the ceasing of business relations with Petronas. We ask him whether or not Petronas is a suitable partner for Daimler. We had posed this question five years previously, and it is the KEY one for us. Should a company that has committed itself to observing a body of rules encompassing the adherence to environmental standards work with a corporation that shares the responsibility for the contamination of the water drunk by hundred thousands of people?

We do not of course get a straight answer to this question. Instead, we are treated to a round of well-polished words. We have heard this all before—in fact, for the last five years, during which nothing has happened except for talks and conferences held in well-appointed premises or on the phone. They have produced non-binding commitments and declarations of intentions supposed to lead to "initial, important steps".

We are forced to recognize that this approach, upon which we embarked with the great hope that it would lead to an alleviation in the suffering of the people in the contaminated area, and which was based on our trust in the integrity of Daimler's managers, will not yield any real progress.

*

We are working in our office in Konstanz. It is the evening of May 11th. An E-mail arrives. It contains the preliminary results of the testing of the hair. The results are devastating. The inhabitants—all of them—show high rates of toxic encumbrance. Klaus Stieglitz sits shocked at his computer. He clicks through the files and reads the victims' names and bar charts, of which many plunge deep into the red.

*

We receive on May 19th an inquiry from Daimler. The company requests our supplying figures on the supply of potable water available to the population in South Sudan. These figures are for "international processing". The inquiry includes a chart. We are to fill it out by providing figures on villages needing wells, and on how much that will cost (estimated), as well as information on their degrees of accessibility in a time of civil war. This information will obviously be incorporated into forthcoming talks with Germany's GIZ agency for international development.

Daimler's inquiry includes two other questions. Both pertain to the Norconsult appraisal. Daimler would appreciate our providing our "top five reasons" why the appraisal is thought not to be of adequate quality, and why our study better describes the matter. We once more compile the information that Daimler and the parties involved have had for many years. The costs of building the wells can be relatively precisely determined: a total of some € 32 million. This immense sum is about as much as the amount supplied by Petronas each year—some € 30 million—to Mercedes' Formula 1 team's annual budget of € 90 million. Instead of going for sponsorship, these funds could give 180,000 people access to safe potable water.[10] When creating water supply by contructing water wells one has to aim for a redundancy of well systems. This will also double the respective costs. A second water well should be able to provide a community with potable water even when the first well fails for example due to problems with the solar system or the water pump. Even when one disregards Petronas' responsibility for the contamination, this constitutes a great example of the schizophrenia shown each day by our entire society when dealing with poverty and with its consequences. Add in the fact that Petronas, which is Daimler's business partner, is directly responsible for the damaging of South Sudan's environment. This makes the compiling of such a comparison of costs and benefits appear quite cynical. The inquiry is a sign of interest on the part of Daimler—that's the way we decide to view its request.

*

Petronas' first "partner garage"—the first of its kind—is commissioned on July 16th in Hamburg.[11] This "Petronas flagship" garage is actually non-affiliated. From now on, it will sport Petronas' logo, and will offer the company's lubricants, which have become known through their use in Formula 1—so the hope in any case of the company's marketers. This claim will enable the lubricants to be distinguished from the everyday ones that can be purchased in any supermarket. Such major manufacturers of automobiles have started selling oil under their own brands.[12] The garages contractually bound to these manufacturers charge up to €30 and even more for a liter of high-performance oil. Automotive suppliers, on the other hand, provide oil meeting the same standards at less than €10 per liter.[13] Oil changes are performed 45 million times a year in Germany alone. This makes the business of providing lubricants highly lucrative.[14]

Nico Rosberg delivers a highly-publicized testimonial at the commissioning of the partnership. He effusively praises Petronas' lubricant to the media. Normal customers are now to benefit from the experiences gained in the Formula 1—this is the marketing message. This is Petronas' way of harvesting the fruits of its expensive involvement in car racing. This involvement in turn is part of the worldwide campaign being pursued by the subsidiary providing lubricants of Petronas, which is owned by the Malaysian government. This campaign is designed to make Petronas' subsidiary "a leading company whose market share makes it one of the top competitors in its field".[15] COO Eric Holthusen has traveled from Kuala Lumpur to Hamburg for the event. Holthusen states: "The Petronas Flagship workshops enable us to create a network in which each garage automatically benefits from the advertising ensuing from our participation in Formula 1."[16]

★

On July 20th, George Clooney presents the "Sentry" project to the media.[17] He is joined by his fellow American John Prendergast, with whom he operates the Satellite Sentinel Project, in setting up this Website, which gathers and distributes information on the national and international-level streams of money flowing into Africa's crisis areas, thus ensuring that these armed conflicts are set forth. The research compiled by Clooney and Prendergast concentrate upon Sudan, South Sudan, Somalia, the Central African Republic and the Republic of the Congo.

★

On July 30th, "Radio Tamazuj" broadcasts a program on the new CEO of Nilepet. Owned by the government of South Sudan, Nilepet holds a 5% stake in the GPOC and DPOC consortia that are operating in South Sudan. In SPOC Nilepet holds an 5% stake. According to the Website of South Sudan's Petroleum Ministry,[18] Nilepet directly reports—as a dedicated department of the Ministry—to Minister Stephen Dhieu Dau. The radio station has been provided with documents. They show that Nilepet has made a large number of payments to friends and political allies who have nothing to do with the businesses pursued by the company.[19] Nilepet's previous CEO had been fired in May. This was due to his murky financial transactions. The new CEO is Joseph Cleto Deng. He is the former head of the office of President Salva Kiir, and he is obviously continuing where his predecessor had to leave off.[20] The documents made public by the radio station cover the first month of Cleto's position as CEO.[21]

★

Sign of Hope receives on August 4th a—long—letter from the managing board of Daimler AG:

"Thank you very much for your letter of March 26, 2015 to Dr. Dieter Zetsche, who has asked us to answer you. Your letter requested our compiling an overview of how we would summarize the state of the charges raised against consortia operating in South Sudan in which Petronas, our Formula 1 partner, participates. We got involved in this at its inceptions. Your letter was employed to occasion another round of discussions with a range of players. It is for that reason that we have not responded to your letter, as had been promised to you, until today.

We are gladly meeting your request to summarize our activities and the state of our knowledge of the matter, and to do such from Daimler's perspective. Please allow us to note that our company itself is not a member of the consortia in South Sudan that are being criticized. Notwithstanding this, Daimler occupied itself with this concern immediately subsequent to your getting in touch with us. This action on our part was based upon our aspiration to do business with business partners that operate in responsible ways. While doing so, we saw our role as primarily being that of an intermediary between Sign of Hope and the parties participating in the facilities in South Sudan. Please allow us to also note that we have always experienced Sign of Hope to be a fair and solutions-oriented partner in our dialogues. This is in turn has been an important precondition for our having worked together in recent times.

This relationship caused us to request information enabling us to assess matters from the consortia in question. A large number of discussions and letters have made it possible for you and the management of the facilities in South Sudan to directly communicate with each other (with this occurring on site there and in Stuttgart). Realizing this was not always easy, in view of the complicated structures of ownership of the facilities in South Sudan, the considerable influence exerted by politicians there, as well as the varying levels of readiness to take part shown by individual participants. Notwithstanding this, we view this communication as being an important precondition for the attaining of further steps. In a further move, our top managers engaged and engage those at Petronas on this topic.

What impairs Daimler's coming to a conclusive assessment of the (geological) facts and its assuming any responsibility ensuing from it is the fact that two appraisals have been made of the issue in question: the Norconsult study that was used as the basis for the decisions reached by the consortia in which Petronas participates, and the analyses made by African Water, which serves as your point of reference. The studies come to opposing conclusions as to the nature of the relationships between causes and effects. This in turn permits us to solely establish which findings we—as a whole—consider 'more plausible'. Regardless of this and speaking in general terms, we do see the necessity to realize the basic aspiration of adhering to environmental standards, and of guaranteeing the local population's access to healthy water.

Turning to the current political situation in South Sudan, we have incorporated the descriptions forthcoming from Petronas, the depictions in the media and your portrayals of the on-site situations into the formulation of our assumption that this situation—due to the civil war prevailing there—remains very difficult. Petronas has informed us that the production facilities in South Sudan were completely abandoned as of the end of 2013. Petronas is not capable of forecasting when operative personnel will be able to return to them. For these reasons, and in accordance with the assessment of the situation in the region compiled at the beginning of our dialogue, there are few ways of realizing on-site initiatives at the moment. This inability is caused by the civil war. Even renowned development aid organizations are advising against undertaking projects in the areas under question.

The above, however, does not deter us from our objective of establishing a direct exchange of information between Petronas and Sign of Hope. Should you consent to this, we will approach you, so as to agree upon with you the conditions of initial talks. This face-face contact will enable the discussion of which on-site initiatives are required today—and once secure access to the area in question is possible. We would support this dialogue by once more having our managers contact Petronas, so as to enlist the support of their top managers. We assume that this will match with your goals.

To the extent possible for us, we will continue to support Sign of Hope's efforts to achieve improvements in the daily lives of the people in question. Should you have any questions, feel free to continue to pose them to ▮▮▮▮▮▮▮▮▮▮▮.

With best regards"

The signature on the left side of the letter is that of Ola Källenius, who was managing director of AMG from 2010 to October 2014. Källenius is regarded as being Zetsche's protégé. Since January 1, 2015, Källenius has been member of Daimler's managing board. He is in charge of the sales and marketing of cars. Christine Hohmann-Dennhardt, the member of the managing board in charge the company's division for integrity and legal affairs—with which we have been in touch—is the renderer of the signature on the right (in the German system, this indicates the signatory's being of lesser importance).

We heard the very same points of view during our visit to Stuttgart in April. Daimler's managers don't even pay lip service to the achieving of actual progress. Rather, they hide behind a study that is obviously inadequate and whose erroneous evaluation of facts is being simply ignored, compelling proof of such notwithstanding. In this case, in which our findings that are substantiated and confirmed by thoroughgoing scientific methods are not understood, as Daimler now implicitly admits, the company should have recruited independently-operating experts and commissioned them with the compilation of an authoritative assessment. But isn't it the case that Daimler does not want to finally make up its mind, because this would enable and force it to observe the precepts contained in its own codes of rules? This, in turn, would have consequences for its partnership with Petronas. At our last meeting Stuttgart, we at Sign of Hope thought that we had made our position perfectly clear. We find Daimler's position to lack merit. The question that we now pose to ourselves is whether or not it makes any sense at all to pursue our relationship with them.

*

Ten days after our receipt of the letter from Daimler, we get an E-mail from South Sudan's Ministry for Petroleum and Mining (MPM).[22] MPM says that its mail is in reference to our press release on the contamination of the drinking water found in Blocks 5A, 1, 2 and 3 by the oil industry.

The MPM seems miffed. The letter attached to the E-mail states that they have managed to check our comprehensive research. While doing so, it learned of our trip to Thar Jath, "which was featured by 'Al Jazeera' and other networks."[23] The MPM is charged with the supervision of the petroleum industry. As such, it has received from a variety of sources complaints about our charges and about the negative campaign being waged against oil companies and, especially, the MPM, which is being accused of not taking appropriate action, the E-mail goes on to say.[24]

In the letter we are summoned—not invited—to attend "as soon as possible" a meeting to be chaired by Mr. Humoon Chol Deng that will "be arranged by Sudd Petroleum Operating Company as the JOC which has been engaging with you at the onset of these allegations".[25] The letter also states: "Note that the two Contract Areas have been under rebel activity since 2013. You are to inform us about how you got there and whom you met."[26]

What has occasioned this letter? Why this tone of voice and why this urgency? Our press conference in Juba was held six months ago. We can only guess what the causes of this E-mail are. Daimler wanted "to contact over the next few days Petronas' top managers." This caused the SPOC apparently to directly contact MPM. Is the paving of the way for the "direct exchange of information" previewed by Daimler?

*

The SPOC's response comes as rapidly. An E-mail invites us to a meeting to be held in Stuttgart. MPM had requested the SPOC's arranging of a meeting with us in Stuttgart, writes a staff member at the SPOC. The date suggested has already obviously been agreed upon by the other parties involved. The August 10th letter from MPM is enclosed. [...]: "You are therefore requested to attend a meeting as soon as possible. It will be led by Mr Humoon Chol Deng [...]"[27] states this not very friendly "invitation". On August 21st, we accept—as a matter of course and displaying the requisite courtesy—the invitation. We suppress the urge to ask why matters are suddenly moving forward.

*

Accompanied by a flurry of media attention, the new "Bobby Benz" is presented at the beginning of September's "Tribute to Bambi" charity event. Sponsored by the "BUNTE" magazine, the event features a Bobby Car designed especially for the purpose by Daimler. The chassis is the same as of that of the special model from 2014. The color is, by way of contrast, quite new. The Bobby Benz no longer displays the elegantly frosted "Monza Gray Magno" but rather the "sporty Petronas green". Nico Rosberg, who has recently become a father, goes on a promotion tour for this special model of Bobby Car. World champion Lewis Hamilton is also filmed taking a Bobby Car for a spin. He does so for "all the children of the world".

Mercedes Benz has always viewed its commitment to society and, specifically, to children as being an especial matter of heartfelt interest. That is why it entered into and maintains a partnership with TRIBUTE TO BAMBI. This year's model of Bobby Car is a limited edition. It features a sporty Petronas green. This Bobby Benz comes with two sets of stickers. These can be applied on individual bases, making these toy cars either a 'Nico Ros-

berg Edition' or a 'Lewis Hamilton Edition'. All of the proceeds from the Bobby Benzes go to TRIBUTE TO BAMBI—assistance for children in emergencies. These little sport cars will be available for purchasing as of the middle of September from your local Mercedes Benz partner."[28]

It takes € 79.90 to get this designer toy car into your child's room. A normal Bobby Car costs less than € 30 at a normal toy store.

★

Nespresso announces on October 7th that coffee will be exported from South Sudan. This is the first time since the founding of the country. This coffee has been classified as being high quality. It will be marketed by Nespresso. This will start during the month. Initial exclusive market will be France. This represents the results of a project initiated by George Clooney to revive the country's longstanding coffee cultivation. Helping realize it are the government of South Sudan, Nespresso and the Technoserve assistance organization.

Some 500 South Sudanese farmers are currently participating in the project. They are organized into three cooperatives. Within 10 years, this number is to be ramped up to 15,000.[29] George Clooney is not suffering under any illusions.[30] This project represents nothing more than a first step.[31] Clooney emphasizes a key message of his coffee project. The diversification of the economy represents an important precondition for the achievement of a lasting peace.[32] What he means by that: the country's unholy dependency upon oil has to be brought to an end. Something else to be considered: the success of this project shows that it is in fact possible to undertake such even during a time of difficulties with security.

On October 11th, Lewis Hamilton finishes first at the Russian Grand Prix. This makes Mercedes the champion among constructors of Formula 1 cars. The USA Grand Prix takes place on October 25th at Austin, Texas' Circuit of the Americas track. If Lewis Hamilton wins here, he will have an invincible lead over the other drivers. He will thus be able to secure his third world championship—and to do so relatively early in the season. His strongest competitor for the title is still Nico Rosberg, his teammate. The race turns out to be one of the most thrilling of the entire season.[33] Rosberg starts from the pole position. But Hamilton gets off to a better start. He takes the inside track along the first curve. He is neck and neck with Rosberg.[34] Centrifugal force sends Hamilton so far to the outside that Rosberg is forced to leave the track to avoid him.[35] Due to this, he falls back two places.[36] Hamilton then jousts for the lead on the rainy track with the two drivers for the Red Bull team.[37] This is followed by Rosberg's comeback, which leads to his once more taking the lead. It takes a mistake on his part to enable Hamilton to forge once more to the front. He is the first to cross the finish line, making him the world champion for the third year. His victory for Mercedes makes it the company's second—after 2014—in the period subsequent to 1955. His victory in Texas enables Hamilton to register a record. He is the first Formula 1 driver to twice (in two seasons) win more than 10 Grand Prix races a year. He responds to questions as to his wishes for the future by saying: "I hope that fans will still remember me 20 years after my career is over, that they will say: there was once a Silver Arrow driver and he was great."[38]

★

It has taken three years, but it's time for another meeting in Stuttgart. On November 10th, in response to an invitation issued by Daimler, we meet once more at Stuttgart's Steigenberger Hotel with representatives of Daimler, of SPOC and of Norconsult, and with senior officials from South Sudan's Petroleum Ministry (MPM). We are being accompanied by two of African Water's experts. The meeting is presided over by the MPM's Humoon Chol Deng.

The presentations and talks at it do not yield anything new. Something striking does happen. We are attacked by the SPOC and by Humoon Chol Deng for having conducted our PA (public affairs) work and for having staged a press conference in Juba. The meeting lacks the friendliness of previous ones. We notice once more something that turned out to be important to the representatives of the consortium from the beginning of our discussions with them: no media. Is that the only thing that was ever really at stake here?

The presentations made by the oil consortium and by the ministry scarcely cover ways in which to join in constructively working to overcome the country's environmental problems. Instead, the two parties inform us that we have to adhere to official regulations. Since 2012, we have been legally obliged to submit all of our investigations to the ministry, which will then decide what is to be published. That's the way the Petroleum Act insists that it has to be, and everybody has to live up to that.

For a number of years, we have requested the SPOC's providing us with the studies and assessments that they have conducted, as it is these that are supposed to prove the lack of perils associated with the oil production processes. We have repeated our requests many times. We have politely and firmly pointed out how important this information is for the local residents. Our opponents now protest: we can't do that, even if we wanted to. Their stance is not entirely new. But it is now backed up a legal justification, at least from the point of view of the consortium. The decision to release or not is to be made solely by the MPM.

The presentations made by the SPOC and by the MPM employ Article 76 of the Petroleum Act to reproach us. International legal experts view this stipulation as constituting a dangerous loophole in the country's otherwise highly praiseworthy legal code, which was created to impart transparency to the oil industry.[39] For several decades, the South Sudanese were prevented from having access to the contracts concluded by and benefiting the North. Immediately after the founding of the Republic of South Sudan, it announced its adherence to the internationally-applicable EITI (The Extractive Industries Transparency Initiative) standard, with which the governments of countries producing raw materials voluntarily commit themselves to attaining the greatest possible transparency as to the economics of the exploitation of such materials.[40]

The Petroleum Act of 2012 is configured to achieve this transparency, and manifests the country's own negative experiences with its lack. The Act fulfills today's expectations for transparency.[41] Once South Sudan had taken over the oil industry, it didn't take very long at all for it to forget about adhering to its own rules on the publication of contracts, of production figures and of public sector revenues and expenditures, and on other activities undertaken by the government and relating to the petroleum industry.[42] In 2012, the parliament of South Sudan passed a highly controversial resolution. It precludes the dissemination to the public of information on contracts, and on amounts of oil pumped and revenues from this.[43] Hillary Clinton, the USA's Secretary of State, warned in 2011 President Salva Kiir: "Nowhere will the transparency and account-ability that President Kiir has promised be more important than in managing South Sudan's abundant natural resources. We know that it will either help your country finance its own path out of poverty or you will fall prey to the natural resource curse, which will enrich small elite, outside interests, corpo-rations, and countries, and leave your people hardly better off then when you started."[44] The object of these concerns was transparency, and how its lack in the country's petroleum in-dustry could impact upon the country's society.[45]

We are an organization providing assistance. This means that this controversial Article of the Petroleum Act does not apply to us. This fact does not interest our critics. We have no plans to produce oil. The brazen audacity which the law is being twisted does manage to astonish us. This loophole was previously used solely to justify secret arrangements, even when they undermine the objectives of the Act.[46] The Petrole-um Act's Article 77 provides each citizen with the right to de-mand information from the government.[47] MPM mistakenly cites this Article 77 in its presentation. Our mentioning of this mistake, which is tantamount to being a Freudian slip, obvi-ously angers our opponents.

We are not the only ones voicing the view that the Petrole-um Act commits the MPM and the oil companies to disclosing their information on the health of the country's environment and population.[48] In April, Humoon Chol Deng and a SPOC co-worker take part in an event staged by the SUDD Institute in Juba. At it, they are publicly summoned to finally meet the legally-stipulated obligation to disseminate information on environmental risks.[49] The SUDD Institute's political analysts use the results of an investigation to reproach the two. None of the measures required by the Petroleum Act and serving to protect the environment have been at all instituted, as revealed by an inquiry placed with the ministries responsible for such.[50]

Our meeting in Stuttgart has actually already come to an end. It is nearly 4 pm. But then Humoon Chol Deng points to the screen, upon which we can now read the "resolutions" issuing from our meeting. It is customary to secure a prior agreement about them. We have, however, not agreed to these. What is now being presented as the results of today's meeting knocks us off our feet. Four points are listed. The first one's gist is that Sign of Hope is not permitted to publish anything containing accusations levied against oil consortia and their owners without having secured the prior consent of South Sudan's MPM. A contravention of this will be considered to be an action taken against the government of South Sudan and to be an endangering of the security of the country. The next two points cover the same ground. To put it concisely, for each step we make in in South Sudan, we are required to secure the approval and be accompanied by its MPM. The fourth point establishes the legal consequences for contraventions of the above stipulations.

The admonition that our activities could endanger the country's security and could be regarded as an aggressive act against it represents a totalitarian system's classic means of repression of opposing viewpoints. These "resolutions" are a clearly-articulated threat. Their goal is force us to keep quiet. And all this is taking place in the presence of Daimler's representatives, and in the green and peaceful climes of Stuttgart, Baden-Württemberg.

*

"I had a hard time breathing after reading what was on the sheet," states Hella Runge (former Rüskamp) of African Water. "We had had a very factual discussion. It was actually rather boring. We had been exchanging well-known facts and re-presented long-held positions."[51] The representatives of African Water decide not to attend the meal.

We consider for quite some time whether or not to accept the invitation to the dinner designed to bring our day of meetings to an end. Everything looks quite different now. We argue intensively internally. Overcoming our reservations, we go with the rest of the participants at the meeting to the Blockhouse restaurant. Daimler's representative asks Klaus Stieglitz and Reimund Reubelt to sit as his table, where Humoon Chol Deng is also present. We are placed across from them.

This is no time for small talk. Perhaps there is still time to find out what caused the afternoon's disturbing events. We ask the representatives of the South Sudan government why he responded at the previous meeting so harshly to the publishing of reports. 'You have been adding fuel to the fire' is his answer. He goes on to say that our publication had occurred a short time after the issuance of a report from the South Sudan government. In this, the report had refuted there being a connection between the cases of illness piling up in the areas of oil production and the production operations themselves. We ask him whether or not we may get a look at this report. To our astonishment, he agrees to such.

Our meals have been served. Deng turns to Klaus Stieglitz, who is sitting across the table. Deng says that a journalist who had criticized the government had been recently shot on the streets in Juba. Whilst relating this, Deng watches us closely. He no doubts sees us wince at that news. As he continues to speak, his lips form themselves into a smug smile. "The president greatly regretted this incident." What this is all about: scaring us. Daimler's representative is sitting right next to him. He gets to hear all of this, but says nothing at all.[52]

We are so taken aback that we fail to respond at the time. It takes our trip back to Konstanz and our talk during it for us to become aware of what we just experienced.

Deng is obviously referring to the murder of Peter Julius Moi, 27 years old, on August 19, 2015 in Juba. Peter Moi was a journalist. Around 8 pm, he left his editorial offices. Two shots in his neck killed him. Neither his money nor his mobile telephone were taken by his killer. Observers thus assumed that this murder was political in nature. Moi was the 7th crusading journalism to have been murdered in South Sudan since 2013.[53] Moi had also worked for "The Citizen". His next stints were as a political reporter for "The New Nation" daily and for the "Corporate Newspaper" weekly.[54] "The Citizen" had been shut down by the security authorities at the beginning of August.[55] "Peter Julius Moi was driven by the need to achieve peace, truth and social justice," wrote his mourning colleagues in his obituary.[56] One of Peter's last articles criticized the government for expending 60% of its budget on the police and the army.[57]

Three days prior to the murder of Peter Moi, President Salva Kiir had said the following to representatives of the media: "The freedom of press does not mean that you work against your country. And if anybody among them does not know this country has killed people, we will demonstrate it one day on them."[58]

*

It is several days after the meeting in Stuttgart. We are taking another look at the presentations shown during it. We notice that the sheet presenting the ominous "resolutions" that was displayed last by Humoon Chol was created by using a template different than the one employed in his previous presentation. This format does not have the logos otherwise all over them.

There is a reason for this weird lack. The stripes crossing the page seem, conversely, familiar to us. This format is one the used in the SPOC presentation. The sheet was thus probably created on November 9th in the hotel in Stuttgart. Is the oil consortium behind the MPM's threat?

*

Our worst fears are confirmed by what we are told by Germany's embassy and by our persons of trust in Juba. They too assess the situation, and tell us that we have to take the threat seriously. The only way for us to communicate with Juba is by E-mail. The telephone connections keep on breaking down. We receive a missive. It informs us that we and the people working for us are in danger of being arrested. MPM would have no trouble enlisting the police and the military to take us on. The governor and commander of the military in Unity operate according to martial law. Germany's embassy advises us to wait until a new administration takes office. A new minister could mean the prospect of a fresh start.

We are skeptical. This is due to our experiences with leading politicians in South Sudan over the last few years. Nearly all of them are primarily motivated by the drive to get into power, and to then control the oil, because this means getting their hands on the money. The government's dependency upon foreign investment remains strong, and has in fact grown stronger. This is caused by the need to reconstruct the pumping rigs in the oil field. These had been destroyed in the civil war. Rebuilding them is expensive. Exacerbating matters is the drop of the price of oil being experienced on world markets. Also falling dramatically has been the willingness of oil companies to invest in such a risky country. And what incentives can one provide them to entice them into returning? Laissez-faire, low costs of production: the vicious cycle remains in force. The speed at which this young country—that intended to be a model democracy—has mutated into a violence-prone autocracy is breathtaking.

*

We stage round-the-clock discussions, in which all options are thoroughly discussed. One of them is adhering to the brutal stipulations imposed by MPM. Our consideration of these is motivated by our staff members in South Sudan, and by the 70,000 patients treated by our two bush clinics each year. What will become of them should we withdraw from the country? And this is precisely what we will have to do should we not want to call off our campaign for clean water. Our days of conferring leads to our reaching the decision to not accept a gag. We will not allow ourselves to be capable of being blackmailed.

After more than 20 years of endeavors, we are forced to evacuate our expatriate staff from South Sudan. We inform in mid-November our on-site staff members of our decision. This decision evokes often conflicting emotions on the part of our colleagues in Nyal. They don't want to leave "their patients" in the lurch. They have built up so many relationships of trust. These are often personal in nature. There is such a joy in having successfully treated them. Our staff members have worked with, felt and hoped with their patients—and, of course, mourned them. They have provided comfort to patients' kin, found the right word to say to each and everyone of them. And this is all now coming to an end simply because the organization they work for has spoken the truth? Our staff members also, conversely, realize that environmental contamination should not be allowed to be swept under the carpet. Many of our staff members belong to the African school of Catholicism.

They have read "Laudato Si", the environmental encyclical of "their Papa Francis". They are aware of the importance placed by the pope upon the preservation of creation. Our staff members thus regret having to leave their places of service, but are conscious of "the big picture's" justifying this step.

*

A hearing is staged on December 10, 2015 in Washington by the Senate's Committee on Foreign Relations. Its topic is "Independent South Sudan: a failure of leadership". John Prendergast is one of the speakers at it. He elucidates the findings disseminated in The Sentry on the systematization of corruption in South Sudan. He reports that the entire country has been hijacked by the elite, whose only interest is enriching itself. The only effective way to achieve a lasting peace is to break up this carousel of corruption, which is being ridden by both the leaders currently in charge and the rebels. To achieve this, a transnational effort has to be made to find the funds stolen from South Sudan by its leaders.[59] The funds have to be frozen and then confiscated and returned to the people of South Sudan. Both the country's political leaders and their opponents form part of a "violent kleptocratic system".

*

The Sentry puts "The Nexus of Corruption and Conflict in South Sudan" on-line on December 17th. This report takes an in-depth look at the corruption plaguing the country's political system.[60] On the very same day, "Manager", a German business magazine, publishes an article on Ola Källenius, who is head of car marketing at Daimler.[61] He is being touted as a probable successor to CEO Dieter Zetsche, who is set to retire in 2019.

"Why Daimler's young Swede is the crown prince" is one of the article's headlines. This confirms our view that the forces within Daimler AG not favoring our cause are gaining power. Ola Källenius signed the letter of July 2015 to us. Its purpose was to play for time.

EPILOGUE 2016

Raising our voice

On January 27th, Transparency International publishes its annual report on corruption. The Republic of South Sudan joins
Angola in occupying the fifth place from the bottom.[1] The two
countries share another "honor". Both are ranked in the top
ten of the world's most violent countries.

★

South Sudan is in the midst of the transition phase specified
in the preliminary peace agreement of Addis Ababa of August
26, 2015. The parties are comprised of the government of South
Sudan and its president Salva Kiir, and the opposition, which
is led by Riek Machar. Both sides realize that the corruption
embraced by the country's elite and military form the heart of
the conflict. That is why the peace agreement ist not a simple
treaty of two parties. In response to an initiative of the Union
of African States, which has been driving the peace process,
a reform program has been developed. Its term is 30 months.
It is designed to transform South Sudan into a transparently
and responsibly operating country.[2] Oil is the main source of
income of this young state. Corruption is most pronounced,
accordingly, in this area. To be revamped are the country's Ministry of Petroleum and the Nilepet (formerly Sudapet—Sudan
National Petroleum Corporation), the petroleum company ow-

ned by the government.[3] The program takes into account the massive conflict of interest plaguing the protection of the environment by this ministry.[4] It is for this reason that experts staffing the SUDD Institute, an independent political think-tank, recommend the creation of a body to be charged with the ensuring of the adherence to environmental regulations.[5] This institution is to examine and disclose all transactions involving the country's petroleum industry since the founding of South Sudan.[6] "Unimpaired transparency" is the slogan to be applied to the reform movement as a whole.[7] The government led by president Salva Kiir is already, however, falling behind the schedule foreseen for the program's implementation.

*

On February 4, 2016 Sign of Hope receives from its contact at the SPOC (Sudd Petroleum Operating Company Ltd.) the minutes of the meeting held on November 10, 2015. This recording of the minutes is in and of itself amazing, as Sign of Hope has always been the one to feel compelled to write down the course and contents of such conferences, and to then distribute the finished product to participants. Even more amazing is that it is also transmitted to us—and that this has been approved by the Petroleum Ministry: the minutes are accompanied by logs of the joint meetings of preparation that took place on November 9th in Stuttgart, and which were attended by the MPM (Ministry of Petroleum and Mining), SPOC and Norconsult, and of the get-together held on November 11 (and thus after our conference) and featuring the same players.

After the meeting in Stuttgart, we noticed that the representative of the Petroleum Ministry had presented his "resolutions" on a sheet whose template—due to its being merely slightly changed—obviously stemmed from the oil consortium. Shaking off our shock at the unconcealed threats voiced during the meeting, we were nearly prepared to regard this discovery as being a strange coincidence, and to consider ourselves slightly paranoid. Our values demand of us that always strive to see the good in others. But the minutes and logs sent to us tell a very convincing and different tale. They detail in official and unmistakable terms the arrangements reached by the SPOC and MPM in order to force us to fall silent. As our "reading material" now informs us, the purpose of the preparatory meeting held on November 9th was nominally to provide the representatives of Norconsult with the opportunity to brief the participants from the SPOC and from the MPM on the latest developments. There's nothing wrong with that. But, according to the minutes, the meeting actually had another, entirely different objective.

The meeting was headed by Emi Suhardi, president of the SPOC. According to Point 1 of the minutes, he emphasized the importance to the other participants of acting as a team. In Point 2, he asked the others whether or not they would be prepared to maintain this approach when confronted with the charges levied by Sign of Hope. In Point 3, Suhardi added that the participants' joining together to give Sign of Hope a key message was necessary. The message: the organization has to submit all its discoveries and findings to the authorities. Point 4 is Suhardi's complaints that the meeting in 2012 in Stuttgart was not attended by a representative of the government of South Sudan, and that the crisis caused the recommendations not to be implemented. Sign of Hope is now being allowed to read Point 5, which states: "That day's meeting [November 9, 2015] was aimed to plan for key resolutions with the leadership of Mr Humoon and the agenda would be finalized."

The SPOC and the MPM work closely and very well together. Conducting a dialogue worthy of the name, one leading to a jointly-desired result and thus yielding true progress, doesn't take this form. This lack is emphasized and exacerbated in Point 6 of the minutes, in which Sign of Hope learns that Mr. Humoon—the Ministry's representative—announced that he agrees with the main point of Mr. Emi—the representative of the SPOC. Mr. Humoon is thus calling for the creation of a "unified front" [...] Mr. Humoon shares the view that the Ministry and the other participants are aware of the recommendations of 2012's not having been implemented due to the onset of the crisis in December 2013.[8]

So that's what the minutes had to say about the preparatory meeting. The representatives of the SPOC and of the Ministry met once more, this time on November 11th. The venue was the same hotel in Stuttgart. The purpose of the meeting was to follow up on the conference. The log of this meeting reveals that the South Sudanese official received two helpings of praise for his efforts on behalf of the "unified front". The SPOC's Emi Suhardi once more presided over the meeting. In Point 1, he thanked Mr. Humoon for chairing the conference and for the "issuance" of the resolutions. The representative of the Ministry being praised thanked Suhardi for the compliments, and, as noted in Point 2 of the minutes, he declared that he welcomed the SPOC's strategy for dealing with Sign of Hope and the consortium's plan of bringing all the participants together to continue to discuss the charges levied by Sign of Hope. In point 6, Emi Suhardi concluded the meeting by thanking the participants for having handled their specific responsibilities and for having made their particular contributions, with his especial thanks going to the representative of the MPM for the "defining resolutions."[9]

What this all means: Emi Suhardi, the president of the SPOC, suggested to Humoon Chol Deng, the representative of the Petroleum Ministry, that he send Sign of Hope a "key message". The core of this is our being gagged. Obviously, this idea stemmed from the SPOC. This message was delivered by a "unified front" comprised of the parties regulating and being regulated in the petroleum industry. The United Nations Environmental Programme had described this collusion, which we had also long suspected of existing. Notwithstanding this, we are completely taken back: We have the feeling to be trapped in a hide-and-seek game.

*

We stumble upon a further sentence in the minutes of the meeting on November 10, 2015: "Daimler representatives were obvious on their support to Sign of Hope but because of MPM directives they believed their role as catalyst was jeopardized."[10]

We ask ourselves what this all means. Then we recall to mind our meeting in Stuttgart. Could the Daimler representative have done more for us? We found him rather restrained. He did seem rather upset at the threats contained in the "Resolutions" and expressed his dismay about the "Resolutions" during the time between the meeting and the dinner. But had he actually voiced his concerns to the MPM and to the SPOC-Petronas group? He said little during the official meeting. During the subsequent dinner, as we and—especially—our staff members in South Sudan were unmistakably being threatened, he did not say a single thing.

We wrote to him on November 23, 2015 that we view our work in South Sudan as being endangered by the "Resolutions". We also referred to the letter from Daimler's managing board on July 27, 2015, and asked what Daimler could do to support

Sign of Hope's operations in South Sudan, in view of the statements contained and implied in the "Resolutions" sheet. It took the company nearly three weeks to reply. Daimler's representative assured us that he had had absolutely no idea of the existence or contents of the "Resolutions" prior to their being presented. Regardless of that, Daimler was finding it difficult to determine what could actually be done in the current situation.

On February 4, 2016, we peruse the printouts of the minutes of the meeting on November 2015 and the letters and E-mails exchanged between Sign of Hope and Daimler. While we do that, we took another look at the purportedly binding guidelines established by Daimler for itself, for its business partners, and for its partners. We reread in Daimler's Integrity Code: "Therefore, we select our direct business partners according to their adherence to the same principles that we have established for ourselves in this Code. In our business relations, we pay heed to the observance of these principles. We reject business partners and customers who violate human rights and workers' rights outlined in the 'Principles of Social Responsibility at Daimler' as well as environmental protection or anti-corruption laws."[11]

*

On the very same day that we receive this highly instructive set of minutes, Daimler announces its having set in financial year 2015 all-high corporate highs.[12] Income rose from 2014's €7.3 billion to 2015's €8.9 billion.[13] This caused the dividend to be increased by 80 cents to the record amount of €3.25 per share.[14]

*

On February 11th, Sign of Hope receives the appraisal rendered by Professor Fritz Pragst of the samples of hair collected in South

Sudan.[15] Pragst is the former head of the Forensic Toxicology Department of the Institute for Criminal Medicine, which itself forms part of Berlin's renowned Charité hospital complex. Pragst is one of the world's leading toxicologists.[16] His area of specialty is the analysis of hair samples. His treatises in this field are considered to form the foundations of this science.[17]

Pragst's appraisal addresses three issues. 1.: He uses the latest scientific literature to cast a searching look at the ability of the findings ensuing from the analysis of hair to indicate levels of environmental contamination, with this especially applying to drinking water's being polluted by toxic metals. 2.: Pragst places the concentrations established in the contexts of normal results, and of those found in especially encumbered populations. 3.: He undertakes an evaluation that is informed by the known contamination of potable water in the region in which the persons whose hairs forming the samples live. Pragst's conclusion: the contamination—taking the form of lead, barium, cobalt and strontium—is directly related to the production of oil. "In the cases of lead and barium, an endangering of health is to be assumed for the residents living in the communities of Koch, Leer and Nyal. The concentration of lead is—with this especially applying to the persons from Koch whose hair was sampled—in a range determined for those working in strongly-contaminated mines and metal processing facilities. A causal connection is yielded by the much lower value established in Rumbeck, which is farther away."[18]

The concentrations of lead found in the residents of Koch are far above those of normal populations living in a wide variety of countries. These concentrations are comparable to those identified in polluted areas in Kosovo, in China's Pearl River Delta, in a village situated immediately next to a zinc and lead mine in China, in a lead mine in southwestern China, in a contaminated flood plain in the Philippines, and in an industrial area in Pakistan.[19] The values in Leer and Nyal are also substantially higher than normal.

According to Pragst, the health-endangering concentrations of barium proven to exist are "indubitably" related to the employment of barites in the drilling fluids.[20] Other conclusions forthcoming from the toxicologist: the higher than normal values for cobalt and strontium are in the same way attributable to the additives used by the oil industry. A toxic endangering is not possible to be established from the hair samples for these elements.[21]

Pragst cites a large number of studies that show the relationship between contamination with toxic metals and wastes —including drilling fluids and produced water—produced by the production of oil.[22] The findings of the appraisal commissioned by Sign of Hope represent a valuable complement to previous research—and constitute an important scientific discovery, says Pragst. This is because Sign of Hope's research has achieved something new. For the first in the world, proof has been delivered of the direct connection between the chemicals employed in the production of oil and the contamination found in human hair. Up until now, the only items thoroughly investigated in this regard were the effects emanating from the noxious materials contained in oil spills. The samples of hair now have enabled the proving of the effects issuing from the use of chemicals in the production of oil.

*

Professor Pragst is joined by the Wolfhagen-based Institute for Environmental Medicine (IFU), in evaluating the contamination of hairs forming the samples. When gathering the background materials to be used by the IFU's scientists, Klaus Stieglitz takes another, even more searching look at the Norconsult study. It had been cited in 2012 by the SPOC and by the MPM as proof of the lack of danger attributable to the conditions of production at Thar Jath. The Norwegians diligently and precisely recorded—using color—all of the values exceeding ceilings in their findings. These values had been extensively discussed at the time. Sign of Hope recognized that the Norwegians had worked honestly and well. Sign of Hope's issue was with the conclusions ensuing from this work. They were unsubstantiated.

Klaus Stieglitz's perusal of the appraisal from Norconsult suddenly encounters a value. Unlike the others, it was not highlighted using a color. It was for that reason not taken into consideration in the discussion of those days. It is only now that Stieglitz, the Sign of Hope's vice chairperson, perceives that the investigation of the tissue of fish taken from the bioremediation plant revealed high values of lead. The Norwegian documented these, but failed to color code them.

*

Klaus-Dietrich Runow is the head of medical studies at the IFU institute of environmental medicine. Runow comes to the same conclusions as Professor Pragst, the Berlin-based toxicologist.[23] The former renders a written report. It states that the amounts and quality of the extant data and of the analyses of hair conducted justify a substantiated statement on the medical impacts of environmental influences.[24] The homogeneity of the results, each showing high pollutant values, support—the low number of 96 providers of samples notwithstanding—the extrapolation of the results to further segments of the local population.[25]

Runow uses the contamination established and factors in that of lead determined in fish tissue by Norconsult to perform the following extrapolation: "A person living in the vicinity of the Central Processing Facility (CPF) who drinks two liters of water a day ingests 1.16 mg of lead in the process. Should the same person eat 500 grams of fish, he is in danger of ingesting a further 1 mg. This would bring the total intake to 2.16 mg. A long-term ingestion of 1.0 mg of lead per day or more causes the consumer to experience chronic illnesses."[26]

Runow establishes that the total toxic contamination of the people in the region determined through the analysis of the hair constitutes a danger to their lives. The first and requisite step to improve the inhabitants' health is the halting of their intake of noxious materials.[27] The highest priority should be given to providing them with access to clean water and uncontaminated food.[28] A further requisite step is the subjecting of each individual in the region to an on-site check-up.[29] Another step to be undertaken in the immediate future should be the gathering of samples of blood from the persons in the regions being investigated and in surrounding areas. To be checked are the concentration of selected toxic elements (heavy metals) in blood and the supply of minerals and trace elements.[30] Persons showing a high level of total toxic encumbrance are to be treated by physicians.[31] Required to be carried out are detoxification measures. These will take three to twelve months for each patient, assuming that they are carried out by appropriately trained medical personnel.[32] Of utmost importance is on-site awareness-raising. The people affected have to be made aware of the damages ensuing and the dangers facing them from the toxic contamination.[33] In further moves, preventive measures leading to the reduction of this toxic contamination on the part of people and the environment in the areas affected have to be developed and implemented.[34]

*

We send on February 26th an E-mail to South Sudan's Ministries of Health, the Environment and Petroleum. In our E-mail, we inform them of the results of the analysis of hairs, and offer them detailed information. We view this step as constituting a way of briefing the local population on-site. We undertook it because we currently do not have any access to the country. This E-mail also represents a way of satisfying the ministries' stipulation of giving priority to informing them first.

*

On March 5th, the "AFP" publishes an article in English on the analyses of samples of hairs collected by Sign of Hope, and on their dramatic findings, and how they relate to South Sudan's oil industry.[35] This article is taken up and spread by international media.

*

On March 8th, the business pages of Munich's "Süddeutsche Zeitung" contain an article on the relationship between the contamination of South Sudan's oil fields and the activities undertaken there by Daimler's partner Petronas (Petroliam Nasional Berhad). The article also covers the Sign of Hope's fruitless efforts to alleviate this contamination by conducting a dialogue with both parties.[36] "ARD" is one of Germany's national TV channels. On the evening of March 8th, its "report from Munich" news broadcast covers Sign of Hope's long and unsuccessful struggle to enlist Daimler in the getting of the parties responsible for the environmental catastrophe in South

Sudan to take corrective actions.[37] "ARD's" reporters have interviewed Fritz Pragst, who states: "You have to either get rid of these perils, or get the people out of these places of danger. But the damages that their neural systems and kidneys have suffered can not be reversed."[38]

Petronas tells "ARD" that the companies managed by it adhere to the strict standards of health, security and environment.[39] Daimler announces that it takes the charges very seriously.[40] The journalists at the "Süddeutsche Zeitung" and "ARD" endorse the view that Daimler should have taken corrective actions a long time ago. "report from Munich" interviews Hartmut Paulsen, who is both a corporate attorney and an expert on corporate ethics. Paulsen states that Daimler should have ascertained, after having been initially contacted by Sign of Hope, the nature and state of compliance rules in force at Petronas, and should have checked to see if these were being adhered to by the company.[41] Paulsen adds that these reports constitute the very last opportunity for Daimler to live up to its obligations of examining its business relationships with Petronas, and, if so required, to put an end to them.[42]

*

The Formula 1 season starts on March 20th. The Mercedes-Petronas team finishes first (Nico Rosberg) and second (Lewis Hamilton).

*

This is where this book ends—but not the story of Sign of Hope, or of its staff members or of the people of South Sudan. We have all paid a high price for our having publicly called attention to the contravening of the fundamental human right to have clean water. This price: we and our employees in South Sudan have been severely threatened. All experts in Germany's Foreign Ministry and in international organizations have given us a clear and unmistakable message: take these threats seriously. This counsel has forced us to evacuate all of our non-South Sudanese staff members from the country. This does not, however, mean that we have imposed a vow of silence upon ourselves. Quite the opposite. We will not stop telling the world who is responsible for damaging the rights and health of the people and environment of South Sudan. And we will not stop demanding of these companies and institutions that they live up to the standards, rules and obligations that they have set for themselves. To the extent possible, we will maintain—using our South Sudanese staff—our school-building and other education projects. We will also continue to operate our bush clinics in the country. We will also cooperate with partner organizations to assist the people of South Sudan.

*

On July 20, 2010, Reimund Reubelt and Klaus Stieglitz went to Daimler's headquarters for their first meeting on this subject. At that meeting, we made our objective very clear. "We are not aiming at getting publicity. Nor do we want to levy charges or incriminate anyone. What we want to achieve: to enlist Daimler's assistance in improving the lives of the people of South Sudan by providing them, once more, with clean water. This, in turn, will enable them to stay in their homeland." Our contact at Daimler emphasized during the meetings and subsequent ones that we at Sign of Hope were on the right track.

Up to now, true progress for the people in South Sudan could not be achieved. Thus we are wondering if we took the right turn. The responses from Daimler and from Petronas, its sponsor and business partner, reported in the "Süddeutsche Zeitung" confirm these doubts.

We are writing these lines in time in which Germany and the rest of Europe are discussing the "refugee crisis", "influx of refugees" and "causes of flight". We are writing them in a time in which "corporate social responsibility" (CSR) is supposedly something to be prized and achieved, and in which every company that considers itself to be important issues a CSR report casting its activities in a positive light.

One key issue requires a thorough discussion in this world of compliance codes, Global Compact phrases and CSR commitments: how binding are actually these pretty words? This is because this case clearly and unmistakably shows that the self-commitments made by companies are obviously not capable of ensuring their adherence to high ethical standards—and that these commitments have to be made legally binding and thus enforceable.[43]

It is high time that the people of South Sudan finally get the help that they so desperately need. It's high time that the parties causing their misery are brought to justice. Sign of Hope is still on the job! When discussing with staff members what actions are to be taken in and for South Sudan, Reimund Reubelt and Klaus Stieglitz repeatedly call to mind the old man with the white hair. Although he had never seen the Berlin Wall and although he was thousands of kilometers away from it, the old man never stopped praying for the Wall's fall.

o El Geneina

Block 17

o Nyala

o Ed Da'ein

Chad

Block C

Block Ea

o Raga

Central African
Republic

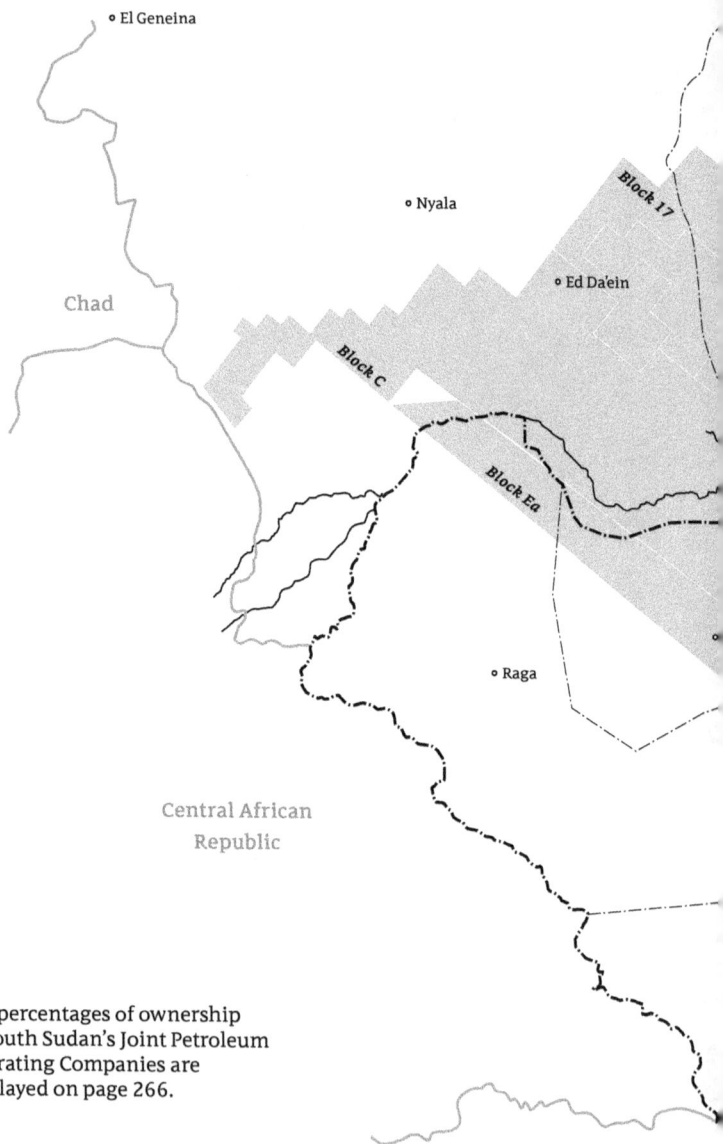

The percentages of ownership
of South Sudan's Joint Petroleum
Operating Companies are
displayed on page 266.

0   km   100

Democratic Repu
of the Congo

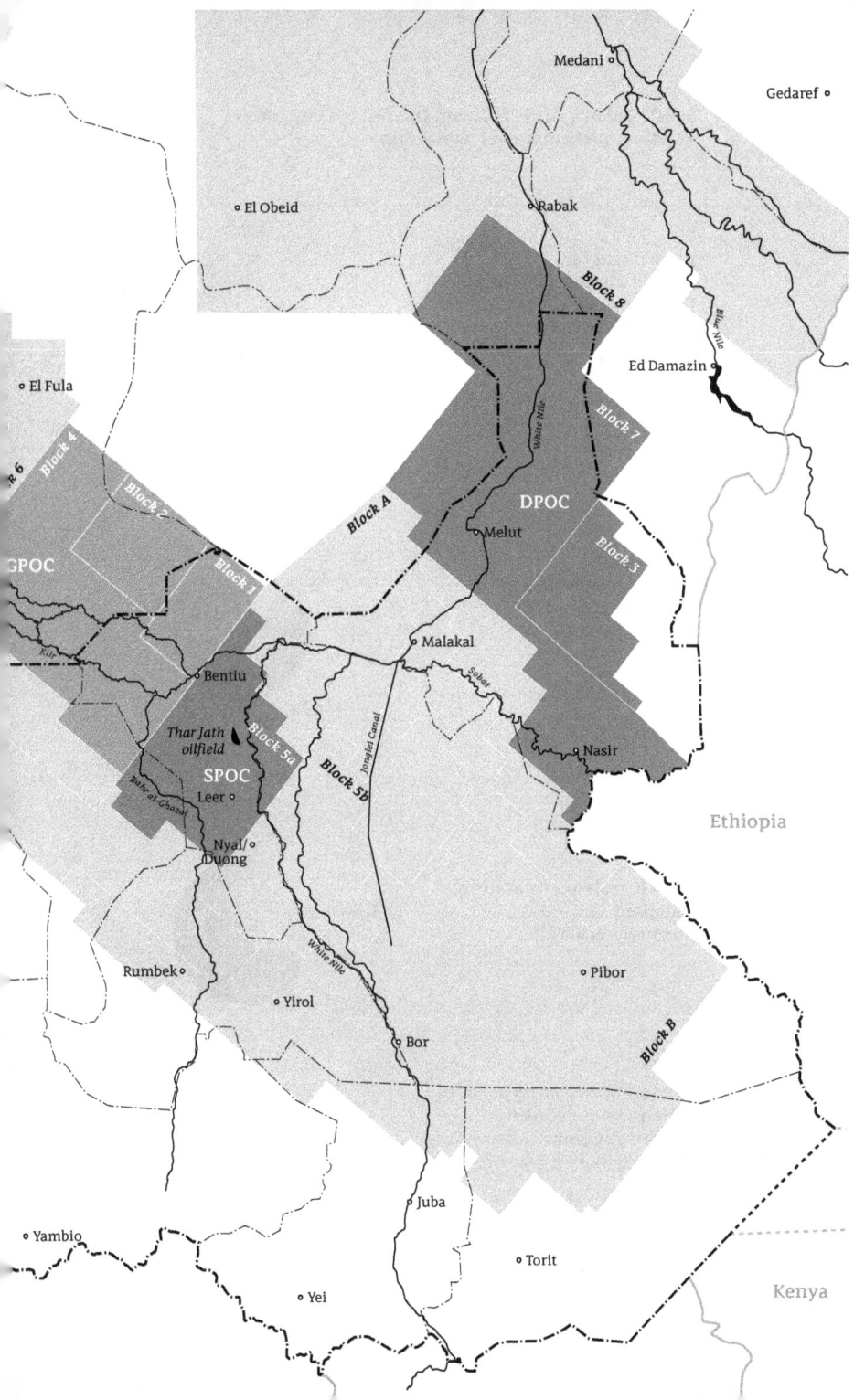

South Sudan's Joint Peroleum Operating Companies and their percentages of ownership

Block 1, 2 and 4:
Greater Pioneer Operating Company Ltd. – GPOC
(formerly GNPOC)

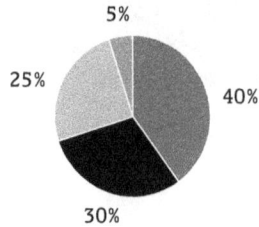

5%
25%
40%
30%

Block 3 and 7:
Dar Petroleum Operating Company Ltd. – DPOC
(formerly PDOC)

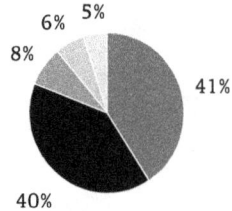

6% 5%
8%
41%
40%

Block 5 a:
Sudd Petroleum Operating Company Ltd. – SPOC
(formerly WNPOC)

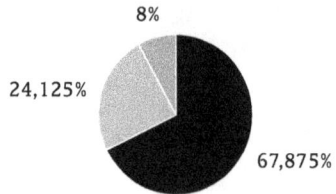

8%
24,125%
67,875%

The concession areas of South Sudan's Joint Petroleum Operating Companies are emphasized in dark gray on pages 264–265.

- CNPC (China)
- Nilepet (South Sudan)
- ONGC Videsh Ltd. (India)
- Petronas (Malaysia)
- Sinopec (China)
- Tri-Ocean (Egypt)

APPENDIX

Chronology of political events in Sudan

---

60 A.D. | Roman Emperor Nero sends troops to find the source of the White Nile.

1821 | Sent from Egypt, Ottoman troops occupy the Sudan and seize control over the country.

1847–1852 | Alfred Brehm participates in an expedition that takes him to what is today Sudan.

1857 | Missionary Daniel Comboni travels to Sudan, where he founds a series of missions.

1899 | Northern Sudan becomes a "condominium". It is jointly administered by the British and the Egyptians. Southern Sudan is run by a British administrator.

1920s | Withdrawal of the Egyptians from northern Sudan. Partition of northern and southern Sudan is pursued by British administration. Northern Sudan's infrastructure is developed; southern Sudan's, neglected.

1947 |At the Juba Conference, the British and the north Sudanese resolve that northern and southern Sudan are to form a single country.

1955 | Northern Sudanese take over administration of the south, causing increase in violent conflict between northern and southern Sudan on the latter's autonomy. This fighting is launched in Torit (located on the border to Uganda).

1956 |On January 1,1956, Sudan achieves its independence from the British-Egyptian colonial powers. The first civil war between north and south begins.

1959 | Prospecting for oil begins in the Red Sea.

1964 | In October, protests cause the deposition of the political leadership under General Ibrahim Abboud.

1969 | General Gafaar Numeiri takes power in a coup d'etat.

1971 | Separatist movements join to form South Sudan Liberation Movement (SSLM).

1972 | Southern Sudan awarded autonomy through peace treaty of Addis Ababa, end of the first civil war.

1974 | Chevron, the US oil giant, awarded concession to territory covering 156,000 square kilometers and located around Muglad and Melut; company begins prospecting for oil.

1979 | Chevron discovers oil in fields in Upper Nile and in Muglad basin.

1980 | Total, the Franco-Belgian oil corporation, receives oil concession, but does not exploit it due to security situation.

1982 | Chevron investigates possible oil fields in Heglig and Unity (in the north of today's South Sudan).

1983 | President Gafaar Numeiri helps cause rupture of peace agreement of Addis Ababa. He dissolves administration of southern Sudan. Islamic-based code of laws—the Sharia—is introduced throughout Sudan, where it is now the law of the land.

> Led by John Garang, the Sudan People's Liberation Army/Movement (SPLAM) is founded. Second civil war starts.

1983 | Subsequent to the attack on oil facilities in Rubkona (located in today's state of Unity), Chevron suspends its production of oil in Sudan.

1985 | In April, President Gafaar Numeiri is deposed.

1986 | Sadiq-al-Mahdi is named Prime Minister.

1989 | General Omar al-Bashir putsches his way into power, and, joined by Hassan al-Turabi, sets up an "Islamic Republic" in Sudan.

1991 | SPLA-Nasir (led by Riek Machar and Lam Akol, both belonging to Nuer ethnic group) splits off from SPLA (led by John Garang, who belongs to the Dinka). Salva Kiir (Dinka) stays with the SLPA. Sudan's provinces are reconstituted as states.

1992 | Armed conflict between SPLA and Sudanese government.

> Chevron sells its oil concessions. Canada's State Petroleum of Vancouver signs contracts foreseeing the production of oil. The company in turn is taken over by Canada's Arakis.

1994 | Sudan's government makes 26 states out of the 9 hitherto in existence.

> Sign of Hope launches its operations in Sudan, with the southern part of the country being its main focus.

1995 | CNPC is an oil company owned by the Chinese government. It receives the concession rights to Block 6 in the Muglad Basin.

1996 | The Sudanese government uses separate peace treaty to co-opt splitter groups of rebels holding sway over the oil fields in southern Sudan.

> Arakis scales down investment and enters into joint venture with the Chinese CNPC, with the Sudanese government's Sudapet and with the Malaysian government's Petronas (representing the latter's first stake in a Sudanese oil concession) through the setting up of the Greater Nile Petroleum Operating Company (GNPOC).

1997 | The WNPOC (renamed SPOC after independence) consortium is formed by the Sweden-based Lundin, Petronas, Austria's OMV and Sudapet; consortium's signing of concession contract with Sudanese government for the production of oil in Block 5A.

> Construction is launched of oil pipeline leading to Port Sudan.

1998 | Arakis purchased by Canada's Talisman Energy.

Arakis' oil production concessions in Blocks 1, 2 and 4 are transferred to GNPOC.

> Sign of Hope publishes an article on human rights in Sudan in the *Internationales Afrikaforum* political science publication. Sign of Hope and a partner organization provide support to a hospital in Lui, a community located in Sudan's state of Western Equatoria.

1999 | Oil starts flowing through pipeline to Port Sudan.

> Sign of Hope sets up an air bridge that dispenses urgently needed supplies to the people living in the Nuba mountains.

2000 | Sign of Hope sends convoys of trucks loaded with emergency supplies to refugees fleeing from the civil war that are living in Mawalkon, a community in Bahr-el-Gazhal state. The organization also provides support to an agricultural project that is to help 6,000 families living in Torit (situated on the Ugandan border).

2001 | Discovery of oil in Thar Jath field in Block 5A.

> Sign of Hope assumes the costs of operating three schools located in the vicinity of Rumbek, a community located in state of Jonglei.

2002 | The SPLA and the Sudanese government agree upon ceasefire in the Nuba mountains, a stronghold of the SPLA.

2003 | Lundin sells its stakes in the concession rights to Thar Jath to Petronas. Talisman sells its stakes to India's ONGC Videsh Ltd. This is viewed as being a cautious step towards achieving detente among the parties fighting the civil war.

> New oilfields are discovered in Blocks 3 and 7.

> Nilepet is founded. This oil company is owned by the state.

> Sign of Hope protests the expulsion of the residents from their home in the oil fields in the state of Unity, which is being fought over by the civil war's parties.

2004 | Amount of oil produced in Sudan comes to more than 300,000 barrels a day.

> OMV sells all of its stakes in the concession rights (Blocks 5A and 5B) to India's ONGC Videsh Ltd.

2005 | Conclusion of Comprehensive Peace Agreement yields extensive autonomy for southern Sudan and ends second civil war. Division of oil revenues between north and south agreed upon.

> John Garang becomes country's vice-president, but dies in helicopter crash.

> In order to foster peace in the north of what is today South Sudan, Sign of Hope and a locally-based partner hold seminars on human rights for local residents.

2006 | Launching in June of oil pumping in Thar Jath.

> Sign of Hope is awarded consultant status by the United Nation's Economic and Social Council, which Sign of Hope briefs on the violation of human rights in South Sudan.

2007 | Sign of Hope learns of the problems with drinking water in and around Thar Jath.

2008 | Sign of Hope collects in February and November samples of water in Thar Jath, and sends letter to WNPOC in Khartoum.

2009 | Revenues from oil pumped in southern Sudan come to $US 2.5 billion a year.

> Further samples of water are collected in April and November. WNPOC publishes declaration on oil-caused contamination on its Website. The declaration contains categorical refutations of Sign of Hope's charges. The latter responds

> Sign of Hope opens in October a clinic in Duong, which is located near Nyal in what is today South Sudan.

2010 | 98.6% of the voters vote for South Sudan's independence in a referendum.

> Southern Sudan receives in March the revenues from oil production in Sudan accruing to it in accordance with the Comprehensive Peace Agreement.

> Sign of Hope contacts in March Daimler AG for the first time. In April Sign of Hope launches construction of a deep well in Bouw, a community in the state of Unity. Another well—this one located in Rier, state of Unity—is completed at the end of the year.

2011 | Meeting in April in Juba are representatives of the WNPOC oil consortium and of Sign of Hope. July 9th. South Sudan becomes an independent country, with Salva Kiir as its first president

> The construction of a deep well is completed in August. It provides water to 2,500 residents of Marial Guit, a community located in the state of Unity.

> The south's secession causes Sudan to lose nearly 75% of its oil fields. South Sudan pumps nearly 350,000 barrels oil a day at the start of independence. In July, in a first, oil from South Sudan is sold to Chinaoil via Port Sudan. Lack of agreement about charges to be paid by South Sudan to Sudan for the use of pipeline. Sudan's president Al-Bashir demands $US 32 per barrel.

> South Sudan's Ministry for Energy and Mining concludes pre-contract with Petronas.

> In November, all state holdings in South Sudan's oil fields that were previously owned by Sudapet in Sudan are transferred to Nilepet.

2012 | SPOC (formerly WNPOC) becomes a registered company in South Sudan.

> Disagreements about transporting fees cause Sudan to block pipeline used by South Sudan to export its oil. South Sudan halts in January production of oil.

> Unrest breaks out in April in disputed oil field of Heglig, which is located on border between South Sudan and Sudan.

> In April Sign of Hope takes over a bush clinic from Malteser International in Rumbek. This clinic receives

its first patients in May. Up to September nearly 6,900 patients are being medically treated in the clinic's outpatients department. In Rumbek Sign of Hope also establishes a logistics center to facilitate its activities in South Sudan. Moreover Sign of Hope strives to improve the conditions of mentally ill patients who are being kept in Rumbek Central Prison.

> Sign of Hope concludes in September the construction of a further three wells in South Sudan.

> On September 27, Sudan and South Sudan sign an agreement in Addis Ababa arranged by the Union of African States on the sharing of oil revenues.

2013 | The president of South Sudan, Salva Kiir, fires vice-president Riek Machar and the rest of the cabinet. Strife breaks out in Bor, a city located in the state of Jonglei, and in the oil fields of the state of Unity.

> Alternatives to exporting oil via Sudan are to be investigated; an agreement is reached between South Sudan and Sudan on the former's exporting of oil via the latter.

> In April, another deep well is commissioned. This one is located in Kuach, a community in the state of Unity.

> In June, Sign of Hope's clinic is moved from Duong to nearby Nyal in the state of Unity.

> In April, the SPOC relaunches the production of oil in Thar Jath.

> On December 15th, bloody battles break out in Juba between the followers of Machar and the Kiir administration. The conflict quickly spreads to other parts of the country. On December 19th, conflict in the Thar Jath oil field kills 11 people. On December 26th, opposition forces control the Thar Jath oil field.

2014 | Bentiu in the state of Unity is plundered during the armed conflicts.

> The United Nations reports that thousands have lost their lives due to the conflicts between South Sudan and Sudan. More than one million people have fled. Five million are dependent upon humanitarian assistance. The government of Sudan and South Sudan join with the groups opposed to the latter in accusing each other in being responsible for the conflicts consuming the border areas and the oil fields in them.

> The decline in oil pumping and transportation cause South Sudan's pound to massively depreciate. During the first half of the year, a mere 120,000 barrels of oil are pumped a day.

> The NPF reports in October on the contamination of the environment through oil spills in and around Thar Jath.

> Sign of Hope informs in June the United Nation's Council on Human Rights of violations of human rights caused by the conflict that broke out in 2013 and of the accompanying lack of constitutional structures.

> Published in November 2014 is a hydro-geological study entitled "Effect of oil exploration and production on the salinity of a marginally permeable aquifer system in the Thar Jath, Mala and Unity oil fields in southern Sudan".

> Sign of Hope launches the building of an elementary school.

2015 | The conflicts roiling the region cause the postponing of elections.

> President Kiir signs—with reservations and due to international pressure—the peace agreement reached with South Sudan's opposition. The agreement returns Riek Machar to being vice-president.

> A number of journalists are murdered in South Sudan during the year. International media criticize the restrictions on freedom of the press.

> At the beginning of the year, South Sudan is paying $US 25 per barrel in pipeline transit fees to Sudan. The price of oil plummets on the world market.

> Fierce fighting rages during May-July in the vicinities of Thar Jath in Unity state and of Malkal in Upper Nile state.

> Sign of Hope presents in February the study of the samples of water collected in the Thar Jath region at a press conference in Juba. To ascertain the contamination by heavy metals, hairs are collected in May and September from 96 residents in Koch, Leer, Nyal and Rumbek.

2016 | The United Nations impose an arms embargo upon South Sudan.

> International media report in March on Sign of Hope's findings of contamination-caused damaging of the health of the people living in the Thar Jath region and resulting from the oil industry. Munich's "Süddeutsche Zeitung" issues a headlining article on March 8th on "Petronas' dirty dealings put the pressure on Daimler". "ARD", Germany's national TV channel, also extensively and prominently covers Petronas, which is the sponsor of the Mercedes Silver Arrows race team, Daimler and their role in the environmental catastrophe in South Sudan.

Sources:

Amnesty International. Erdöl. http://amnesty-sudan.de/ amnesty-wordpress/erdoel (last retrieved on 10.3.2016).

Batruch, Christine. 2003. Lundin Petroleum's experience in Sudan. www.lundin-petrole um.com/Documents/ot_su dan_experience_24-11-03.pdf (last retrieved on 15.3.2016).

BBC World. 2015. South Sudan profile-Timeline. BBC World, www.bbc.com/news/world-africa-14019202 (last retrieved on 2.3.2016).

BR24: *Silberpfeil-Sponsor Petronas* Daimler und die Umweltkatastrophe im Sudsudan. Munich. 8.3.2016. www.br.de/

nachrichten/petronasdaimler-suedsudan-100.html (last retrieved on 15.3.2016).

CNPC 2009. Review of Years of Sino-Sudanese Petroleum Cooperation. www.cnpc.com.cn/en/csr2009en/201407/8fc23f51afa74701a14b3453211cb6eb/files/139ad08f4a204b79ac5cff82972e37e5.pdf (last retrieved on 14.3.2016).

Ecos Online 2014. ECOS Oil Map. http://sudanreeves.org/wp-content/uploads/2014/09/Sudan_ECOS_Oil_Map.jpg (last retrieved on 15.3.2016).

European Coalition on Oil in Sudan: The Legacy of Lundin, Petronas and OMV in Block 5A, Sudan 1997–2003. Utrecht. Available online: www.ecosonline.org/reports/2010/UNPAID_DEBT_fullreportweb.pdf (last retrieved on 10.3.2016).

Gallab, Abdullahi A. *The first Islamist republic: Development and disintegration of Islamism in the Sudan.* Ashgate Publishing, Ltd., 2008.

Hoffnungszeichen | Sign of Hope e.V. 2014. Legal System, Conflict and Human Rights ins South Sudan. Human Rights Council. A/HRC/26/NGO/72. 5.6.2014.

Human Rights Watch 2003. Sudan, Oil, and Human Rights. New York, www.hrw.org/reports/2003/sudan1103/sudanprint.pdf (last retrieved on 5.3.2016).

Natsios, Andrew S. 2012. Sudan, South Sudan & Darfur. What everyone needs to know. New York: Oxford University Press.

Rueskamp, Hella, et al. 2014. "Effect of oil exploration and production on the salinity of a marginally permeable aquifer system in the Thar Jath-, Mala-and Unity Oilfields, Southern Sudan". *Zentralblatt für Geologie und Paläontologie,* Part I: 95–115.

Simon, Tobias. 2016. Südsudan. LiPortal. Das Länder-Informations-Portal (Country Information Portal). Bonn, Eschborn: GIZ GmbH, www.liportal.de/suedsudan (last retrieved on 2.3.2016).

Stieglitz, Klaus 1998: Zur Lage der Menschenrechte im Sudan vor dem Hintergrund des anhaltenden Bürgerkrieges. *Internationales Afrikaforum* 34(1): 71–79.

Sudan Update 2016. Chevron and Nimeiri. Hebden Bridge, Großbritannien. www.sudan update.org/REPORTS/Oil/08 cn.html (last retrieved on 14.3.2016).

Süddeutsche Zeitung 2016. Petronas' schmierige Geschäfte setzen Daimler unter Druck. Stuttgart. 8.3.2016. www. sueddeutsche.de/wirtschaft/ oel-konzern-schmierige-geschaefte-1.2895544 (last retrieved on 15.3.2016).

Understanding Sudan. A Teaching and Learning Resource 2015. http://understanding sudan.org/Oil/OilResources/ L2FS2-HistoryofOilinSudan. pdf.

Von der Mehden, Fred R., Troner Al. 2007. In commission James A. Baker III Institute for Public Policy u. Japan Petroleum Energy Center. Rice University. Houston, Texas. https://bakerinstitute.org/ media/files/page/9dd51576/ noc_petronas_tronervdm. pdf (last retrieved on 14.3.2016).

Abbreviations employed

AFP | Agence France Presse

BBC | British Broadcasting Corporation

BMZ | Germany's Ministry of Development

CAA | Civilian Aviation Authority

CNN | Cable News Network

CNPC | China National Petroleum Corporation

CPA | Comprehensive Peace Agreement

CPF | Central Processing Facility (in Thar Jath, Sudan)

CSR | Corporate Social Responsibility

dpa | Deutsche Presse Agentur (news agency)

DPOC | Dar Petroleum Operating Company

DTM | Germany's Touring Car Competition

ECOS | European Coalition on Oil in Sudan

EIA | Energy Information Administration

EITI | The Extractive Industries Transparency Initiative

FAZ | Frankfurter Allgemeine Zeitung (newspaper)

FIA | Fédération Internationale de l'Automobile

GDES | General Directorate of Environment and Safety

GIZ | Germany's Agency for International Development

GNPOC | Greater Nile Petroleum Operating Company

GONU | Government of National Unity

GPOC | Greater Pioneer Operating Company

HSE | Health, Safety and Environment Standards

ISO | International Organization for Standardization

JIU | Joint Integrated Units, Sudan (units comprised of soldiers from the SPLA and SAF)

MEM | Ministry of Energy and Minerals, Sudan

MPM | Ministry of Petroleum and Mining (South Sudan)

Norad | Norwegian Agency for Development Cooperation

NPC | National Petroleum Commission

OAG | Other Armed Groups

OECD | Organization for Economic Cooperation and Development

OMV | Österreichische Mineralölverwaltung AG (Austrian oil company)

ONGC | Oil and Natural Gas Corporation (ONGC) Videsh Ltd.

Petronas | Petroliam Nasional Berhad

SPLA | Sudan People's Liberation Army

SPOC | Sudd Petroleum Operating Company Ltd.

SOH | Sign of Hope

Sudapet | Sudan National Petroleum Corporation

TAZ | Tageszeitung, Berlin (newspaper)

TDS | Total Dissolved Solids

UNAMID | African Union/United Nations Mission in Darfur

UNEP | United Nations Environment Programme

UNMISS | United Nations Mission in the Republic of South Sudan

USAID | United States Agency for International Development

WNPOC | White Nile Petroleum Operating Company

Comments

Prologue

1 See Budge, E.A. Wallis: The Egyptian Sudan, its history and monuments, Philadelphia 1907, p. 172ff.

2 Brehms Weltreisen zwischen Nordkap und Äquator. Von ihm selbst erzählt. Ausgewählt und mit biographischen Zwischentexten versehen von Helmut Bode ("Brehm's travels throughout the world, between Norway's North Cape and the Equator. Told by himself. Selected and with biographical inserts provided by Helmut Bode"), Mannheim 1956, p. 76.

3 Ibid., p. 73.

4 See www.comboni.de/comboni/heilig/texte/redesayer.php, retrieved on 20.12.2015.

5 Ibid.

6 Ibid.

7 Guido Knopp, ZDF-History: Rennen in den Tod ("Race to the death"). Die Katastrophe von Le Mans 1955 ("The catastrophe of Le Mans 1955"), Documentation, Germany 2011.

8 See ibid.

9 Ibid.

10 Ibid.

11 Ibid.

12 Interview with Uwe Day ibid., in full length at: Silberpfeil und Hakenkreuz. Automobilrennsport im Natonalsozialismus ("Silver arrows and swastikas. Automobile racing in the Nazi era"), Berlin 2006.

13 Knopp, as previously cited.

14 Extensively and with critical annotations concerning the

review of the "Miracle of Bern": Bruggemeier, Franz-Josef: Das "Fussballwunder" von Bern, In: Informationen zur politischen Bildung, Heft 290 v. 4.5.2006, available online: www.bpb.de/izpb/8767/das-fussballwundervon-1954?p=1, last retrieved on 16.12.2015.

15 Day, Uwe: Silberpfeil und Hakenkreuz. Autorennsport im Nationalsozialismus ("Silver arrows and swastikas. Automobile racing in the Nazi era"), Berlin 2011, p. 253.

16 See Ibid., p. 252f.

17 See Knopp, Guido, as previously cited.

18 Knopp, as previously cited.

19 "Gibt es höhere Gewalt?" ("Does force majeure exist?", In: Der Spiegel of June 22, 1955, p. 31.

20 Ibid.

21 Interview with Edzard Reuter, Knopp as previously cited.

22 Schimpf, Eckard: Vom Mäzen zum Sponsor ("From donor to sponsor"), In: Die Geschichte des Rennsports ("The history of automobile racing"), Wissenschaftliche Schriftenreihe des Daimler-Chrysler Konzernarchivs ("Series of scientific documents from the archives of the DaimerChrysler Group"), Pub. Harry Niemann, Wilfried Feldenkirchen, Armin Hermann, Volume 5, p. 273. This prohibition never applied in the USA, ibid. p. 274.

23 Mücküsch, Andreas: Der erste Bürgerkrieg und die schwierige Unabhängigkeit 1956 bis 1983 ("The first civil war and the difficult achieving of independence"), In: Chiari, Bernhard (Pub.): Sudan. Wegweiser zur Geschichte, Paderborn et al ("Guide to history"), 2008, p. 39.

24 Pahl, Magnus: Zeit der Fremdherrschaft (1820–1955) ("Time of foreign rule"), In: Chiari as previously cited, p. 35.

25 Ibid.

26 Ibid.

27 See ibid.

28 Ibid.

29 Ibid.

30 Ibid.

31 Ibid.

32 Ibid., p. 36.

33 Ibid.

34 Ibid.

35 Ibid., p. 37.

36 See www.sudantribune.com/ spip.php?article28325, retrieved on 18.12.15.

37 Mücküsch as previously cited, p. 39.

38 See Human Rights Watch Report Sudan 2003 "Sudan, Oil and Human Rights", p. 45. Retrievable online: www.hrw.org/reports/2003/ sudan1103/sudanprint.pdf.

39 See ibid.

40 Patey, Luke: State Rules: Oil Companies and Armed Conflict in Sudan, p. 5. Complete version available in: Third World Quarterly, Volume 28, Issue 5, Juli 2007. Without annotations on: www.sudantribune.com/ spip.php?article22901, last retrieved on 23.12.2015.

41 Cf. www.auswaertiges-amt. de/DE/Aussenpolitik/Regio naleSchwerpunkte/Afrika/ Sudan/Darfur_node.html, Background information relating to the conflict in Darfur, (North-) Sudan. Last retrieved on 23.12.2015.

42 Feldenkirchen, Wilfried: Unternehmenspolitische Aspekte in der Geschichte des Motorsports bei der Daimler-Benz AG, In: Nieman et. al., Geschichte des Rennsports, loc. cit., p. 146.

43 Ibid.

44 Ibid.

45 Ibid.

46 Ibid., p. 148ff.

47 Ibid.

48 Ibid., p. 155 for 2002 and presently: www.auto-news. de/auto/fotoshows/anzeige_ Die-beliebtesten-Autofarben -Welche-Marke-faehrt-in- welchem-Lack_id_27850& picindex=12, last retrieved on 14.2.2016.

49 Patey, loc. cit., p. 6.

50 Ibid., p.7.

51 Ibid.

52 Ibid.

53 Background information in detail: ibid., p. 7f.

54 Ibid.

55 Ibid.

56 Ibid.

57 "Thar Jath"—is a Nuer expression and means: "Place under the tree". The place "under the tree" is of high importance in the social life in South Sudan. In the shade of big trees, people play, teach, discuss, intermediate and hold court.

58 Cf. elaborately: ECOS (Ed.): Unpaid Debt. The Legacy of Lundin, Petronas and OMV in Sudan 1997–2003.

59 Ibid.

60 Ibid.

61 Cf. York, Geoffrey: Malaysia's Petronas confirms dispensing of fuel for Sudanese military, air flights, In: The Globe and Mail on 25.10.2013.

62 Patey, p. 15.

63 Cf. e.g. Petronas Annual Report 2012, p. 47, www.petronas.com.my/investor-relations/Documents/PETRONAS AnnualReport2012.pdf.

64 Figures taken from: Human Rights Report Sudan loc. cit., p. 36 and passim.

2008

1 www.unesco.de/wissenschaft/wasser/un-und-wasser/wasserdekade.html, retrieved on 7.1.15.

2 Ibid.

3 Ibid.

4 Ibid.

5 Ibid.

6 Text of the Comprehensive Peace Agreements is to be found at: https://unmis.un missions.org/Portals/UNMIS/ Documents/General/cpa-en. pdf, retrieved on 3.1.2016.

7 Ibid., p. 48, 1.10.

8 Ibid., p. 51, 3.1.1 a).

9 Ibid., 3.1.1 b).

10 Ibid., 3.1.1 c).

11 Ibid., 3.1.1 d).

12 Ibid., 3.4.1ff.

13 See for instance www.hrw. org/reports/2003/sudan1103/ 25.htm, retrieved on 18.11.15.

14 CPA as previously cited, 4.1.

15 Norwegian Directorate for Nature Management: Environmental and Social Impacts of the Petroleum Activities in Southern Sudan, Report, Trondheim 2009, Summary, first page (unnum.) (unpublished).

16 "Western Gazelle River".

17 See for instance www.women undersiegeproject.org/con flicts/profile/darfur-sudan, retrieved on 5.2.2016.

18 An in-depth elucidation of the history: Eve M. Troutt Powell: A Different Shade of Colonialism. Egypt, Great Britain and the mastery of the Sudan, Berkeley 2003.

19 A good overview: Prender-gast, John; Clooney, George: Sudan's silent suffering is getting worse, https://news. vice.com/article/sudans-silent-suffering-is-getting-worse, retrieved on 10.1.2016.

20 Human Rights Watch: Report Sudan 2003, as pre-viously cited, p. 41f.

21 See above.

22 See: Kahurananga, James: South Sudan's Conservation Potential, www.awf.org/ blog/south-sudan%E2%80% 99s-conservation-potential, retrieved on 20.1.2016.

23 For further information: www.ramsar.org/about/the-ramsar-convention-and-its-mission, retrieved on 10.1.2016.

24 www.ramsar.org/news/ sudans-designation-of-the-sudd-marshes-on-world-environment-day-2006, retrieved on 10.1.2016.

25 Extensively: Riak, K.M.: Sudd Area as Ramsar Site: Biophys-ical features.

26 Ibid.

27 See ibid.

28 Zimmer, Carl: In Sudan, an Animal Migration to Rival Serengeti, New York Times of 12.6.2007.

29 Ibid.

30 Ibid.

31 Ibid.

32 There are by now providers of safaris. These include www.bahr-el-jebel-safaris. com/parks---reserves-of-south-sudan-a-summary. html. It has impressive photos.

33 Zimmer, as previously cited.

34 Ibid.

35 Begley, Sharon: Big Business: Wildlife Trafficking, In: Newsweek of 1.3.2008, http:// europe.newsweek.com/big-business-wildlife-traffick ing-83865?rm=eu, retrieved on 20.1.2016.

36 Ibid.

37 Zimmer, as previously cited.

38 See Hamilton Johnson, Douglas: The Root Causes of Sudan's Civil Wars, Peace or Truce, revised version, Kampala 2001, p. 48f.

39 Sign of Hope knows the name of the person interviewed.

40 Brief overview on http://de.wikipedia.org/wiki/Riek_Machar, last retrieved on 21.1.2016.

41 Oil and the Future of Sudan, Conference Report, 1.–2.11.2006, Juba, Southern Sudan, p. 10., www.ecosonline.org/reports/2006/Oil_and_the_future_of_Sudan.pdf, retrieved on 21.1.2016.

42 www.epa.gov/dwstandards regulations/secondary-drinking-water-standards-guidance-nuisance-chemicals, retrieved on 9.2.2016.

43 See: Petronas Annual Report 2007, p. 74. www.nioclibrary.ir/free-e-resources/Petronas/annual%20report%202007.pdf, retrieved on 21.1.2016 and www.ecosonline.org/news/2006/white_nile_celebrates_first_commercial_lifting_of_crude_oil, retrieved on 21.1.2016.

44 This and all further elucidations are from the unpublished appraisal created by Dr. Hella Rüskamp and commissioned by Sign of Hope in 2008. The appraisal was completed in 2010.

45 Ibid, p. 20.

46 "Rock" is the geological term for the entirety of the layers in the ground.

47 C. E. Clark and J.A. Vail: Produced Water Volumes and Management Practices in the United States, Argonne National Laboratory, September 2009, p.13.

48 Introduction to radioactive contamination resulting from oil pumping: Strahlende Ölquellen. Industrie verschweigt Gefahren durch radioaktive Rückstände ("Radiant oil wells. Industry conceals dangers of radioactive residues"): www1.wdr.de/themen/archiv/oelquellen-industrie100.html, retrieved on 20.1.2016.

49 C. E. Clark and J.A. Vail: Produced Water Volumes and Management Practices in the United States, Argonne National Laboratory, September 2009, p. 16.

50 See Report Oil and the future of Sudan, as previously cited, p. 8, 10, 17ff. and passim.

51 Ibid, p. 20.

52 www.lundin-petroleum.com /Press/pr_sudan_28-04-03_e. html, retrieved on 16.1.2016.

53 See www.ecosonline.org/ news/2006/white_nile_cele brates_first_commercial_ lifting_of_crude_oil, retrieved on 21.1.2016.

54 www.lundin-petroleum.com /Press/pr_sudan_28-04-03_e. html, retrieved on 21.1.2016.

55 Main consumer is China. The stakes held by Chinese companies in the consortia are smaller than those held by the Malaysian ones.

56 Extensive: Barlow, Maude: Blaue Zukunft. Das Recht auf Wasser and wie wir es schützen ("Blue future. The right to water and how we protect it") Kunstmann, Munich 2014.

57 All of the facts contained in this paragraph are from: Schallenberg, Jörg: Hamilton rast in letzter Minute zum WM-Sieg ("Hamilton's race to a last-minute victory"), In: spiegelonline of 2.11.2008, www.spiegel.de/sport/for mel1/formel-1-drama-hamil ton-rast-in-letzter-minute- zum-wm-sieg-a-587970. html, retrieved on 20.1.2016.

58 The processing facility in which the crude oil is separated from the produced water (and from which it is transported via a pipeline northwards for further processing) was originally and erroneously regarded by the Sign of Hope's staff as being a refinery.

2009

1 Norwegian Directorate for Nature Management: Environmental and Social Impacts of Petroleum Industry in Southern Sudan, Trondheim 2009, p. 2f. Unpublished. Hereafter referred to as the "Trondheim Report".

2   Ibid., p. 3.

3   Ibid., p. 2.

4   Ibid.

5   Ibid., p. 47.

6   Ibid.

7   www.oceans-esu.co.uk/wp-content/uploads/2012/02/Produced-Water-Bioremediation-with-Beneficial-Reuse.pdf, retrieved on 29.1.2016.

8   See Petronas Sustainability Report 2007, p. 19.

9   Ibid.

10 Trondheim Report, p. 47.

11 Ibid., p. 50.

12 Ibid.

13 Ibid., p. 47, 56.

14 UNEP Sudan. Post-Conflict Environmental Assessment, Nairobi 2007.

15 Ibid., p. 150.

16 Ibid.

17 Ibid.

18 Ibid.

19 See, as above, the sustainability report from Petronas 2007.

20 UNEP Report as previously cited, p. 154.

21 Ibid.

22 Ibid.

23 Ibid., p. 156.

24 Ibid.

25 Trondheim Report, p. 47.

26 The correspondence with the WNPOC was carried out in English.

27 See www.gupf.tu-freiberg.de/geologie/geo_minerale.html, retrieved on 13.12.2015.

28 The Cenomanian is the oldest age of the Late Cretaceous epoch. It began some 96 million years ago, and ended 93 million years ago. See www.mineralienatlas.de/lexikon/index.php/Cenoman, retrieved on 13.12.2015.

29 All of the information mentioned in this section is from: Unpaid Debt, as previously cited, p. 3.

30 See www.urbaniana.edu/tesi/archivio_06.htm, retrieved on 13.02.2016.

31 Herve Bar: AFP Feature—From blood to oil, the curse of a Sudanese village. Nov. 19, 2009.

32 Boswell, Alan: German Rights Group Says Oil Company Spoiling Water in Southern Sudan, VOA news, www.voanews.com/

english/2009-11-16-voa37.
cfm?renderforprint=1, re-
trieved on 19.11.2009.

33 Greste, Peter: Oil polluting
    Sudan water, BBC News,
    http://news.bbc.co.uk/go/
    pr/fr/-/2/hi/africa/8363024.
    stm, published on 16.11.2009,
    retrieved on 19.11.2009.

34 www.theguardian.com/
    environment/gallery/2009/
    nov/18/oil-water-pollution-
    sudan, retrieved on 8.2.2016.

35 Eveleens, Ilona: Durst: Es gibt
    Zyanid Chrom Blei ("Thirsty?
    There's cyanide, chrome and
    lead to drink") in: TAZ of
    22.11.2009, www.taz.de/nc/1/
    zukunft/umwelt/artikel/1/
    durst-es-gibt-zyanidchrom-
    Blei, retrieved on 23.11.2009.

36 http://business-humanrights.
    org/en/sudan-german-ngo-
    says-white-nile-petroleum-
    operating-joint-venture-pe
    tronas-sudapet-contaminat
    ing-drinking-water#c103318,
    retrieved on 8.2.2016.

37 WNPOC press release on
    24.11.2009, www.ecosonline.
    org/news/2009/WNPOC_res
    ponse, last retrieved on
    13.1.2016.

38 Iwersen, Sönke: Henkel und
    Daimler streiten um die
    Formel 1 ("Henkel and Daim-
    ler are fighting about the
    Formula 1") www.handels-
    blatt.com/sport/motorsport/
    betrugsskandal-henkel-und-
    daimler-streiten-um-formel-
    1/3326142.html, retrieved on
    8.2.2016.

39 Ibid.
40 Ibid.
41 Ibid.
42 Ibid.
43 Ibid.
44 Ibid.
45 Ibid.
46 Ibid.

47 www.who.int/water_sanita
    tion_health/dwq/fulltext.
    pdf, p.392, retrieved on
    13.03.2016.

48 Press release from Daimler,
    cited according to www.mer
    cedes-seite.de/motorsport/
    formel-1/2009/12/petronas-
    wird-titelsponsor-von-merce
    des-gp, retrieved on 8.2.2016.

49 Ibid.
50 Ibid.
51 Ibid.
52 Ibid.

53 Ibid.

54 Hecker, Arno: Petronas steigt bei Mercedes GP ein ("Petronas joins the Mercedes GP team"), FAZ online of 21.12.09, www.faz.net/aktu ell/sport/formel-1/formel-1-petronas-steigt-bei-merce des-gp-ein-1899984.html, retrieved on 8.2.2016.

55 Ibid.

56 See press release from Daimler as previously cited.

57 FAZ see above.

58 Ibid.

59 Schilling, Frieder: Die Schumacher-Dekade. Regengott reloaded ("The Schumacher Decade. Rain man reloaded"), Spiegel online of 22.12.2009, www.spiegel.de/sport/formel 1/die-schumacher-dekade-regengott-reloaded-a-663371. html, retrieved on 8.2.2016.

60 See for instance bulletin on Spiegel online of 23.12.2009, www.spiegel.de/sport/for mel1/formel-1-comeback-mercedes-plant-drei-jahre-mit-schumacher-a-668774. html, retrieved on 8.2.2016.

61 dpa v. 22.12.2009, retrievable at: www.heise.de/autos/ar tikel/Michael-Schumacher-faehrt-wieder-in-der-Formel-1-892136.html, retrieved on 8.2.2016.

2010

1 www.focus.de/sport/formel1/ formel-1-schumachers-neu-er-silberpfeil_aid_473922. html, retrieved on 9.2.2016.

2 Ibid.

3 Ibid.

4 Ibid.

5 Ibid.

6 Bundestagsdrucksache (parliamentary document) 17/722 from 15.2.2010.

7 Ibid.

8 Bundestagsdrucksache (parliamentary document) 17/878 from 2.3.2010.

9 Ibid.

10 Ibid.

11 Ibid.

12 www.unglobalcompact.org/ what-is-gc, retrieved on 9.2.2016.

13 See the report issued by Daimler AG on the Global Compact: 2008 Communica-

tion on Progress (COP) for the Global Compact, unnumbered, last page and passim, retrievable at: www.unglobalcompact.org/system/attachments/3574/original/COP.pdf?1262614908, retrieved on 9.2.2016.

14 The new point system in the Formula 1, starting in 2010: www.speed-magazin.de/formel1/news/formel-1-2010-neues-f1-punktesystem-f%C3%BCr-die-rennsaison-2010-soll-jetzt-fix-sein_20057.html.

15 All of the information in this section is from: Schmidt, Michael: Wie gut ist Michael Schumacher? ("How good is Michael Schumacher?"), in: Auto, Motor und Sport from 16.3.2010, www.auto-motor-und-sport.de/formel-1/f1-analyse-michael-schumacher-comeback-wie-gut-ist-michael-schumacher-1784779.html, retrieved on 17.2.2016.

16 www.justice.gov/criminal-fraud/case/united-states-v-daimlerchrysler-china-ltd-court-docket-number-10-cr-066-rjl, retrieved on 2.2.2016.

17 Ibid.

18 www.zeit.de/wirtschaft/unternehmen/2010-03/daimler-korruption-usa, retrieved on 12.1.2016.

19 See Hawranek, Dietmar: Im Würgegriff der USA ("In the choke-hold of the USA"), In: Der Spiegel Nr. 50/2011, p. 82–84.

20 See www.speed-magazin.de/formel1/news/formel-1-mercedes-motorsportchef-norbert-haug-„ein-erstklassiges-rennen-von-nico-und-unser-erster-podiumsplatz_21074.html.

21 The PDF is to be downloaded at: www.ecosonline.org/reports/2010/%5Eindex.html/UNPAID_DEBT_fullreportweb.pdf.html, retrieved on 12.11.2015.

22 Ibid., p. 5.

23 Ibid.

24 E. g.: Abend, Lisa: Was a Swedish Firm Complicit in Sudan's War? In: Time from 4.7.2010, content.time.com/time/world/article/0,8599,2001197,00.html, retrieved on 20.1.2016.

25 Collection of articles available at: www.bloodhound.dk.

26 Abend, Lisa, as previously cited.

27 UN-Resolution 64/292 from 28.7.2010.

28 Ibid.

29 Ibid.

30 Ibid.

31 Winkler, Inga: Wasser für Alle. UNO-Gremien haben Wasser und Sanitärversorgung als Menschenrecht anerkannt ("Water for all. UNO commissions have recognized water and sanitary facilities to be a human right"), In: Amnesty Journal December 2010, retrievable at: www.amnesty.de/journal/2010/dezember/wasser-fuer-alle, retrieved on 9.2.2016.

32 Ibid.

33 www.gnpoc.com/mission.asp?glink= GL001&plink= PL001,retrieved on 21.2.2016.

34 dpa from 16.11.2010: Organization: Ökologisches Desaster im Sudan ("Organization: Ecological Disaster in Sudan").

35 In this context, the number of affected persons consisted of the inhabitants of areas around the oilfield of Thar Jath, Mala, Unity, Toma South, El-Nar, El-Toor and Munga.

2011

1 Perry, Alex: George Clooney, South Sudan and How the World's Newest Nation Imploded, In: Newsweek of 10.2.2014.

2 Ibid.

3 Ibid.

4 Ibid.

5 Ibid.

6 Nienhaus, Lisa: Eine rote Dame für Daimler ("Lefty lady for Daimler"), In: FAZ of 23.1.2011 www.faz.net/aktuell/wirtschaft/unternehmen/richterin-hohmann-dennhardt-eine-rote-dame-fuer-daimler-1580020.html, retrieved on 20.2.2016.

7 Ibid.

8 Ibid.

9 Ibid.

10 Ibid.

11 Ibid.

12 Ibid.

13 Hamilton, Rebecca: Looming challenge for southern Sudan: Regulating oil companies, in: Washington Post of 12.2.2011, Section A, A.6.

14 Ibid.

15 Ibid.

16 Ibid.

17 Ibid.

18 Ibid.

19 Ibid.

20 Ibid.

21 Daimler, press release of 15.2.2011, http://media.daimler.com/dcmedia/0-921-65618 6-49-1368689-1-0-0-0-0-1-127 59-614216-0-0-0-0-0-0-0.html ?TS=1455990211497, retrieved on 20.2.2016.

22 See Die drei Probleme des Autokonzerns ("The three problems of the automobile manufacturer"), in: Manager Magazin of 7.6.2011, www.manager-magazin.de/foto strecke/fotostrecke-68872.html, retrieved on 20.2.2016.

23 Ibid.

24 Ibid.

25 WNPOC press release of 24.11.2009, www.ecosonline.org/news/2009/WNPOC_res ponse, retrieved on 13.1.2016.

26 See above.

27 See above.

28 Petronas neuer Teamsponsor von Mercedes-Benz ("Petronas to sponsor Mercedes-Benz's race team"), www.motorsport-total.com/dtm/news/2011/04/Petronas_neu er_Teamsponsor_von_Mer cedes-Benz_11042902.html, retrieved on 20.2.2016.

29 Ibid.

30 Ibid.

31 Ibid.

32 Ibid.

33 Ibid.

34 www.dailymail.co.uk/tv showbiz/article-2038638/ George-Clooney-stars-Mercedes-Benz-advert.html# comments, retrieved on 21.2.2016.

35 Ibid.

36 Daimler. Richtlinie für integres Verhalten ("Directive on integrity-based conduct") 2012, p. 3.

37 Ibid.

2012

1 See Südsudan dreht den Öl-hahn zu ("South Sudan turns

off the oil tap"), via news agencies on 29.1.2012, in: NZZ of 29.1.2012.

2   In 2011, Petronas' financial year began on April 1st. This has by now been changed to January 1st.

3   Petronas, Sustainability Report 2011, p. 36.

4   Ibid.

5   Ibid.

6   Ibid.

7   Ibid.

8   Ibid.

9   Ibid.

10 Ibid.

11 Ibid.

12 Ibid.

13 http://edition.cnn.com/2012/03/16/us/washington-clooney-arrest/, retrieved on 27.2.2016.

14 Ibid.

15 www.spiegel.de/panorama/leute/protest-gegen-menschenrechtsverletzungen-im-sudan-george-clooney-in-washington-festgenommen-a-821859.html, retrieved on 27.2.2016.

16 Bach, Ralf: Formel1. Sieg für einen Spätbremser ("Victory for a late braker"), in: spiegel online of 15.4.2012, www.spiegel.de/sport/formel1/formel-1-in-china-nico-rosberg-jubelt-ueber-ersten-sieg-im-mercedes-a-827647.html, retrieved on 27.2.2016.

17 Summary of agency reports on 15.4.12, www.welt.de/sport/formel1/article106184661/Historischer-Sieg-fuer-Rosberg-Vettel-Fuenfter.html, retrieved on 27.2.2016.

18 Ibid.

19 Ibid.

20 Ibid.

21 See above, prologue.

22 http://sites.tufts.edu/reinventingpeace/files/2012/09/Oil-Agreement-between-SudanSouth-Sudan0001.pdf, retrieved on 24.2.2016.

23 www.spiegel.de/sport/formel1/formel-1-mercedes-trennt-sich-offenbar-von-schumacher-a-858450-druck.html, retrieved on 9.3.2016.

24 Integrity Code. Common Guiding Principles at Daimler. Our Principles of Behaviour and Guidelines for

Ethical Conduct. November 2012, p. 3.

25 Ibid.

26 Ibid., p. 6.

27 Ibid.

28 Ibid.

29 Daimler, Ethical business. Our shared responsibility.

30 Ibid., p. 8.

31 Ibid., p. 9.

32 Ibid.

33 Ibid.

34 Ibid., p. 16.

35 Involved are ISO 14001:2004 and BSI-OHSAS 18001–1999.

36 Petroleum Act 2012, Art. 61 Section 2.

37 Ibid., Chapter XIV of above.

38 Rio Declaration on the Environment and Development, Principle 16, www.un.org/depts/german/conf/agenda 21/rio.pdf, retrieved on 26.2.2016.

39 See www.lac.org.na/projects/grap/Pdf/epupa_debate.pdf, retrieved on 25.1.2016.

40 www.internationalrivers.org/resources/letter-of-protest-to-norad-norconsult-on-their-role-in-epupa-dam-3284, retrieved on 25.1.2016.

41 Ibid.

42 Ibid.

43 See ibid.

44 Ibid.

45 Ibid.

46 Rønning, Morten: Genocide foretold: Norconsult hopes to get contracts, In: Norwatch of 15.7.1997, www.framtiden.no/english/other/genocide-foretold-norconsult-hopes-to-get-contracts.html, retrieved on 25.1.2016.

47 Ibid.

48 See https://gfbvberlin.wordpress.com/2009/12/08/namibia-himba-am-kunene-flus-droht-aus, retrieved on 25.1.2016. The blog entry from the Society for Threatened Peoples covers the revival of the dam plans.

49 Davidson, Desmond: Norwegian firm linked to Sarawak dams refuses to meet 3 activists, In: The Malaysian Insider of 22.5.2014, retrievable at: www.themalaysianinsider.com/malaysia/article/norwegian-firm-linked-to-sarawak-dams-refuses-to-meet-3-activists.

50 www.sarawakreport.org/
2014/05/pr-blunder-by-nor
ways-norconsult, retrieved
on 25.1.2016.

51 Norwegian Consultant
admonished over Sarawak
dams, Bruno Manser Fonds,
press release of 24.6.2015.

52 Ibid. letter from Norconsult
CEO John Nyheim to FIVAS
of 13.5.2014.

53 See "PR Blunder by Norway's
Norconsult" as cited above.

54 Ibid.

55 Extensively: Bruno Manser
Fonds: Complicit in Corruption. Taib Mahmud's Norwegian Power Man, Basel, May
2013, retrievable at: www.
bmf.ch/upload/berichte/
bmf_report_complicit_in_
corruption.pdf.

56 See www.hydro.com.au/
about-us/news/2012-08/
hydro-tasmania-rejects-sa
rawak-dam-building-claims
and http://ens-newswire.
com/2012/12/05/hydro-tas
mania-to-withdraw-from-
sarawak-dam-building-
program.

57 See www.sarawakreport.org/
2014/07/misrepresenting-

the-facts-we-publish-more-
documents, retrieved on
26.1.2016.

58 www.theborneopost.com/
2015/11/19/baram-dam-
project-halted-indefinitely,
retrieved on 26.1.2016.

59 This was confirmed by the
oil consortium to Sign of
Hope. This is in accordance
with the legal code of South
Sudan. It smacks however
of a misdeed. This is due to
the personal ties between
officials of the Petroleum
Ministry and the oil con-
sortium. These causes the
mechanisms of control not
to do the jobs foreseen for
them, as remarked in the report issued by UNEP in 2006.
See farther above.

60 See for instance www.face
book.com/cmadenansatem/
posts/899746186766235,
publication of the head of
government of Sarawak on
17.8.2015.

2013

1 Bach, Ralf: Schlecht abge-
stimmt, spiegelonline on
12.5.2013.

2   Ibid.

3   Ibid.

4   Bach, Ralf: Wir fühlen uns betrogen ("We've been cheated"), spiegel online of 27.5.2013.

5   Ibid.

6   Ibid.

7   Ibid.

8   Ibid.

9   Ibid.

10 Ibid.

11 Ibid.

12 See www.motorsport-total. com/f1/splitter/2013/06/Mer cedes_-AND-_Pirelli_Fans_ hatten_haerteres_Urteil_ erwartet_13062104.html, retrieved on 1.3.2016.

13 Ibid.

14 Dudek, Anna Lena: "Prominente als Markenbotschafter. Chancen, Risiken und Herausforderungen" ("Headliners as ambassadors for brands. Opportunities, risks and challenges"), Hamburg 2014, p. 29.

15 See www.technoserve.org/ blog/technoserves-coffee- work-in-south-sudan-high lighted-in-the-globalpost/

tag/South+Sudan, retrieved on 9.3.2016.

16 Ibid.

17 Ibid.

18 Waakhe, Simon Wudu: Parliament Orders Environmental Audit In Oil Producing States, In: Gurtong of 18.9.2013.

19 Ibid.

20 Ibid.

21 Ibid.

22 Machel, Amos: South Sudan oil extraction causing environmental damage, www. africareview.com/Business-- -Finance/South-Sudan-oil- extraction-causing-environ mental-damage/-/979184/200 3940/-/ghn2fi/-/index.html, retrieved on 3.12.2015.

23 Ibid.

24 Ibid.

25 Ibid.

26 Ibid.

27 USAID/South Sudan. Economic Governance Project in South Sudan (Pub.): Bradley, Claudine: Health, Safety and Environment Management Systems under the Petroleum Act 2012, Juba 2013.

28 Bradley, as indicated, p. 4.

29 Ibid.

30 Ibid.

31 Ibid.

32 Ibid.

33 Ibid.

34 Ibid.

35 Ibid., p. 5.

36 Ibid.

37 Ibid.

38 Ibid.

39 Ibid.

40 Ibid.

41 Ibid.

42 Ibid., p. 6.

43 Ibid., p. 5.

44 Ibid.

45 Ibid., p. 6.

46 York, Geoffrey: Major Player in Canadian energy sector accused of violating Sudan arms embargo, in: The Globe and Mail of 22.10.2013.

47 Ibid.

48 Ibid.

49 Ibid.

50 Ibid.

51 Ibid.

52 Ibid.

53 Ibid.

54 Ibid.

55 See O'Neil, Peter: Petronas must comply with UN sanctions before investing in Canada: Amnesty International, In: Vancouver Sun of 23.10.2013.

56 Petronas Media Relations Department: Press Statement—Petronas' Fuel Supply Services in Sudan of 25.10.2013.

57 Ibid.

58 Ibid.

59 Ibid.

60 Ibid.

61 Ibid.

62 Ibid.

63 Ibid.

64 Ibid.

65 York, Geoffrey: Malaysia's Petronas confirms dispensing of fuel for Sudanese military, aid flights, In: The Globe and Mail v. 25.10.2013.

66 Ibid.

67 Ibid.

68 Ibid.

69 Wani, Clement: Official: We must have oil pollution laws, eyeradio of 28.10.2013, http://eyeradio.org/official-oil-pollution-laws/, retrieved on am 1.3.2016.

70 Ibid.

71 Ibid.

72 Ibid.

73 Ibid.

74 Ibid.

75 Ibid.

76 Ibid.

77 Unity State to take action against oil companies over pollution, www.sudantri bune.com/spip.php?article 48681, retrieved on 3.12.2015.

78 Ibid.

79 Ibid.

80 Ibid.

81 Ibid.

82 Ibid.

83 http://in.reuters.com/article/ southsudan-unrest-fighting-idINL6N0JY2UB20131219, retrieved on 2.3.2016.

84 http://in.reuters.com/article/ southsudan-unrest-oil-idIN L6N0K51SQ20131226, re-trieved on 2.3.2016.

2014

1 Nimmervoll, Christian: Millionenvertrag gesichert: Mercedes verlängert mit Petronas ("Contract worth millions secured—Mercedes and Petronas extend their agreement"), www.motor sport-total.com/f1/news/2014 /05/millionenvertrag-gesi chert-mercedes-verlaengert-mit-petronas-14052405.html, retrieved on 16.12.2015.

2 Ibid.

3 See ibid.

4 Ibid.

5 Ibid.

6 Ibid.

7 Ibid.

8 www.gwf-wasser.de/pro dukte/?tx_acmproducts_ps %5Bproduct%5D=6780&cHa sh=389b33b5aa2e38c38d3c 3164b5ea1b37, retrieved on 2.3.2016.

9 Rueskamp, Hella et al.: Effect of oil exploration and production on the salinity of a marginally permeable aquifer system in the Thar Jath, Mala and Unity oil fields, Southern Sudan, In: Zentralblatt für Geologie und Paläontologie Part I, year 2014, Issue 1, p. 95-115, retrievable under: www. schweizerbart.de/papers/ zgp1/detail/2014/84542/ Effect_of_oil_exploration_

and_production_on_the_sa
linity_of_a_marginally_per
meable_aquifer_system_in_
the_Thar_Jath_Mala_and_
Unity_Oilfields_Southern_
Sudan?af=search.

10   See Rencken, Dieter;
Fritzsche, Mario: 2014: Die
Rekordsaison von Mercedes
("The record season of Mercedes"), Motorsport Total of
29.11.14, www.motorsport-to
tal.com/f1/news/2014/11/2014-
die-rekordsaison-von-mer
cedes-14112921.html, re-
trieved on 2.3.2016.

11   Ibid.

12   Ibid.

2015

1   Broadcast on 25.2.2015,
Transcript of the broadcasts
published at: https://unmiss.
unmissions.org/Portals/un
miss/Miraya%20News/2015/
February%202015/25%20
February%202015%20-%20
0100%20pm%20News%20
Bulletin.doc, retrieved on
28.1.2016.

2   See http://radio-miraya.org/
about, retrieved on 28.1.2016.

3   All of the facts and figures
contained in this section are
from the above-mentioned
transcript published by the
UNMISS on the 1 pm broad-
cast on 25.2.2015.

4   See transcript of 5 pm broadcast on 25.2.15, published by
the UNMISS, https://unmiss.
unmissions.org/Portals/un
miss/Miraya%20News/2015/
February%202015/25%20Feb
ruary%202015%20-%205pm.
doc, retrieved on 28.1.2016.

5   https://radiotamazuj.org/en/
article/study-%E2%80%98
direct-link%E2%80%99-bet
ween-oil-exploration-and-
water-pollution-unity,
retrieved on 9.3.2015.

6   See Müchler, Benno: Diesel
für die News-Hütte ("Diesel
for the news hut"), in Süddeutsche Zeitung on 22.12.11.

7   "Oil production makes Unity
water unsafe for consump-
tion: study", in: The Citizen
on 2.3.2015.

8   "Soaked in Oil: The cost of
war in South Sudan", Al
Jazeera on 4.3.2015.

9   Letter from Sign of Hope to
Dieter Zetsche, Chairman

of the managing board at Daimler AG, on 26.3.2015.

10 When constructing drinking water boreholes one has to plan for a redundancy of supplying systems. This redundancy affects the cost calculation. A second water well should be available to supply the local population with drinking water even if the first water well system becomes inoperative e.g. due to a failure of the solar panels or the water pump.

11 Wenz, Konrad: Formel 1 in der freien Werkstatt ("Formula 1 in the non-affiliated garages"), kfz-betrieb of 17.7.2015, www.kfz-betrieb. vogel.de/service/articles/498 113, retrieved on 18.1.2016.

12 See www.mercedes-benz.de/ content/germany/mpc/mpc_ germany_website/de/home_ mpc/passengercars/home/ servicesandaccessories/ge nuine_partsandaccessories/ motor_oil.html, retrieved on 31.1.2016.

13 See www.focus.de/auto/ ratgeber/kosten/tid-34671/

13-spar-tipps-fuer-autofah rer-so-sparen-sie-beim-oel wechsel-viel-geld_aid_1158 478.html, retrieved on 31.1.2016.

14 See: Das Geschäft mit dem Ölwechsel ("The business of oil changes"), broadcast on 15.8.2015 at Plusminus, ARD, www.daserste.de/informa tion/wirtschaft-boerse/plus minus/sendung/12082015- plusminus-autoinspektion- 100.html, retrieved on 31.1.2016.

15 See www.petronas.de/Un ternehmensportrait/Vision.

16 "Nico Rosbergs Werkstätte" ("Nico Rosberg's garage"), In: Auto und Wirtschaft, 9/2015, www.autoundwirt schaft.at/news.php?id=9107, retrieved on 18.1.2016.

17 See www.theguardian.com/ film/2015/jul/21/george-cloo ney-seeks-to-expose-those- who-fund-and-profit-from- wars-in-africa, retrieved on 31.1.2016.

18 http://mpmisouthsudan.org/ AboutMPM.html, retrieved on 18.02.2016.

19   https://radiotamazuj.org/en/
     article/nilepet-boss-secretly-
     diverting-funds-friends-
     and-political-allies, retrieved
     on 31.1.2016.

20   See www.globalwitness.org/
     en/blog/safe-pair-hands-
     change-top-south-sudans-
     national-oil-company, re-
     trieved on 31.1.2016.

21   Ibid.

22   Letter from the MPM to Sign
     of Hope via SPOC—sent by
     E-mail of 10.8.2015.

23   Ibid.

24   Ibid.

25   Ibid.

26   Ibid.

27   Letter from the First Under-
     secretary of the Ministry
     of Petroleum and Mining,
     Machar Aciek Ader, to Sign
     of Hope on August 10, 2015.

28   www.tributetobambi.de/
     aktionen.html, retrieved on
     11.11.15.

29   Smith, David: South Sudan
     to export coffee for the first
     time, In: The Guardian of
     8.10.2015.

30   See Baker, Aryn: Why George
     Clooney is supporting coffee
     farming in South Sudan,

In: Time v. 12.6.2015, http://
time.com/3918857/george-
clooney-south-sudan, re-
trieved on 9.3.2016.

31   Ibid.

32   Ibid.

33   www.spiegel.de/sport/for
     mel1/formel-1-hamiltons-
     party-rosbergs-aerger-a-105
     9548.html, retrieved on
     27.12.2015.

34   Ibid.

35   Ibid.

36   Ibid.

37   Ibid.

38   Ibid.

39   See Global Witness Report:
     Blueprint for Prosperity.
     How South Sudan's new laws
     hold the key to a transparent
     and accountable oil sector,
     November 2012, p. 9.

40   Overview: www.bmz.de/de/
     themen/transparenz/eiti/
     eitistandards/index.htm,
     retrieved on 1.2.2016.

41   See ibid.

42   See for instance www.global-
     witness.org/en/reports/will-
     star-shine-south-sudan.

43   See www.sudantribune.com/
     spip.php?article42153, re-
     trieved on 1.2.2016.

44 Ibid.

45 Ibid with further criticisms.

46 Global Witness as cited above.

47 Extensively: www.suddinsti tute.org/publications/show/ understanding-the-enforce ment-of-environmental-pro visions-of-petroleum-act- 2012-and-why-environmen ta, retrieved on 1.2.2016.

48 See www.suddinstitute.org/ news-and-events/events/ transparency-and-accoun tability-in-the-south-suda nese-petroleum-industry, retrieved on 1.2.2016.

49 www.suddinstitute.org/ news-and-events/events/ understanding-the-enforce ment-of-environmental- provisions-in-south-sudan- s-petroleum-act-2012, re- trieved on 1.2.2016.

50 Ibid, Policy Brief.

51 Talk on 10.1.2016.

52 Sign of Hope, minutes of discussion on 11.11.2015.

53 www.mict-international.org/ projects/mourning-peter- julius-moi, retrieved on 15.11.2015.

54 Ibid.

55 Ibid.

56 Ibid.

57 Ibid.

58 Ibid.

59 Zeitvogel, Karin: Fueled by corruption, South Sudan war enters third year, 17.12. 2016, www.irinnews.org/ report/102304/fuelled-by- corruption-south-sudan- war-enters-third-year, re- trieved on 31.1.2016.

60 https://thesentry.org/re- ports/south-sudan, retrieved on 31.1.2016.

61 Eckl-Dorna, Wilfried: Was Daimlers jungen Schweden zum obersten Kronprinzen macht, In: Manager-Maga- zin of 17.12.2015, retrievable: www.manager-magazin.de/ unternehmen/autoindustrie/ daimler-ola-kaellenius-ist- heissester-anwaerter-auf- vorstandsposten-a-1068196. html, retrieved on 30.1.2016.

2016

1 www.visionofhumanity.org/ #page/indexes/global-peace- index/2015/SSD/OVER re- trieved on 31.1.2016.

2   See Global Witness 2015: Turning the Tide. Building a clean oil sector through South Sudan's peace agreement, p. 4.

3   See Ibid., p. 10.

4   Tiitmamer, Nhial: Understanding the Enforcement of Environmental Provisions of Petroleum Act 2012 and Why Environmental Ruin Continues, SUDD Institute, Policy Brief of 21.4.2015, p. 14.

5   Ibid.

6   Global Witness loc. cit., p. 10.

7   Ibid., p. 4 and passim.

8   Ministry for Petroleum and Mining: Engagement with Sign of Hope, Stuttgart, November 2015, Summary of Notes, p. 4 of 19, unpublished.

9   Ibid, p. 19 of 19.

10 Ministry of Petroleum and Mining, Engagement with Sign of Hope, Stuttgart, November 2015, Summary of Notes, p. 17.

11 Integrity Code. Common Guiding Principles at Daimler. Our Principles of Behaviour and Guidelines for Ethical Conduct. p. 17 (www.daimler.com/documents/sustainability/integrity/daimler-integritycode.pdf, last retrieved on 7.4.2016).

12 www.finanzen.net/nachricht/aktien/Daimler-hebt-die-Dividende-nach-Rekordgewinn-kraeftig-an-4721107, retrieved on 17.2.2016.

13 Ibid.

14 Ibid.

15 Pragst, Fritz: Toxikologisches Gutachten – Haarproben Südsudan ("Toxicological appraisal—samples of hair from South Sudan"), Charité-Centrum für diagnostische and präventive Labormedizin. Institut für Rechtsmedizin. Abteilung Forensische Toxikologie of 11.2.2016, unpublished.

16 See www.dgrm.de/die-dgrm/ehrungen/aktuelle-preistraeger/2010, retrieved on 11.3.2016.

17 Ibid.

18 Ibid., p. 20.

19 Ibid., p. 15.

20 Ibid., p. 19.

21 Ibid.

22 Ibid., p. 19.

23 Runow, Klaus-Dietrich: Gutachterliche Stellungnahme. Ermittlung der toxischen Belastung durch Analysen menschlicher Haarproben of 96 Probanden aus Ortschaften in unterschiedlicher Entfernung zu einem Erdölgebiet im Südsudan ("Appraisal of the determination of toxic contamination through the analysis of human hair from 96 persons living in communities located varying distances from an oil field in South Sudan"), IFU, 2016, unpublished.

24 Ibid., p. 5.

25 Ibid.

26 Ibid., p. 18.

27 Ibid., p. 19.

28 Ibid.

29 Ibid.

30 Ibid.

31 Ibid.

32 Ibid.

33 Ibid.

34 Ibid.

35 AFP—South Sudan oil production pollution threatens thousands March 4, 2016.

36 Langhans, Katrin, Hägler, Max: Petronas' schmierige Geschäfte setzen Daimler unter Druck ("Petronas' dirty deals put Daimler under pressure"), in: Süddeutsche Zeitung of 8.3.2016. www.sueddeutsche.de/wirtschaft/oel-konzern-schmierige-geschaefte-1.2895544, retrieved on 11.3.2016.

37 See www.br.de/nachrichten/petronas-daimler-suedsudan-100.html, retrieved on 11.3.2016.

38 Ibid.

39 Report from Munich, broadcast on 8.3.2016, www.br.de/mediathek/video/sendungen/report-muenchen/report-umweltkatastrophe-suedsudan-daimler-petronas-100.html, retrieved on 11.3.2016.

40 Ibid.

41 Ibid.

42 Ibid.

43 Cf. Hilty, Reto M.; Henning-Bodewig, Frauke (Ed.): Corporate Social Responsibility: Verbindliche Standards des Wettbewerbsrechts?, Berlin 2014. (Congress paper of the Max Planck-Institute for Innovation and Competition).

Picture credits

Cover: © Aleksandra Kovac/
   Stocksy
P. 6: © Saskia Noll
P. 9: © Sign of Hope
P. 32: © Sign of Hope
P. 51: © Sign of Hope
P. 66: © Saskia Noll
P. 80: © African Water
P. 83: © Sign of Hope
P. 106: © The Cahier Archive/
   Corbis
P. 115: © Sign of Hope
P. 127: © Sign of Hope
P. 145: © Sign of Hope
P. 147: © Sign of Hope
P. 162: © Sign of Hope
P. 175: © African Water
P. 184: © KEYSTONE/AP/
   Pete Muller
P. 189: © Sign of Hope
P. 192: © Sign of Hope
P. 202: © Sign of Hope
P. 207: © Sign of Hope

P. 210f.: © African Water,
   Saskia Noll
P. 212: © Sign of Hope
P. 220: © Sign of Hope
P. 248: © Jakub Krechowicz/
   123rf.com
P. 264ff.: © ECOS/PAX/Sign of
   Hope/Saskia Noll

Hoffnungszeichen | Sign of Hope e. V.

is an organization that has dedicated itself to helping the world's threatened by protecting their human rights and by providing them with humanitarian assistance. Sign of Hope is not affiliated with any confession.

Our Christian beliefs constitute the basis of our motivation for our actions, which are guided by the belief's principles of compassion for and love of fellow human beings and of solidarity with them. Our credo is:

> *"Whatever you did for one of the least of these brothers and sisters of mine, you did for me!" Matthew 25.40*

Sign of Hope started its life in Bonn in 1983. Its original name was CSI-Deutschland e.V. In 1993, its headquarters were moved to Singen, a city in the southwestern corner of Germany. In 1999, the organization ended its cooperation with CSI International. That caused the organization's general assembly to resolve to change its name and logo. Since 2013, Sign of Hope has maintained its offices in Konstanz, the city located on the lake of the same name. These offices coordinate the organization's worldwide operations. This association's organization comprises a foundation of the same name.

Sign of Hope has been since 1997 a member of Deutscher Spendenrat (Germany'a Association of Donors). It also is an active member of VEN-RO, which is Germany's association of NGOs that are active in development work and in the provision of humanitarian assistance. Sign of Hope has signed the self-commitment formulated by Germany's Initiative Transparente Zivilgesellschaft (Initiative for a Transparent Society). Sign of Hope has been awarded consultative status by the UN.

Hoffnungszeichen e.V. has been recognized by Germany's taxation authorities as an organization serving the public welfare and providing charitable assistance. This recognition makes all donations tax deductible.

Contact

Hoffnungszeichen e.V.
Schneckenburgstr. 11 d
78467 Konstanz
Germany
Tel. +49 7531 9450160
mail@hoffnungszeichen.de

For donations

Hoffnungszeichen e.V.
Bank für Sozialwirtschaft
IBAN: DE31 6602 0500 0008 7173 00
BIC: BFSWDE33KRL

Our deepest thanks go to

our donors and other friends whose support and encouragement enable Sign of High to carry out its work. We also wish to thank the members of our association and supervisory board: Gerhard Heizmann, Manfred Steiner, Father Wilhelm Olschewski, Ute Felgenhauer-Laier and Stefan Daub.

As this book's co-author, I wish to thank Reimund Reubelt, who is the chairperson of Sign of Hope and thus my cherished colleague, for the way he kept this book on track by finding the ideas driving it forward, for his great support of and his work on it. Reimund and I join to thank Dirk Rumberg for his tireless devotion to this project.

My thanks and great appreciation are accorded to Dr. Sabine Pamperrien, my co-author. Thanks for your keen perception of the big picture and of the important details comprised in it. Your perceptiveness and adeptness have decisively shaped this book.

A big "thank you" goes to Anne Rüffer, my publisher, and her team, with this especially applying to Saskia Noll, for the incredible energy that she mobilized and deployed in the realization of this book.

I also want to express my gratitude to our colleagues at Sign of Hope, with this especially including Hanna Fuhrmann, Martin Hofmann, Anna Hüncke, Ines Jörger, Marcel Kipping and Dr. Lucia Sorrentino. It is great to be able to work with such dedicated people, with this applying to this book and to all other aspects of our working relationship.

And last but absolutely not least I want to take this opportunity to thank Dr. Hella Runge and Christian Runge of African Water for the scientific expertise and the outstanding cooperation that they have supplied during our many years of working together for and in South Sudan. The two of them have lived and hoped and prayed with and for the people in this country.

Other interesting books

www.ruefferundrub.ch

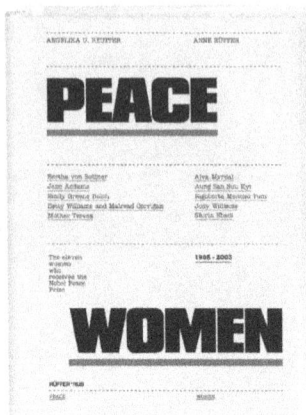

Anne Rüffer
Angelika U. Reutter

Peace Women
The eleven women
who received the
Nobel Peace Prize

256 pages I hardcover
ISBN 978-3-907625-20-0

Bertha von Suttner – Jane Addams – Emily Greene Balch – Betty Williams & Mairead Corrigan – Mother Teresa – Alva Myrdal – Aung San Suu Kyi – Rigoberta Menchú Tum – Jody Williams – Shirin Ebadi

War is always the result of fear and violence. Conflict is supposed to resolve what was not resolved in dialogue and negotiations—for lack of good will to solve it. What remains are misery and destruction, anger and impotence, and last but not least breeding-grounds for renewed violence. Those who were conquered by force of arms want revenge, want justice for themselves and their cause—again, through violence.

The examples of the eleven women who were awarded the Peace Nobel Prize up to 2003 show that other approaches are possible. They decided to stand up for their ideals without identifying with fear, violence, and brutality. Their motivation grew out of an attitude that gives life, an inner attitude that trusts life and will not give up.